PORTFOLIO BY
VALENTIN JECK, 2016–2017

I

Revolution Square (today Republic Square), Ljubljana,
Slovenia. 1960–74. Edvard Ravnikar (1907–1993).
View of the East Office Tower and NLB Bank building

II   Revolution Square (today Republic Square), Ljubljana,
            Slovenia. 1960–74. Edvard Ravnikar (1907–1993).
←   Northern view

III   Jasenovac Memorial Site, Jasenovac, Croatia.
          1959–66. Bogdan Bogdanović (1922–2010)

IV   Monument to the Uprising of the People of Kordun and Banija,
Petrova Gora, Croatia. 1979–81.
Architect: Berislav Šerbetić (1935–2017) and Zoran Bakić (1942–1992).
Sculptor: Vojin Bakić (1915–1992). Exterior view

V   S2 Office Tower, Ljubljana, Slovenia. 1972–78.
Milan Mihelič (b. 1925). Exterior view

VI   Danube Flower restaurant, Belgrade, Serbia. 1973–75.
Ivan Antić (1923–2005). Exterior view

VII   Aeronautical Museum, Belgrade, Serbia. 1969–89.
Ivan Štraus (b. 1928). Exterior view

VIII   Block 23, New Belgrade, Serbia. 1968–74.
Božidar Janković (b. 1931), Branislav Karadžić (1929–2007),
Aleksandar Stjepanović (b. 1931), and Milutin Glavički
(1930–1987). View of buildings 1 to 4

IX   Block 23, New Belgrade, Serbia. 1968–74.
Božidar Janković (b. 1931), Branislav Karadžić (1929–2007),
Aleksandar Stjepanović (b. 1931), and Milutin Glavički
(1930–1987). View of the entrance to Slab 5

X   West Gate of Belgrade (Genex Tower), Belgrade, Serbia. 1977–80.
      Mihajlo Mitrović (b. 1922). View of the northwestern facade

XI   Monument to the Fighters Fallen in the People's
Liberation Struggle, Ilirska Bistrica, Slovenia. 1965.
Architect: Živa Baraga (b. 1931).
Sculptor: Janez Lenassi (1927–2008)

XII   Apartment Building of the Military Directorate,
Zagreb, Croatia. 1953–57. Drago Galić (1907–1992).
View of the facade

XIII   Apartment Building of the Military Directorate,
Zagreb, Croatia. 1953–57. Drago Galić (1907–1992).
Interior view of the staircase

XIV   Hotel Adriatic II, Opatija, Croatia. 1970–71.
Branko Žnidarec (b. 1937). Exterior view

XV   Braće Borozan building block in Split 3, Split, Croatia. 1970–79.
Dinko Kovačić (b. 1938) and Mihajlo Zorić (b. 1939)

XVI   Memorial and Cultural Center, and Town Hall,
Kolašin, Montenegro. 1969–75.
Marko Mušič (b. 1941). Exterior view

XVII Macedonian Opera and Ballet, Skopje, Macedonia. 1968–81.
Biro 71 (est. 1971; Štefan Kacin [b. 1939], Jurij Princes [b. 1933],
Bogdan Spindler [b. 1940], and Marjan Uršič [b. 1934]).
View of the foyer

XVIII   Monument to the Battle of the Sutjeska, Tjentište, Bosnia and Herzegovina. 1965–71. Sculptor: Miodrag Živković (b. 1928). Engineer: Đorđe Zloković (1927–2017)

XIX   Šerefudin White Mosque, Visoko, Bosnia and Herzegovina. 1969–79. Zlatko Ugljen (b. 1929). Interior view

XX   Museum of People's Revolution (today History Museum
       of Bosnia and Herzegovina), Sarajevo, Bosnia and
       Herzegovina. 1958–62. Boris Magaš (1930–2013),
       Edo Šmidihen (1930–2015), and Radovan Horvat (d. 2016).
       Exterior view of the entrance

XXI   Haludovo Hotel complex, Malinska, Krk, Croatia. 1969–72.
Boris Magaš (1930–2013). Interior view

XXII   Haludovo Hotel complex, Malinska, Krk, Croatia. 1969–72.
Boris Magaš (1930–2013). Exterior view

XXIII   Hotel Creina, Kranj, Slovenia. 1964–73.
Edvard Ravnikar (1907–1993). Southern facade

XXIV   Council Assembly Building, Kranj, Slovenia. 1954–60.
Edvard Ravnikar (1907–1993). Interior view of the auditorium

XXV   Diagnostic and Therapeutic Wing of the University
Medical Center, Ljubljana, Slovenia. 1967–76.
Stanko Kristl (b. 1922). Interior view of the entrance hall

XXVI   Sava Center, Belgrade, Serbia. 1976–78.
        Stojan Maksimović (b. 1934). Interior view

XXVII   Sava Center, Belgrade, Serbia. 1976–78.
Stojan Maksimović (b. 1934). Interior view

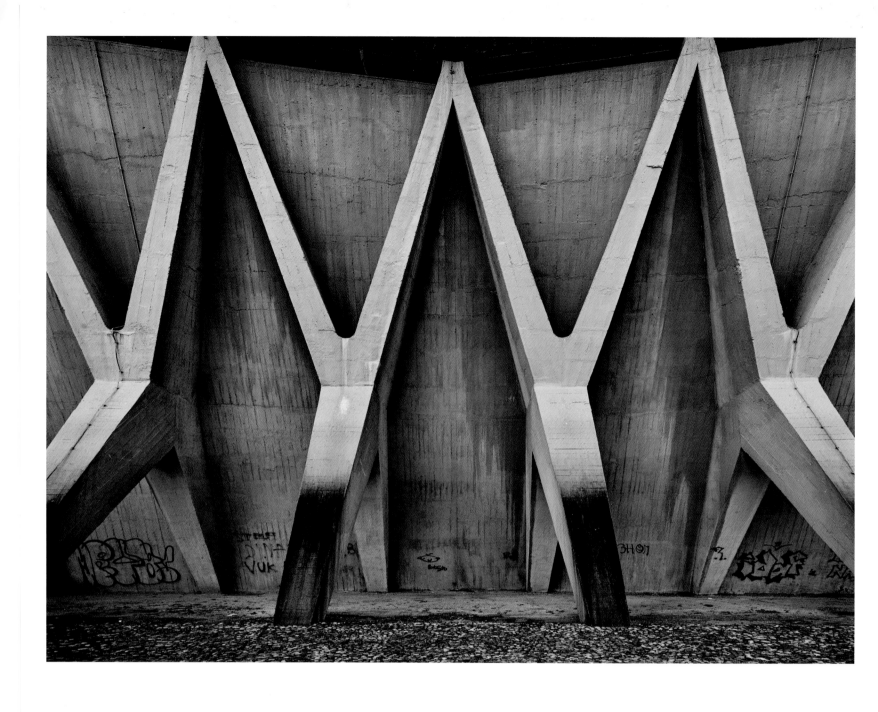

XXX   Pavilion of West Germany, Zagreb Fair, Zagreb, Croatia. 1957.
Architect: Ivan Vitić (1917–1986).
Engineer: Krunoslav Tonković (1911–1989).
View of the northeastern facade

XXXI   Battle of the Sutjeska Memorial Center, Tjentište,
Bosnia and Herzegovina. 1968–74.
Ranko Radović (1935–2005). View of the entrance

XXXII   Necropolis for the Victims of Fascism,
Novi Travnik, Bosnia and Herzegovina. 1971–75.
Bogdan Bogdanović (1922–2010)

XXXIII   Monument to the Ilinden Uprising, Kruševo, Macedonia.
          1970–73. Iskra Grabul (1936–2008) and
          Jordan Grabul (1925–1986). Exterior view

XXXIV   Avala TV Tower, Mount Avala, near Belgrade, Serbia.
          1960–65. Destroyed in 1999 and rebuilt in 2010.
          Architects: Uglješa Bogunović (1922–1994) and Slobodan Janjić (b. 1928).
   →   Engineer: Milan Krstić (1914–1974). Exterior view

XXXV	Podgorica Hotel, Podgorica, Montenegro. 1964–67.		XXXVII	Telecommunications Center, Skopje, Macedonia. 1968–81.
	Svetlana Kana Radević (1937–2000).			Janko Konstantinov (1926–2010).
←	Exterior view of the balconies		→	View of the southwestern block facade

XXXVI	Telecommunications Center, Skopje, Macedonia. 1968–81.		XXXVIII	Medical High School, Skopje, Macedonia. 1969–73.
	Janko Konstantinov (1926–2010).			Janko Konstantinov (1926–2010).
↑	Exterior view of the main hall		→ →	Detailed view of the facade

TOWARD A CONCRETE UTOPIA: ARCHITECTURE IN YUGOSLAVIA 1948–1980

Martino Stierli
Vladimir Kulić

With a photographic portfolio by
Valentin Jeck

and essays by

Tamara Bjažić Klarin
Vladimir Deskov, Ana Ivanovska Deskova,
  and Jovan Ivanovski
Andrew Herscher
Sanja Horvatinčić
Theodossis Issaias and Anna Kats
Jelica Jovanović
Juliet Kinchin
Martina Malešič
Maroje Mrduljaš
Arber Sadiki
Luka Skansi
Łukasz Stanek
Matthew Worsnick
Mejrema Zatrić

**The Museum of Modern Art
New York**

CASE STUDIES

FOREWORD

Glenn D. Lowry

Toward a Concrete Utopia: Architecture in Yugoslavia, 1948–1980 brings to the fore a body of work that has rarely been considered outside of the region for which it was originally conceived. The Museum of Modern Art embraced this exhibition as an opportunity to shine a light on a unique mid-century architecture culture at the intersection of East and West—one that, through Yugoslavia's leading role in the Non-Aligned Movement, had repercussions on a global scale. More than merely a historical investigation into largely uncharted territory, *Toward a Concrete Utopia* provides a lens through which to historicize and provide context to our contemporary age of globalization. In this vein, the exhibition also builds upon and expands the tenets of MoMA's interdisciplinary C-MAP (Contemporary and Modern Art Perspectives) research program, which investigates multiple art histories beyond North America and Western Europe in an effort to arrive at a better understanding of the complex and multivalent history and legacy of modernism around the globe.

  While the history of Yugoslavia ended relatively quickly after the end of the Cold War, the country, which offered a "Third Way"—an alternative to capitalist West and Communist East—enjoyed an outsize international presence for a time, thanks to its unique geopolitical situation at the intersection of a bifurcated world. MoMA's interest in the nation's cultural production is longstanding, as evidenced by a series of programs in the 1960s, including, most notably, the exhibition *Yugoslavia: A Report* from 1969, which brought to an American public forty-five contemporary prints by twenty-four Yugoslav artists, among them figures such as Ivan Picelj, whose work is amply documented in the Museum's collection. Two film series, in 1961 and 1969, respectively, investigated the country's rich experimental cinema of the day.

  In keeping with this history, *Toward a Concrete Utopia* also includes select works from contemporary architects and artists represented in the Museum's collection that comment on modern architecture in Yugoslavia, including the stunning architectural drawings of the American visionary Lebbeus Woods and work by the Croatian artist David Maljković, whose video piece *Scenes for a New Heritage* (2004)—which lent its name to a group show at MoMA in 2015—addresses the legacy of some of the memorials and monuments on display in the current exhibition.

  To facilitate the groundbreaking research behind *Toward a Concrete Utopia*, the curatorial team of Martino Stierli, The Philip Johnson Chief Curator of Architecture and Design, and Vladimir Kulić (with Anna Kats, Curatorial Assistant) assembled an advisory board of locally based scholars and architects. These participants brought not only regional expertise to the project but also access to a multitude of institutions and individuals, many of whom became generous lenders to the exhibition. As the Museum moves toward exploring similarly uncharted non-Western geographies, this spirit of collaboration may serve as a model.

  We are grateful to those lenders and to The International Council of The Museum of Modern Art and the Graham Foundation for Advanced Studies in the Fine Arts, without whose support this exhibition would not have been possible. Finally, we are thankful for the generous funding of this volume by the Jo Carole Lauder Publication Fund of The International Council of The Museum of Modern Art.

Glenn D. Lowry, Director, The Museum of Modern Art

INTRODUCTION

Martino Stierli
Vladimir Kulić

Toward a Concrete Utopia examines, by means of a large survey exhibition and the present volume, the architectural production of a country that ceased to exist more than twenty-five years ago and whose violent demise haunts the Western Balkans region to the present day. Despite, or precisely because of this trauma, we believe such a consideration of Yugoslav architecture culture—from the break with Stalinism in 1948 up to the death, in 1980, of Tito, the country's long-term authoritarian leader—is both a timely and a necessary undertaking. The year 1980 also marked the beginning of an economic and political crisis, as well as the emergence of the concept of postmodernism in Yugoslav architectural discourse, which together heralded considerable changes in architectural production going forward. During the period bracketed by these two historical turning points, Yugoslav architects produced a massive body of work that can be broadly identified as modernist for its social, aesthetic, and technological aspirations, but at the same time they added varied novel dimensions to that general category. However, as with many innovative, postwar architectural cultures in Eastern Europe, Yugoslavia's has, until quite recently and with few exceptions, received little sustained attention. Indeed, Eastern European architecture as a whole has largely been left out of the discipline's modern canonical history, an oversight that not only underscores an ongoing Eurocentric (Western) bias, but also reflects the prolongation of the cultural logic of the Cold War long after its end.[1] A Western perception of the Balkans region as Europe's "Orient"—an exotic, "other" territory between East and West—has further hindered a serious evaluation of cultural production in the region on par with the Western canon.[2] *Toward a Concrete Utopia* sets out to fill one of the gaps that have resulted from such a myopic perspective. To do so seems particularly timely in an age of rapid globalization and an increasing awareness—not only in academia but also in a larger cultural conversation—that the old bipolar model of center and periphery of cultural production has produced a skewed and deeply problematic outlook onto history. What is needed instead is a fundamental recharting of the world map and an investigation into the many channels of cultural—and, by extension, architectural—exchange that have intensified between cities and regions outside the traditional cultural centers, but have been active and productive all along. Such a methodological recalibration would provide, as it were, a prehistory of that age of globalization, allowing us to critically reconsider the assumptions that led to that previous, flawed model of cultural production in the first place. As a major agent in the genesis and dissemination of that canonical history, The Museum of Modern Art has a special responsibility in its revision.

  The former Yugoslavia provides a particularly promising inroad into such a recharting mission. After a short alliance with the Eastern Bloc and a break with Joseph Stalin's USSR in 1948, the socialist state went on to pursue a relatively independent brand of socialism based on workers' self-management, becoming the torchbearer of a "Third Way" in the bifurcated world of the Cold War. Tito's Yugoslavia deliberately defied the geopolitics of the East-West divide, pursuing friendly relations, cultural connections, and economic exchange with both rival blocs. From the early 1960s onward, as a founding nation of the Non-Aligned Movement, it also forged economic and political bonds with partner nations across Africa, the Middle East, and Asia, many of them entering a process of decolonization after newly gained independence. The ensuing network of global relationships—many of which have only recently moved into the focus of serious research[3]—provided manifold opportunities for the exchange of architectural knowledge outside of the Western world's established systems of communication.

If the Non-Aligned Movement enabled the emergence of networks of knowledge and material exchange within a specifically postcolonial framework, the federal and multiethnic state provided a structure for cultivating internal multiculturalism, another distinctive feature of the postwar Yugoslav project. Comprising numerous ethnicities, some of which had been engaged in bitter conflict during World War II, the country sought to acknowledge the various identities of its constituent groups. Architecture became one of the most visible bearers of the process, tapping not only into the repositories of *longue durée* traditions but also into the more recent lineages of local modernism, present in the region since the turn of the twentieth century. The result was a range of early and coherent regional(ist) cultures on par with other similar, simultaneous phenomena elsewhere. That many of the local modernists involved in this process were already allied with leftist politics prior to World War II was certainly beneficial to the socialist project. When socialism finally arrived, they and their disciples thus invested a great deal of effort in adapting the existing manifestations of modern architecture to the specificities of the new Yugoslav society. Affordable mass housing, new civic and social institutions, public spaces for interaction and participation, tourism facilities, and even commemorative structures all became grounds for experimentation, giving rise to some extraordinary, internationally relevant results.

Since the dissolution of Yugoslavia in the early 1990s, many of the buildings and projects featured in this selection have fallen into disrepair. The commons—from urban public spaces to the various civic, educational, and cultural facilities—have been subject to shady privatization schemes, reduced to mere real estate. Many of the monuments commemorating the victims of fascism and the antifascist struggle of World War II have been vandalized or completely destroyed, now discredited as "Communist." Though the vast majority of buildings and structures continue to be used and inhabited, they—as with postwar and brutalist architecture in other parts of the world—have suffered from neglect due to a general lack of appreciation of the architectural propositions and concerns of that period. One objective of our exhibition and catalogue is to bring attention to the outstanding architectural and spatial qualities of many of these buildings and the ensuing need for their long-term preservation and care. This concern is expressed—explicitly and implicitly—in the portfolio of photographs by the Swiss photographer Valentin Jeck that preludes the catalogue, as well as in select contemporary photography throughout the book. Jeck's photographs capture a sense of the temporality of works of architecture, an aspect that is all too often forgotten when we talk about architecture's presence in the world.

Postwar Yugoslavia legitimized itself by claiming to pursue emancipation along intersecting axes: internally, from class oppression and ethnic rivalry, and externally, by supporting anticolonialism. It is due to such wide-reaching ambitions that we may consider the country, for better or worse, a paradigm of a utopian project, one geared toward the creation of a pluralistic, secular, and idealistic society. Hence the title of our exhibition and book, which echoes German philosopher Ernst Bloch's theorization of utopia as a hopeful, future-oriented process in a perpetual state of emergence.[4] Translated into an architectural context, Bloch's "concrete utopia" becomes more than merely a pun evoking the ubiquitous material of Europe's postwar reconstruction; rather, it highlights architecture's power and responsibility to give material shape to a larger social project. In an age beholden to a global "star" system, when architecture in many parts of the world has ceased to contribute to the common good and is seen instead as a luxury commodity, Yugoslavia serves as a reminder that architecture culture can only thrive in the presence of a strong social and political consensus about its capacity to transform society.

As we now know, Yugoslavia's utopian vision was sadly doomed to fail, perhaps not so much because the project itself was at fault but because the divisionist rhetoric of emerging nationalism ultimately discredited it. However, the architecture produced during the country's short existence still testifies to its aspirations and achievements. We hope that

Toward a Concrete Utopia will not only help to recover the memory of these achievements, but also contribute to reviving architecture's potential for, and commitment to, social responsibility. This is crucial for architecture as a discipline and for the multifold movements of emancipation that continue to shape our contested present.

1   One major noteworthy exception in the early Western reception of Eastern European architecture is Udo Kultermann, *Zeitgenössische Architektur in Osteuropa* [Contemporary Architecture in Eastern Europe] (Cologne: DuMont, 1985).

2   Maria Todorova, *Imagining the Balkans,* rev. ed. (Oxford, U.K.: Oxford University Press, 2009). Before Todorova, Larry Wolff argued that the entire Eastern Europe was long subject to a "demi-Orientalization"; Wolff, *Inventing Eastern Europe: The Map of Civilization on the Mind of the Enlightenment* (Stanford, Calif.: Stanford University Press, 1994).

3   See, among other sources, "Cold War Transfer: Architecture and Planning from Socialist Countries in the 'Third World,'" ed. Łukasz Stanek, special issue, *Journal of Architecture* 17, no. 3 (2012); Christina Schwenkel, "Traveling Architecture: East German Urban Designs in Vietnam," *International Journal for History, Culture and Modernity* 2, no. 2 (2014): 155–74; Dubravka Sekulić, "Energoprojekt in Nigeria: Yugoslav Construction Companies in the Developing World," *Southeastern Europe* 41, no. 2 (2017): 200–29; Vladimir Kulić, "Building the Non-Aligned Babel: Babylon Hotel in Baghdad and Mobile Design in the Global Cold War," in "Socialist Networks," special issue, *ABE Journal,* no. 6 (2014), available online at https://abe.revues.org/924.

4   Ernst Bloch, *The Principle of Hope,* vols. 1–3 (Cambridge, Mass.: MIT Press, 1995 [1954, 1955, 1959]).

Fig. 1

NETWORKS AND CROSSROADS:

THE ARCHITECTURE OF SOCIALIST YUGOSLAVIA AS A LABORATORY OF GLOBALIZATION IN THE COLD WAR

Martino Stierli

Viewed through a contemporary Western lens, the Balkans region, and the former Yugoslavia more specifically, is hardly considered a hotspot of cultural or architectural innovation. Despite the worldwide resonance of artists such as Belgrade-born Marina Abramović or several young Slovenian and Croatian architects, little has changed the notion that Yugoslavia and its successor states have been peripheral to the cultural mainstream; the region is still mainly associated with the disintegration of the Socialist Federal Republic of Yugoslavia in the early 1990s and the ensuing, violent wars of separation along lines of ethno-national divisions. Indeed, as historian Maria Todorova asserts in her groundbreaking study, a view of the Balkans as only peripherally associated with the project of Enlightenment in the Western world—as Europe's internal "other"—dominates the history of the region's representation in Western art, literature, and culture.[1]

However, if one carefully considers Yugoslav architects' production and networks of exchange between the years 1948 and 1980, a very different picture emerges. Rather than being a backwater of the modern world, Yugoslavia was instead at the forefront of international architectural discourse during that period, due in large part to the country's diverse associations with architects on both sides of the Iron Curtain as well as in Africa and the Middle East. While the political, economic, and cultural processes of globalization accelerated rapidly after the fall of the Berlin Wall and the end of the Cold War in 1989, Yugoslavia's leadership in the Non-Aligned Movement provided local architects (and engineers) a broad stage on which to exchange architectural knowledge and ideas across ideological divisions, political borders, and cultural gaps—a unique position that anticipated the current age of globalism. A climate of relative ideological openness allowed these architects—as well as artists more broadly—to look for inspiration in East and West, and to apply notions of modernism to specific local conditions, both topographically and culturally. Situated at the crossroads of geopolitical poles, Yugoslav architects had a double agency in the postwar project of global modernity: as absorbers of the prewar legacy of Western and Central European modernism, on the one hand, and on the other, as carriers and promoters of notions of modernity in many newly independent postcolonial nations.

LOOKING WEST AND ELSEWHERE: CENTERS OF EDUCATION AS NETWORKS OF EXCHANGE

Despite the Western misconception that Yugoslavia's postwar architecture culture operated largely in the orbit of the Soviet Union—and its massive quest for standardization and prefabrication—Yugoslav architects maintained strong bonds to centers of architectural discourse in Western Europe and North America. The Yugoslav regime had in fact broken with Stalinism

Fig. 1   International Trade Fair, Lagos. 1973–77.
Zoran Bojović (1936–2018) for Energoprojekt (est. 1951).
Entrance hallway. 1977. Personal archive of Zoran
Bojović. Photograph: Zoran Bojović

in 1948, only three years after the end of World War II and the foundation of the Socialist Federal Republic of Yugoslavia. Thus, architects were freed from the eclectic, historical mandate of socialist realism—even as it was concurrently installed in East Berlin and Warsaw as the singular architectural style of socialist society. Instead, Yugoslav architects looked to the modernist legacy of the interwar period. Architectural magazines played a particularly significant role in the internationalization of the country's design discourse after its geopolitical recalibration. The editorial policies of *Arhitektura*, the leading Zagreb-based architectural journal, exemplify the rapid response to this ideological about-face.[2] Starting with its first issue in 1947, the journal published a table of contents and captions in both French and Russian as well as in the native Serbo-Croatian. Russian was dropped in the last issue of 1949, coinciding with the publication of a feature on Le Corbusier's Unité d'Habitation in Marseilles. This multifunctional building typology converged easily with notions of communal living in the fledgling socialist state. The prominence granted to Le Corbusier's work also underscored the westward recalibration of the country's political outlook, while anticipating a veritable Corbusier fever, which ultimately produced a number of prominent buildings in Belgrade, Zagreb, and Ljubljana directly inspired by the Unité paradigm. *Arhitektura* continued to include translated feature texts from foreign journals, and from mid-1951 onward, the magazine adopted English as its second foreign language, signaling a conclusive turn of the regime's political compass needle to the West.

Education proved an even more decisive arena for facilitating a continuous dialogue with Western modernism. Throughout the 1920s and 1930s, many Yugoslav architects who would become leading figures in the postwar period studied or worked in offices abroad. Given the long-standing political and economic ties of the northern parts of the country to Central Europe, it is not surprising that various prominent Yugoslav architects trained in Vienna or other major cities of the former Austro-Hungarian empire. Nikola Dobrović (1897–1967), for example, often regarded as one of the most influential Serbian modernist architects (and Bogdan Bogdanović's [1922–2010] teacher at the Faculty of Architecture in Belgrade), undertook his training in Budapest and at the Technical University in Prague before coming to Yugoslavia in the 1930s. Muhamed (1906–1983) and Reuf Kadić (1908–1974), who would advance to become the defining figures of modernism in the 1930s in Bosnia, also studied at the Technical University in Prague in the late 1920s. Likewise, the prominent Slovene architects Max Fabiani (1865–1962) and Ivan Vurnik (1884–1971) both received their degrees from the Technical University in Vienna. The tradition revived in the 1950s and 1960s, this time within the framework of grant and aid programs funded by Western nations to curry political influence and strategic partnership with a country that had distanced itself from the Soviet Union.

Among these various workshops for learning abroad, Le Corbusier's Paris studio at rue de Sèvres arguably had the most impact. Though fed through a variety of competing traditions and increasingly informed by American postwar architecture, the lure of Paris was strong for postwar Yugoslav architecture culture, particularly for students of the Ljubljana Faculty of Architecture. Established in 1919, the school would become one of the leading centers of architectural discourse in Central-Eastern Europe under the leadership of Vurnik and, especially, Jože Plečnik (1872–1957). Among Plečnik's graduate students who left for Paris in the interwar period was Edvard Ravnikar (1907–1993), who would become one of the most prolific and influential architectural figures in postwar Yugoslavia. Equally, Croatian architects Ernest Weissmann (1903–1985) and Juraj Neidhardt (1901–1979), who were paid assistants in Le Corbusier's studio from 1927 to 1930 and 1933 to 1935, respectively, facilitated the influx of younger Yugoslav colleagues to the atelier.[3] And another prominent Corbusier student, Milorad Pantović (1910–1986), later designed the much-celebrated Belgrade Fair.

Ravnikar and Neidhardt, in particular, through their built work and theoretical contributions, were both key in defining Yugoslav modern architecture in the postwar period. Neidhardt had been initiated into the gospel of modern architecture as early as 1920, when he started his four-year architectural education at the Viennese Academy of Fine Arts under Peter Behrens, whose Berlin office he joined for another eighteen months in 1930.[4] In Le Corbusier's studio later that decade, he worked mainly on urbanist projects such as La Ville Radieuse and the plan for Algiers. After Neidhardt returned to Yugoslavia, a steel company in the Bosnian town of Zenica hired him in 1939 to design housing stock for its workers; he made his home in Sarajevo and taught at the Faculty of Architecture there.[5] He would go on to become the most important Bosnian architect of the postwar period. Though few of his projects were executed—among them the seat of Parliament of Bosnia and Herzegovina and two apartment blocks on Sarajevo's Đure Đakovića Street (fig. 2), both of which interpreted Le Corbusier's Five Points for a New Architecture in a regionalist, texture-rich register—Neidhardt's most seminal contributions were theoretical. His book *Architecture of Bosnia and the Way to Modernity*, published in 1957 and written during the emergence of a modernist "regionalism" in the 1930s,[6] is considered the apogee of Neidhardt's architectural thinking. It was co-authored by the Slovene architect Dušan Grabrijan (1899–1952), another Plečnik disciple gone modernist during a yearlong stint in Paris, though he did not work for Le Corbusier. Based on a thorough ethnographic analysis of the legacy of Ottoman building typologies and notions of urbanism in the region, Neidhardt and Grabrijan articulated what they saw as proto-modernist features in traditional Ottoman houses, underscoring the abstract cubic volumes, large horizontal windows, whitewashed walls, and, perhaps

Fig. 2   Residential buildings on Đure Đakovića Street, Sarajevo, Bosnia and Herzegovina. 1952–53. Juraj Neidhardt (1901–1979). Exterior view. 2010. Photograph: Wolfgang Thaler

Fig. 3   Sketch of a *divanhana* from Dušan Grabrijan and Juraj Neidhardt, *Arhitektura Bosne i put u suvremeno/Architecture of Bosnia and the Way to Modernity* (Ljubljana: Državna založba Slovenije, 1957), 169.

13

Fig. 2

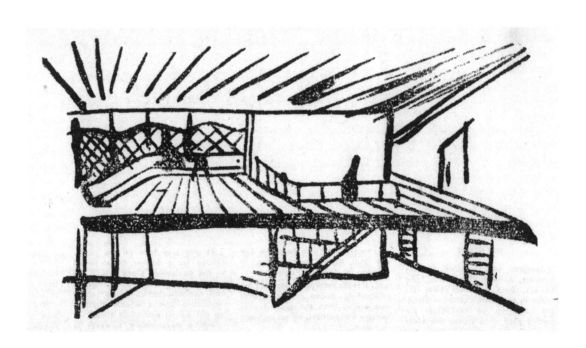

Fig. 3

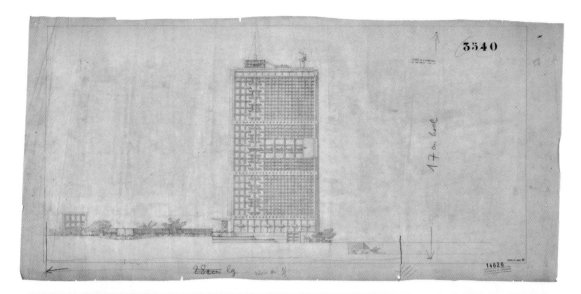

Fig. 4

Fig. 5

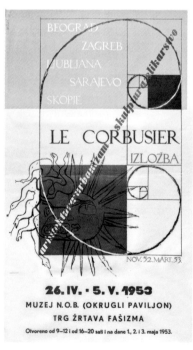

Fig. 6

Fig. 7

decisively, the interaction between exterior and interior spaces in traditional features such as the *divanhana*, an open porch wrapping around the core of the house (fig. 3). Despite being published bilingually in Serbo-Croatian and English, however, the book was largely ignored outside of Bosnia and has only recently been reconsidered as an important source text of Yugoslav modern architecture.

Ravnikar, too, became one of the leading dramatis personae in Yugoslav architecture culture and one of the most prolific and innovative architects of his generation. Much like his Swiss mentor, Ravnikar produced a great many projects and was also an avid writer and theorist.[7] Though Ravnikar's employment in Le Corbusier's studio lasted only a few months in 1939, it would prove to be a transformative experience for the young Slovene. During his tenure at the studio, Ravnikar worked on an unexecuted high-rise for Algiers, for which he produced a number of drawings, among them a spectacular large-scale rendering of the elegant structure indicative of his artistic capacity (fig. 4).

Many of Ravnikar's projects display an idiosyncratic ambiguity between an allegiance to Plečnik's predilection for classicist elements and exploration of material textures, on the one hand, and a reference to Le Corbusier's abstract and sculptural thinking on the other. This unique synthesis of competing architectural aesthetics was already evident in Ravnikar's Modern Gallery in Ljubljana (1936–51) (fig. 5). The building's liberal interpretation of the classical language of architecture, the texturally rich handling of the facades, and the organization of the spaces all clearly reference Plečnik's precedent. However, the ceremonial canopy framing the main entrance, reminiscent of Le Corbusier's white villas of the 1920s, clearly speaks a different language. If Corbusian thinking here appears to be little more than an afterthought, his principles had clearly registered fully by the time Ravnikar started to work on the regulatory plan for the new city of Nova Gorica in 1948 (p. 60, fig. 4), an urban plan he modeled after the Athens Charter, with a clear division of differing functions (working, dwelling, leisure, circulation), a civic center with ample public spaces, and an open, parklike landscape into which high-rise slabs are loosely placed following an underlying orthogonal grid. Similarly, at the Memorial Complex at Kampor (1953) (p. 108, figs. 6 and 7), which commemorates the

victims of the Croatian island's former Italian Fascist concentration camp, Ravnikar synthesized Corbusian principles (such as the organization of the complex into a ritualized sequence according to the notion of the *promenade architecturale*) with Plečnik's sensibility for materiality and texture, taking its cue from eminent German architect and theorist Gottfried Semper's widely influential *Stoffwechseltheorie* (theory of material transformation).[8] The dialectic allegiance to both a Germanic understanding of architecture as an atectonic art of dressing and the constructive rationalism in the French tradition would become a hallmark of much of Ravnikar's later work and is the core of his unique and idiosyncratic oeuvre.[9]

Le Corbusier's studio not only established a sense of continuity with the "heroic" period of prewar modern architecture, but his work also became a very direct source of reference for architectural modernism in and for the fledgling socialist state in the postwar period. A traveling exhibition on the work of the Swiss master—the very first international architectural exhibition to come to Yugoslavia after the end of World War II and the country's break with Stalin in 1948—provided an opportunity for direct contact and learning (fig. 6). The political significance of this embrace of Le Corbusier's ideas in the context of shifting tectonics in the Cold War landscape should not be underestimated. While his architecture was deemed "bourgeois" and unfit to serve as a model for the construction of a new socialist society during the short years of Yugoslavia's alignment with the Soviet Union, its championing in the early 1950s underscored Yugoslavia's political realignment and commitment to modernism as opposed to the dictums of socialist realism. (Except for a few important government competitions for administrative buildings in New Belgrade—none of which were built—socialist realism never took hold in Yugoslavia.) Originally organized by the Boston Institute of Contemporary Art in 1948, the exhibition traveled to several venues in North and South America before arriving in Europe in the fall of 1952.[10] There it was shown only in the divided city of Berlin and in Yugoslavia (at the request of the country's Committee for Science and Culture). The symbolism inherent in the exhibition's appearance in two highly contested territories in the early Cold War context cannot go unnoticed. In Yugoslavia, notably, the exhibition received wide exposure, with stops in Belgrade, Skopje, Sarajevo, Split, Ljubljana, and Zagreb between December 1952 and May 1953, drawing large audiences and multiple reviews in the professional and general press.

The country's architects showed particular interest in Le Corbusier's Unité d'Habitation mass-housing typology, which had only just been completed in Marseille, hailing it as a model for communal living that combined a strong modernist assertion with an adaptability to the social standards of the newly emerging socialist state. Within a few years, the major urban centers of Belgrade, Zagreb, and Ljubliana all received their own simplified and adapted versions of the Unité, many of which were located at key urban nodes. Among these, two apartment buildings in Zagreb by the architect Drago Galić (1907–1992) stand out (fig. 7; p. 93, fig. 6).

Against this backdrop, the tenth (and final) conference of the International Congresses for Modern Architecture

Fig. 4   Skyscraper at the quartier de la Marine, Algiers. 1938–39. Le Corbusier (1887–1965). Drawing: Edvard Ravnikar (1907–1993). Longitudinal elevation. 1939. Pencil on tracing paper, 20 1/16 × 42 7/16 in. (51 × 108 cm). Fondation Le Corbusier

Fig. 5   Modern Gallery, Ljubljana, Slovenia. 1936–51. Edvard Ravnikar (1907–1993). Perspective of the central hall. c. 1940. Ink on tracing paper, 9 15/16 × 19 7/16 in. (25.2 × 49.3 cm). Museum of Architecture and Design, Ljubljana

Fig. 6   Exhibition poster, *Le Corbusier: Architecture—Urban planning—Sculpture—Painting*. 1952. Color lithography, 33 7/16 × 24 in. (85 × 61 cm). Poster collection of the Department of Prints and Drawings, Croatian Academy of Sciences and Arts

Fig. 7   Apartment Building of the Military Directorate, Zagreb, Croatia. 1953–57. Drago Galić (1907–1992). View of the piloti. c. 1964. Tošo Dabac Archive, Museum of Contemporary Art, Zagreb. Photograph: Tošo Dabac

(CIAM), which took place in Dubrovnik in August 1956, could have been the triumphant acknowledgment of the country's full integration into Western modernism. However, the CIAM was already disintegrating at this point, and none of the protagonists of the old guard (Le Corbusier, Walter Gropius, Alvar Aalto) participated in the conference.[11] The meeting became a swan song to the first generation of modern architects and produced little lasting effect on Yugoslavia's contemporary and thriving architecture culture. Under the rubric of Team 10, whose thinking would greatly inform architectural production in Yugoslavia in the following years, the young guard was in the process of taking over the discursive leadership. That same year, in 1956, the young Croatian architect Radovan Nikšić (1920–1987) spent half a year studying and working in the Netherlands through a program of technical aid to Yugoslavia. There, he was employed in the Rotterdam studio of Johannes van den Broek and Jacob Bakema, the latter one of the leaders of Team 10, whose thinking would greatly inform architectural production in Yugoslavia in the following years—evidenced most prominently in the Moša Pijade Workers' University in Zagreb (see Kulić, pp. 124–27) that Nikšić designed together with Ninoslav Kučan (1927–1994) upon his return home.[12]

YUGOSLAV ARCHITECTURE IN COLD WAR POLITICS

The break with Stalin in 1948 had left the fledgling socialist Yugoslavia with uncertain prospects and without any ideological or financial support to construct a socialist society. However, this crisis also paved the way for the disproportionately large role that the small country was to assume in the Cold War. Under Presidents Harry S. Truman and Dwight D. Eisenhower, the United States quickly sought to step in, viewing Yugoslavia as a possible "wedge" to be driven into the Communist bloc, a spearhead of Western influence that would potentially destabilize the USSR's firm grip on Eastern Europe.[13] Throughout the 1950s, the US generously supported the country with economic and military means, while Yugoslavia's authoritarian leader and long-term president, Josip Broz Tito (commonly known as Tito), succeeded in sustaining both Yugoslavia's independence from NATO and commitment to a socialist system—according to its own terms and the decentralized ideology of "socialist self-management."[14]

It is well known that the US fought the Cold War to no small degree with the soft power of cultural politics, seeking to disperse American values throughout Europe, and architecture played a prominent role in this endeavor. Art historian Serge Guilbaut and others have described how the mostly leftist social agenda of the prewar avant-gardes was refashioned and aesthetically neutralized into a program of abstraction that celebrated an unbridled freedom of artistic expression that conveniently aligned with the political tenets of Western liberal democracies.[15] In this context, it is interesting to note a heightened interest in Yugoslavia's artistic and architectural production on the part of Western cultural institutions, including The Museum of Modern Art. At the same time, Yugoslavia conversely sought to promote Western artistic production, of which the

Le Corbusier retrospective was a prominent first example. Demonstrating the country's new prominence on the world stage, the Yugoslav section won two awards at the Bienal do São Paulo. In reviewing the exhibition, *New York Times* critic Aline Louchheim explicitly referenced the political context in her assessment of the work of prize-winning Montenegrin painter Petar Lubarda (fig. 8):

> One country in particular realized how emphatically art can make a point. Yugoslavia, keenly aware that the Western World queries how philosophically deep the break with Russia is, shrewdly eschewed the over-life-size bronze of Tito … which dominated the Yugoslav pavilion in the Venice international show three years ago. Here all the eggs were put into the modern basket—the work of Petar Lubarda. It was perfectly clear that these semiabstract, expressionist works indicated a freedom of expression and a modern idiom, which … would not have been acceptable in the Soviet Union.[16]

Another *New York Times* article, published in 1957, specifically addressed the architecture of New Belgrade and again underscored the allegiance of Yugoslav cultural politics to a Western corollary. Its author, Harrison Salisbury, drew clear lines between what he saw there and what was favored in the USSR in terms of architecture:

> To a visitor from eastern Europe a stroll in Belgrade is like walking out of a grim barracks of ferro-concrete into a light and imaginative world of pastel buildings, "flying saucers," and Italianate patios. Nowhere is Yugoslavia's break with the drab monotony and tasteless gingerbread of "Socialist Realism" more dramatic than in the graceful office buildings, apartment houses and public structures that have replaced the rubble of World War II…. Simplicity, airiness, pastel pinks, blues, and yellows are the hallmark of the new Belgrade school, sharply contrasting not only with the mixed baroque of Stalinist style but with the heavy, dark constructions that were typical of the pre-war city.[17]

Recognizing how instrumental such statements were in securing international support, the Yugoslav government increasingly used modernist architecture and progressive cultural politics for its own aims. Croatian

Fig. 8   Petar Lubarda (1907–1974). *Guslar*. 1952. Oil on canvas, 64 3/16 × 58 in. (163 × 147.5 cm). Museum of Contemporary Art, Belgrade

Fig. 9   Yugoslav Pavilion at the XIII Milan Triennial. 1963. Vjenceslav Richter (1917–2002). Two black-and-white photographs of the model on panelboard, 43 5/16 × 39 3/8 in. (110 × 100 cm). Vjenceslav Richter Archive, Museum of Contemporary Art, Zagreb. Photo: Branko Balić

Fig. 10   Vjenceslav Richter (1917–2002). *Reliefometar* (Relief-meter). 1964. Frame holding adjustable aluminum rods, 43 5/16 × 43 5/16 × 4 3/4 in. (110 × 110 × 12 cm). Vjenceslav Richter and Nada Kareš Richter Collection, Zagreb

Fig. 8

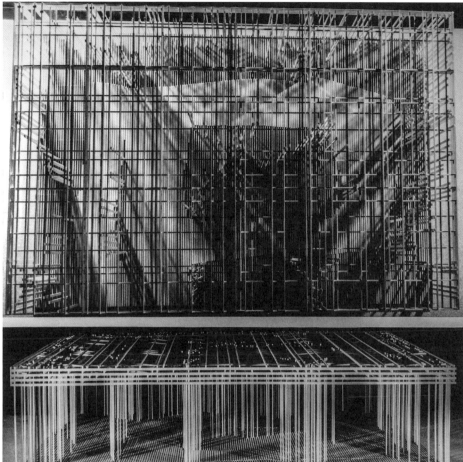

Fig. 9

Fig. 10

Fig. 11

Fig. 12

Fig. 13

architect Vjenceslav Richter's (1917–2002) split-level, transparent pavilion, which represented Yugoslavia at the 1958 World's Fair in Brussels (see Kats, pp. 132–35), underlined this strategy most effectively while also providing an opportunity to present the country's distinct system of socialist self-management to an international audience.[18] Both Richter's pavilion and a 1959 exhibition, *Contemporary Yugoslav Architecture*, which traveled to Oslo, Copenhagen, Stockholm, Warsaw, London, Glasgow, and Liverpool, received flattering reviews.[19] Richter was also responsible for the radically innovative design of the official national pavilions at the International Labor Exhibition in Turin, in 1961, and at the XIII Milan Triennial in 1963 (fig. 9). In subsequent years, he increasingly gravitated toward the visual arts,[20] becoming one of the leading international exponents of Yugoslav avant-garde art,[21] first as a co-founder and chief ideologue of the EXAT 51 (Experimental Studio 51) group and later through his membership in the Zagreb-based New Tendencies movement (fig. 10).[22]

Throughout the 1950s, the United States forcefully spread the blessings of Western culture—both high and low—in Yugoslavia. The Museum of Modern Art and its international program played an important part in this undertaking. At the invitation of the Yugoslav Committee on Foreign Cultural Relations and in cooperation with the American Embassy, the traveling exhibition *Modern Art in the United States* presented a selection of works from MoMA's permanent collection to audiences in various European cities, including Belgrade in the summer of 1956 (figs. 11 and 12).[23] The exhibition featured an architecture section with sixteen buildings. Shown at the local Fresco Museum, the checklist included works by, among others, Mies van der Rohe; Philip Johnson; Frank Lloyd Wright; Eero Saarinen; Skidmore, Owings, and Merrill; and Harrison & Abramovitz.[24] The exhibition catalogue was translated into Serbo-Croatian and included an essay by Henry-Russell Hitchcock and Arthur Drexler on postwar American architecture. (Hitchcock and Drexler adapted their text from the catalogue for the 1953 MoMA exhibition *Built in the USA: Post-War Architecture*, which was exhibited in its entirety in Yugoslavia in 1958–59.) In his foreword to the 1956 exhibition, the Museum's director, René d'Harnoncourt, underscored the significance of cultural initiatives in the context of Cold War politics:

The cooperation of Yugoslavia in the art activities of UNESCO, her participation in international exhibitions around the world, and the lively program of exhibitions brought from other countries through the enterprise of the Yugoslav Commission for Cultural Relations with Foreign Countries all testify to her conviction that artistic exchange is one of the most potent instruments for fostering understanding among the peoples of the world.[25]

With over 24,000 visitors in only one month, *Modern Art in the United States* was the most popular art exhibition in Belgrade since the war,[26] and was received very positively in the press. Bogdan Bogdanović, who would emerge as one of the defining figures of postwar Yugoslav architecture culture, reviewed the architectural section for *Politika*. Bogdanović described the show as mainly focused on functionalist architecture and lamented what he viewed as an underrepresentation of Frank Lloyd Wright, even though two of the sixteen projects were by him (the Johnson Wax Laboratory and Office and the V. C. Morris store) and another one by his son Lloyd (the Wayfarers' Chapel).[27] The 1956 exhibition also marked the end of the Corbusier fever that raged in Yugoslavia a few years earlier, only to be replaced by a preference for American postwar modernism and its attributes of transparency, slab buildings, and curtain walls.

MoMA's aforementioned exhibition *Built in the USA* arrived in its entirety in Yugoslavia in 1958 and toured, through the efforts of the Yugoslav Association of Architects, to Niš and Subotica in Serbia, Skopje in Macedonia, and Titograd in Montenegro. This dissemination of postwar American modernism to audiences in regional centers further sustained a shift in architectural aesthetics and a taste for "American facades." In 1963, *Visionary Architecture*—another highly popular, MoMA-produced architectural exhibition from 1960—traveled to Zagreb and Belgrade. As before, a catalogue was produced in Serbo-Croatian,[28] but the exhibition reviews were not unequivocally positive.[29]

The extent of American cultural investment in Yugoslavia is exemplified in the 1957 Zagreb Fair (the same year in which MoMA's *The Family of Man* photo exhibition was also displayed in Belgrade to enormous success [fig. 13]). The United States contributed a fully blown supermarket meant to promote Western consumerism—in pointed contrast to the USSR's concurrent display of industrial machinery. While the US pavilion's ultimate effect on Yugoslav socialism is hard to determine, the self-service supermarket introduced a new retail model into the country, which would quickly spread across Yugoslavia in the following years.[30] The confrontation between Soviet productivism and American consumerism anticipated the famous "Kitchen Debate" fought between US Vice President Richard Nixon and Soviet Premier Nikita Khrushchev on the occasion of the American National Exhibition in Moscow in 1959.

Perhaps the most striking symbol of the Western orientation of Yugoslav architecture and cultural politics was the Belgrade Museum of Contemporary Art (1959–65) by Ivan Antić (1923–2005) and Ivanka Raspopović (1930–2015) (see Kulić, pp. 137–39). While

Fig. 11   *Modern Art in the United States: Selections from the Collections of the Museum of Modern Art, New York*, Belgrade, Serbia, July 6–August 6, 1956. View of the exhibition's architecture section at Muzej Fresaka. IC/IP, I.A.517. MoMA Archives, NY

Fig. 12   Cover of the exhibition catalogue *Savremena umetnost u SAD. iz zbirki Museum of Modern Art New York* [Modern Art in the United States: Selections from the Collections of The Museum of Modern Art, New York]. Belgrade: Komisija za kulturne veze s inostranstvom FNRJ, 1956. IC/IP, I.A.517. MoMA Archives, NY

Fig. 13   *The Family of Man*, Belgrade, Serbia, January–February 1957. View of the queue outside the exhibition venue, Cvijeta Zuzorić Art Pavillion. IC/IP, I.A.517. MoMA Archives, NY

the museum's architecture—six interconnected volumes rotated by 45 degrees on an underlying structural grid—seems not to be directly informed by any contemporary Western museum buildings (although the diagonals as well as the brutalist handling of surface materials in the original conception may relate to Louis Kahn's contemporary work), the institution's organization was explicitly modeled after The Museum of Modern Art. The Belgrade museum was founded by the local artist, critic, and curator Miodrag Protić, who had spent two months in New York in 1962 on a Ford Foundation grant and was keenly interested in MoMA director Alfred Barr's vision of how to showcase contemporary art in a museum setting. Protić sought to translate MoMA's curatorial mission for the specific Yugoslav context. In a first for a Yugoslavian museum, his Museum of Contemporary Art instituted permanent departments for education, public programs, international exchange, and so forth, an organization clearly informed by what he had seen and learned in New York. The building's successful completion in 1965 did not go unnoticed. MoMA architecture curator Ludwig Glaeser considered including the building in his *Architecture of Museums* exhibition in 1968 but eventually decided against it.[31] The opening made it to the international news, however, with *Newsweek* magazine once again underscoring the significance of the achievement in terms of Cold War cultural politics, calling the structure "an ultramodern monument to artistic freedom" and even—rather imprecisely—"a modern and joyful tombstone to socialist realism."[32]

While such international recognition culminated in the late 1950s, Western and American interest quickly waned in the following years, and articles in the press became increasingly scant. The USSR's readjustment of cultural politics in the wake of de-Stalinization had severe consequences for Yugoslavia, which was faced with the loss of its special status and strategic role as a "wedge" into the Eastern Bloc. Looking for new geopolitical alliances, in 1956 Tito, together with the leaders of India and Egypt (Jahawarlal Nehru and Gamal Abdul Nasser, respectively) signed the Brioni Declaration, which is generally seen as the founding document of the Non-Aligned Movement (NAM) (fig. 14). The NAM, an alliance that sought to establish a third way between the two dominant opposing blocs of the Cold War, was formalized in the first conference of the Non-Aligned countries in Belgrade in 1961. The loose association of nations, predominantly from Africa and the Middle East (many of which had just recently won independence and embarked on decolonization processes), provided Yugoslavia with a powerful platform for securing economic independence from both East and West while also opening up a multitude of opportunities for exporting its modernist architecture and engineering expertise overseas.

ENTER THE UN: THE ARCHITECTURE OF INTERNATIONAL RELATIONS

Socialist Yugoslavia's engagement on the world stage is exemplified in the figure of Croatian-born architect Ernest Weissmann. Weissmann had worked in Le Corbusier's atelier in the late 1920s and later became a founding member of the Croatian CIAM group.[33] After

the end of World War II, he took a job in the newly founded UN Secretariat's Department of Economic and Social Affairs, a position that would prove pivotal in directing attention and resources to his homeland in the aftermath of the devastating earthquake that struck the Macedonian capital of Skopje in 1963. In the wake of the earthquake, the international community committed to an ambitious reconstruction initiative, with many countries in both East and West actively involved in the project. Weissmann became Chair of the International Consulting Team in charge of the reconstruction and in 1965 helped facilitate an international competition, jointly organized by the UN and the Yugoslav government, for the rebuilding of Skopje's city center (fig. 15).[34] Of the eight invited teams, the somewhat unlikely winner was the Japanese architect Kenzō Tange. The first major commission for a Japanese architect outside of Japan, Tange's Skopje project, if fully executed, would also have been one of the prime examples of Japanese Metabolism on an urban scale (see Deskov et al., pp. 72–77).[35] The list of Tange's collaborators in the Skopje competition reads like a who's who of Japanese architecture of the late twentieth century, including, among others, the young Arata Isozaki as well as Yoshio Taniguchi, who would, many years later, design MoMA's 2004 expansion project.

Even though Tange's winning scheme was only partially implemented, Skopje's reconstruction did produce a significant number of buildings and projects by major international architects from both sides of the Iron Curtain, making the city an "international architectural exhibition of sorts."[36] The Johann Heinrich Pestalozzi Elementary School, funded by the Swiss government and designed by Alfred Roth,[37] was a particularly successful project (fig. 16). And once again, the opportunity for young architects to study abroad introduced fundamental changes to the local profession. Instead of funding specific buildings, the US sponsored a program that allowed seven young Macedonian architects to pursue graduate studies in leading American universities, all of whom became involved in the reconstruction upon returning home. Among them, Georgi Konstantinovski (b. 1930) deserves to be singled out for both the number of buildings and quality of his work. Konstantinovski studied with Paul Rudolph at Yale University and then interned in the New York office of I. M. Pei. The Macedonian architect's buildings for Skopje clearly reference the aesthetic predilection for exposed concrete

Fig. 14   Leaders of the Non-Aligned Nations. 1960. Original caption: "New York, Sept. 30—Neutralist Leaders Meet—Leaders of five key neutralist nations met in New York last night at headquarters of Yugoslav delegation to the United Nations. From left are Indian Prime Minister Nehru, President Kwame Nkrumah of Ghana, President Gamal Abdel Nasser of United Arab Republic, President Sukarno of Indonesia and President Tito of Yugoslavia, host at the meeting." Associated Press

Fig. 15   "United Nations Technical Assistance Mission in Yugoslavia: Earthquake Reconstruction Programme Skopje, 1965–1968." United Nations Archives and Records. S-0175-2221-05

Fig. 16   Pestalozzi Elementary School, Skopje, Macedonia. 1965–69. Alfred Roth (1903–1998). Perspective drawing. Diazotype copy with colored pencil, 11 13/16 × 32 11/16 in. (30 × 83 cm). gta Archives, Institute for the History and Theory of Architecture, Zurich

Fig. 14

Fig. 15

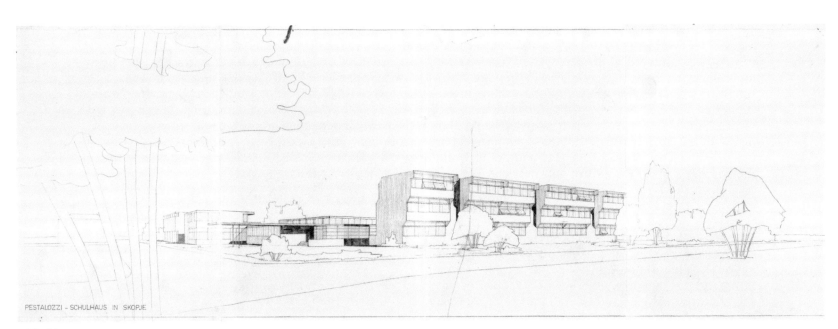

PESTALOZZI - SCHULHAUS IN SKOPJE

Fig. 16

of his American brutalist masters while at the same time adapting to the local construction technologies and particular spatial programs of a socialist society. This is most evident in Konstantinovski's celebrated Goce Delčev Student Dormitory (1969–77) as well as his building for the City Archive of Skopje, both of which feature the corrugated concrete facades first introduced into the vocabulary of modern architecture in Rudolph's Yale Art and Architecture Building. (Konstantinovski received his degree at Yale shortly after the building's completion in 1963.) (See Deskov et al., pp. 160–63.) The reconstruction of Skopje thus amounted to a unique synthesis of Japanese Metabolism with Western (mainly US) brutalism, which became a blueprint for subsequent architecture in all of Yugoslavia, as evidenced for example in the work of Belgrade-based Mihajlo Mitrović (b. 1922) or the Croatian Boris Krstulović (1932–2014) (see Skansi, pp. 64–71).

Studying and working in the West continued to be a defining feature in the education of many Yugoslav architects. Montenegrin Svetlana Kana Radević's (1937–2000) project for the Podgorica Hotel (1964–67) betrays a debt to the Structuralist thinking of Louis Kahn—with whom she would study in the early 1970s—and achieves a haptic quality on the facade through the application of local pebbles (see Portfolio, xxxv). It is interesting to note that Kana Radević would work for Kishō Kurokawa for some time after graduating from the University of Pennsylvania, underscoring the far-reaching global connections of Yugoslav architecture culture. Mimoza Nestorova-Tomić (b. 1929), another prominent female figure in Yugoslav architecture and the designer of the Museum of Macedonia in Skopje (1970), had traveled extensively throughout Western Europe in the early 1960s before receiving a stipend to study at the University of California, Berkeley, in 1964 (see Issaias and Kats, pp. 96–103).[38] Marta (1920–2009) and France Ivanšek (1922–2007), the architects of the Murgle neighborhood of individual family houses in Ljubljana (1965–80), lived in Sweden for five years from 1954 to 1959, where they worked in various architectural offices.[39] The Murgle settlement is clearly informed by the Scandinavian "New Empiricism" of the 1950s and proposed a "humanized" version of modernism through detailing and the use of "warm" materials with haptic qualities (fig. 17). The model of the Scandinavian welfare states proved particularly attractive from a Yugoslav point of view and the country's quest for a third way between Western capitalism and Eastern communism.

If Skopje served as an open-air classroom for a younger generation of Yugoslav architects, the UN's involvement equally set an example for further international collaboration. Following the Skopje competition, the UN, again in tandem with local authorities, was directly involved in the elaboration of regional development plans for the Adriatic coast, laying the groundwork for the creation of an extensive tourism infrastructure along the coast and rapidly accelerating the country's transition from a formerly agrarian to a developed service economy catering to international audiences (see Mrduljaš, pp. 78–83). Among the most successful resulting projects was the Haludovo Hotel (1969–72) on the Croatian island of Krk (see Portfolio

XXI and XXII). Designed by Boris Magaš (1920–2013), the hotel was partly financed by Bob Guccione, then editor and publisher of *Penthouse* magazine, who successfully marketed the resort to American and Western European audiences. Haludovo was remarkable in pairing Magaš's interest in modular systems with the desire to create a playful, exuberant, and immersive vacation environment for the (sophisticated) mass market.[40]

EXPORT ARCHITECTURE

Yugoslav architecture culture was not just the "recipient" of ideas generated abroad. As previously mentioned, through its leading role in the Non-Aligned Movement and the ensuing economic contacts to many countries in Africa and the Middle East, in particular, also became a major agent in disseminating modern architecture to newly independent states in the wake of postcolonialism. Given Yugoslavia's relatively advanced standards in construction and engineering, the architecture and building sectors counted among the country's most successful exports, providing a steady stream of revenue and foreign currency back to the domestic economy.

Though the NAM and the various economic, political, social, and cultural networks and exchanges it generated may be seen as an early instance of contemporary globalization, there were other consequential processes afoot. The NAM's foundation should equally be considered within, and as a direct consequence of, the decolonization of Africa, which reached its peak in 1960, the year in which seventeen nations declared their independence. This situation not only created the need for new alliances but also an enormous opportunity for economic investment. Yugoslavia would appear to be something of an exotic outlier in this group of newly independent nations. However, as Tito declared in a visit to Guinea in 1961 (one of many journeys that the Yugoslav leader undertook in this period with the aim to bond politically and facilitate economic investment), his country could be seen as "an example of how a country, enslaved and underdeveloped in the past, is able to rise to such a level Yugoslavia has attained nowadays."[41] In comparing Yugoslavia's independence after World War I to the postcolonial situation, Tito suggested that the newly independent nations could learn historically from his country's experience and further advocated contemporary socialist Yugoslavia as a model for these countries to emulate.

Fig. 17   Murgle estate, Ljubljana, Slovenia. 1965–80. Marta (née Ravnikar) Ivanšek (1920–2009) and France Ivanšek (1922–2007). View from the garden. France and Marta Ivanšek Foundation

Fig. 18   Milica Šterić (1914–1998) at work. c. 1977. Energoprojekt Archive

Fig. 19   Ministry Complex, Kano, Nigeria. 1978. Milica Šterić (1914–1998) and Zoran Bojović (1936–2018) for Energoprojekt (est. 1951). Detail view. c. 1978. Personal archive of Zoran Bojović

Fig. 20   Experimental Housing Block, Luanda, Angola. 1978. Lead architect: Ivan Petrović (1932–2000), for the IMS Institute of Belgrade. Elevation. 1:100. Diazotype, 7 × 11 5/8 in. (18 × 29.5 cm). Personal archive of Ivan Petrović

23

Fig. 17

Fig. 18

Fig. 19

Fig. 20

In this context, is his hardly coincidental that the first summit of NAM leaders was held in Belgrade in 1961. New Belgrade, then the largest active construction site in Europe, was effectively used as an advertisement for the local construction sector.[42] The message was received, and in subsequent years several Yugoslav companies were hired to execute ambitious infrastructure projects, including dams, railways, and roads across Africa, with the Belgrade-based firm of Energoprojekt being the most prominent example.[43] Nor was the scope of action limited to infrastructure. Under the leadership of Milica Šterić (1914–1998), Energoprojekt's Department for Architecture and Urbanism (founded in 1971) successfully established itself in the design of large-scale projects (figs. 18 and 19). (Šterić, like so many of her colleagues, had studied abroad for some time, having spent six months on a stipend from the Dutch government in the office of Van den Broek and Bakema in 1957).[44] Energoprojekt's projects for Nigeria are particularly noteworthy. The master plan for seven cities in the state of Kano exported lessons from the UNESCO-sponsored Development Plan of the South Adriatic (where the Greek architect Constantinos A. Doxiadis had served as an adviser) to Western Africa, adapting the methodology to the local conditions through a careful analysis of traditional building techniques in vernacular mud architecture.[45] The Kano master plan in turn served as a blueprint for the ambitious Lagos Trade Fair complex, whose layout was directly influenced by traditional settlement typologies in Kano (fig. 1; see also Stanek, pp. 84–89). Similar to the contemporary globalized building industry, cheap labor was imported from South Asian NAM member states such as Pakistan and Bangladesh.[46]

Meanwhile, Yugoslav architectural exports were by no means limited to Western Africa. After the success of the Lagos Trade Fair, Energoprojekt was hired for the Al Khulafa street development project in Baghdad in anticipation of the NAM summit in the Iraqi capital in 1982. (The summit never materialized due to the outbreak of the first Iran-Iraq War.) In the same city, Edvard Ravnikar's design for the Babylon Hotel was realized after the Iraqi government bought the scheme, which had originally been developed in the early 1970s for the Adriatic coast.[47] Prefabricated building systems proved another export success: In 1957, the engineer Branko Žeželj introduced a prestressed skeletal system of precast columns and slabs, which he continued to develop at the Serbian Institute for the Testing of Materials (IMS Institute) (fig. 20). The IMS Žeželj system was not only widely used across Yugoslavia but also applied in more than 150,000 apartment units in places such as Italy, Hungary, Cuba, Angola, and the Philippines,[48] further underscoring the exceptional presence of Yugoslavian architectural innovation and production on a world stage.

The aforementioned relationships with Western architectural discourse are only one facet of the agency of Yugoslav architecture in an international network of exchange, one that has so far been largely overlooked and whose significance for a more nuanced understanding of the cultural dynamics in the Cold War has only recently started to surface. A more sustained investigation than is possible in this short essay would have to address the flows of information, knowledge, and ideas between non-aligned Yugoslavia and the Soviet bloc. A comparative analysis between Yugoslav internationalism in architecture and that of other Eastern European countries would also appear to be an illuminating undertaking. However, the specific global networks briefly highlighted here clearly point to the exceptionalism of Yugoslav architecture culture. The density and diversity of these networks of exchange was only possible under the unique geopolitical conditions Yugoslavia found itself in during the Cold War. Indeed, history tells us that this model was not sustainable beyond the limits of a bifurcated world order. But in its time, it contributed to a proliferation of architectural ideas whose contribution to the world history of modern architecture we are only now beginning to understand.

I am indebted to Vladimir Kulić, whose scholarship has greatly contributed to this essay, as have countless conversations over the years in preparation of the exhibition that this catalogue accompanies. My thanks go also to the various members of our Curatorial Advisory Board, whose contributions have greatly enhanced my understanding of specific aspects of Yugoslav architecture culture. Several curatorial and research assistants at The Museum of Modern Art have helped gather information that went into the present essay. I am particularly indebted to Anna Kats, Theodossis Issaias, Matthew Worsnick, and Joana Valsassina Heitor for their assistance.

1   See Maria Todorova, *Imagining the Balkans,* rev. ed. (New York: Oxford University Press, 2009).
2   Vladimir Kulić, "Land of the In-Between: Modern Architecture and the State in Socialist Yugoslavia, 1945–65" (Ph.D. diss., University of Texas at Austin 2009), 195–96.
3   For a detailed discussion of Le Corbusier's impact on the Ljubljana school of architecture, see Bogo Zupančič, "Plečnik's Students in Le Corbusier's Studio," in *Unfinished Modernisations Between Utopia and Pragmatism: Architecture and Urban Planning in the Former Yugoslavia and the Successor States,* ed. Maroje Mrduljaš and Vladimir Kulić (Zagreb: Croatian Architects' Association, 2012), 391–94; for the impact on Croatian architecture, see Tamara Bjažić Klarin, "Ernest Weissmann and Juraj Neidhardt," in Mdruljaš and Kulić, *Unfinished Modernisations,* 395–98.
4   Dijana Alić, "Historical Materialism: The Fabric of Communist Yugoslavia's Architectural Aspirations," in *Materiality and Architecture,* ed. Sandra Karina Löschke (London: Routledge, 2016), 100–1.
5   Jelica Karlić Kapetanović, *Juraj Neidhardt. Život i djelo* (Sarajevo: Veselin Masleša, 1990), 99.

6   Jean-François Lejeune and Michelangelo Sabatino, eds., *Modern Architecture and the Mediterranean: Vernacular Dialogues and Contested Identities* (London: Routledge, 2010).

7   A selection of the most important of Ravnikar's writings has been translated and published in Aleš Vodopivec and Rok Žnidaršič, eds., *Edvard Ravnikar: Architect and Teacher* (Vienna: Springer, 2010).

8   On Kampor, see William J.R.Curtis, "Abstraction and Representation: The Memorial Complex at Kampor, on the Island of Rab (1952–53) by Edvard Ravnikar," in Vodopivec and Žnidaršič, *Edvard Ravnikar*, 33–50; on the relationship of Ravnikar and Plečnik, see also Aleš Vodopivec, "Ljubljana: Jože Plečnik und Edvard Ravnikar," in *Die Architektur, die Tradition und der Ort: Regionalismen in der europäischen Stadt*, ed. Vittorio Magnago Lampugnani (Stuttgart: Deutsche Verlags-Anstalt, 2000), 329–59.

9   Vodopivec, "Ljublijana," 346 and passim.

10 Kulić, "Land of the In-Between," 199.

11 Kulić, ibid., 197.

12 On this and the relationship of Croatian archtitects to CIAM in general, see Tamara Bjažić Klarin, "CIAM Networking—International Congress of Modern Architecture and Croatian Architecture in the 1950," *Život Umjenosti: Magazine for Contemporary Visual Arts* 99, no.2 (2016): 40–57.

13 On the "wedge strategy," see Lorraine M.Lees, *Keeping Tito Afloat: The United States, Yugoslavia, and the Cold War* (University Park: Pennsylvania State University Press, 1997). For a detailed discussion of the impact on Cold War politics on Yugoslav architecture culture in the 1950s, see Kulić, "Land of the In-Between," 213ff.

14 For a detailed discussion of self-managment, see Maroje Mrduljaš's essay in this volume "Architecture for a Self-Managing Socialism," pp.41–55.

15 Serge Guilbaut, *How New York Stole the Idea of Modern Art: Abstract Expressionism, Freedom, and the Cold War,* trans. Arthur Goldhammer (Chicago: University of Chicago Press, 1983).

16 Aline B.Louchheim, "Cultural Diplomacy: An Art We Neglect," *New York Times*, January 3, 1954, SM16.

17 Harrison E.Salisbury, "Building Pattern Set by Belgrade," *New York Times*, August 22, 1957, 8.

18 On the pavilion see Vladimir Kulić, "An Avant-Garde Architecture for an Avant-Garde Socialism: Yugoslavia at Expo 58," *Journal of Contemporary History* 47, no.1 (2012): 161–84.

19 Kulić, "Land of the In-Between," 227.

20 For a preliminary survey of Richter's artwork, see Marijan Susovski, ed., *Zbirka Richter* (Zagreb: Museum of Contemporary Art, 2003).

21 For a recent account of the New Tendencies movement, see Armin Medosch, *New Tendencies: Art at the Threshold of the Information Revolution (1961–1978).* (Cambridge, Mass.: MIT Press, 2016).

22 In the United States, Richter was the subject of a 1968 solo show at Staempfli Gallery in New York City; his work was published in exhibition catalogues by the Albright-Knox Art Gallery in Buffalo, New York, and by the Los Angeles County Museum of Art, though the latter institution did not show his work for technical reasons.

23 For the press release of this exhibition see https://www.moma.org/momaorg/shared/pdfs/docs/press_archives/2100/releases/MOMA_1956_0081_71.pdf?2010.

24 Memo from Arthur Drexler, Curator and Director of the Department of Architecture and Design, to Porter McCray, Director of the International Program, The Museum of Modern Art, January 11, 1955. International Council and International Program Records, I.A.544. The Museum of Modern Art Archives, New York.

25 René d'Harnoncourt, "Text of Introduction to Catalogue." IC/IP, I.A.518. MoMA Archives, New York.

26 Letter from Robert G.Hooker, Jr., Counsellor of Embassy, to William A.M.Burden, President, The Museum of Modern Art, October 16, 1956. IC/IP, I.A.517. MoMA Archives, New York.

27 Bogdan Bogdanović, "The exhibit 'Modern Art in the United States': Modern Architecture," *Politika*, July 22, 1956, 11. IC/IP, I.A.516. MoMA Archives, New York.

28 *Vizionarna arhitektura,* exh. cat. (Zagreb: Museum of Decorative Arts, 1963). IC/IP, I.A.1062. MoMA Archives, New York.

29 The most important reviews were translated into English for MoMA; see IC/IP, I.A.1062. MoMA Archives, New York.

30 Dennison Rusinow, "The Supermarket Revolution," in *Yugoslavia: Oblique Insights and Observations* (Pittsburgh: University of Pittsburgh Press, 2008), 26–42; see also Vladimir Kulić, Maroje Mrduljaš, and Wolfgang Thaler, *Modernism In-Between: The Mediatory Architectures of Socialist Yugoslavia* (Berlin: Jovis 2012), 173–74.

31 The Museum of the History of Bosnia and Herzegovina in Sarajevo by Boris Magaš and Edo Šmidihen was under consideration as well but was ultimately not included.

32 "Slavs Without Marx," *Newsweek*, February 7, 1966, 40.

33 See Tamara Bjažić Klarin, *Ernest Weissmann: Socially Engaged Architecture, 1926–1939* (English/Croatian) (Zagreb: Croatian Academy of Sciences and Arts, 2015).

34 For a detailed account, see Deskov et al. "The Reconstruction of Skopje," pp.72–77 in this volume. For the official UN report see Derek Senior, *Skopje Resurgent: The Story of a United Nations Special Fund Town Planning Project* (New York: United Nations, 1970).

35 For a discussion of Skopje's reconstruction within the international context in the Cold War see Ines Tolić, *Dopo il terremoto: La politica della recostruzione negli anni della Guerra Fredda a Skopje* [After the Earthquake: The Politics of Reconstruction During the Cold War Years in Skopje] (Venice: Edizioni Diabisis, 2011); Kulić, Mrduljaš, and Thaler, *Modernism In-Between*, 44–46; Mirjana Lozanovska, "Kenzo Tange's Forgotten Master Plan for the Reconstruction of Skopje," *Fabrications* 22, no.2 (2012): 140–63; Lozanovska, "Brutalism, Metabolism and its American Parallel: Encounters in Skopje and in the Architecture of Georgi Konstantinovski," *Fabrications* 25, no.2 (2015): 153–75; and Ines Tolić, "Ernest Weissmann's 'World City': The Reconstruction of Skopje within the Cold War Context," *Southeastern Europe* 41 (2017): 171–99.

36 Kulić, Mrduljaš, and Thaler, *Modernism In-Between*, 45.

37 "Schulhaus 'Heinrich Pestalozzi' Skopje, Jugoslawien," *Werk* 58, no.8 (1971): 524–26.

38 Mirjana Lozanovska, "Perfoming Equality: The Exceptional Story of Mimoza Nestorova-Tomić in the Post-1963 Earthquake Reconstruction of Skopje," in *Ideological Equals: Women Architects in Socialist Europe, 1945–1989*, ed. Mary Pepchinski and Mariann Simon (London: Routledge, 2017), 123–38.

39 Martina Malešič, "Murgle Housing Estate," in Mrduljaš and Kulić, *Unfinished Modernisations*, 338–51.

40 For a detailed history of Adriatic tourism development, see Maroje Mrduljaš, "Building the Affordable Arcadia: Tourism Development on the Croatian Adriatic Coast Under State Socialism," in *Holiday After the Fall: Seaside Architecture and Urbanism in Bulgaria and Croatia*, ed. Elke Beyer, Anke Hagemann, and Michael Zinganel (Berlin: Jovis, 2013), 171–207.

41 Quoted in Dubravka Sekulić, "Energoprojekt in Nigeria: Yugoslav Construction Companies in the Developing World," *Southeastern Europe* 41 (2017): 200–29, 207.

42 Dubravka Sekulić, "Constructing the Non-Aligned Modernity," in Andrej Dolinka, Katarina Krstić, and Sekulić, eds., *Tri tačke oslonca / Three Points of Support: Zoran Bojović*, exh. cat. (Belgrade: Museum of Contemporary Art, 2013), 164–65.

43 Sekulić, "Energoprojekt in Nigeria."

44 Ibid., 212.

45 Sekulić, "Constructing the Non-Aligned Modernity," 170–75.

46 Ibid., 177.

47 On the history of the project, see Vladimir Kulić, "Building the Non-Aligned Babel: Babylon Hotel in Baghdad and Mobile Design in the Global Cold War," in "Social Networks," special issue, *ABE Journal: Architecture Beyond Europe*, no.6, ed. Łukasz Stanek (December 30, 2014).

48 Kulić, Mrduljaš and Thaler, *Modernism In-Between*, 176.

Fig. 1

BUILDING BROTHERHOOD AND UNITY:

ARCHITECTURE AND FEDERALISM IN SOCIALIST YUGOSLAVIA

Vladimir Kulić

The sprawling modernist structure at the center of New Belgrade is still colloquially known by the acronym SIV (*Savezno izvršno veće*—Federal Executive Council), even though the federation that was once governed from it no longer exists. As the administrative heart of socialist Yugoslavia, the enormous, H-shaped complex also physically embodied the political imaginary that held the country together, most poignantly in a sequence of ceremonial rooms on the second floor of the building's central pavilion. Suspended on *pilotis* above the main entrance, the opulent space is organized around a top-lit hall adorned with a massive mosaic commemorating the 1943 Battle of the Sutjeska, one of the legendary events of the People's Liberation War of Yugoslavia. Surrounding the hall is an enfilade of six "salons" dedicated to the former Yugoslavia's constituent republics—Bosnia and Herzegovina, Croatia, Macedonia, Montenegro, Serbia (with its two autonomous provinces, Vojvodina and Kosovo), and Slovenia—each designed by an architect from the respective republic to communicate an imagined sense of ethno-national identity. From vernacular to neo-avant-garde, the design of these spaces conjures an image of a diverse mosaic of cultures, which reaches a triumphant synthesis under the gigantic crystal chandelier of the final room—the vast salon of Yugoslavia. Lavishly appointed with an abundance of artworks of diverse styles as well as custom-designed modernist furniture, rugs, and wall treatments, the entire sequence of rooms exemplifies an impressive realization of the postwar ideal of the synthesis of the arts conceived to celebrate a socialist federation (figs. 1–4).[1]

Taken together, these spaces read as an apt metaphor for the Yugoslav socialist state: a modern container for the collection of distinct traditional ethnicities, brought together by their common struggle for liberation from fascism, class oppression, and underdevelopment, an idea succinctly expressed through the slogan "brotherhood and unity." Not only was the SIV building designed to convey this message, it was itself a product of trans-federal collaboration that assembled architects, artists, builders, artisans, and materials from different parts of the country.[2] Conceived as the focal point of New Belgrade, the new federal capital erected after World War II, even its siting carried a special symbolism. The capital that arose out of former marshlands at the confluence of the country's two largest rivers, the Danube and the Sava, emphatically defied the area's history as a no-man's-land between foreign empires that for centuries had divided native populations.[3]

Indeed, the history of fluctuating geopolitical divisions that cut through the region stretched back to antiquity: between the Eastern and Western Roman Empires, between Eastern and Western Christianity, between the Ottomans and the Habsburgs, and between Christianity and Islam. The result was a dizzying mosaic of

Fig. 1   New Belgrade in the mid-1960s. In the foreground: Federal Executive Council Building (SIV–*Savezno izvršno veće*), Belgrade, Serbia. 1947–50, 1954–62. Vladimir Potočnjak (1904–1952), Antun Ulrich (1902–1996), Zlatko Neumann (1900–1969), and Dragica Perak (1917–1998) (original design); Mihailo Janković (1911–1976) (redesign). Aerial view. Private archive of Mihailo Janković

Fig. 2

Fig. 3

Fig. 4

dialects, ethnicities, and religions, as well as of varied architectural and artistic traditions brought together into close physical proximity, if not always in direct contact.[4] Consequently, socialist Yugoslavia's leading intellectuals frequently invoked the trope of a "kaleidoscope of cultures," which became both a mode of self-perception and of self-representation to foreign audiences.[5] The ideology of brotherhood and unity sought to reconcile this kaleidoscopic image with the universalizing juggernaut of socialist modernization. The federation's six republics roughly corresponded to the six constituent nations, as opposed to only three acknowledged in the prewar state, and they became the bearers of the modern architectural profession: its organizations, educational institutions, etc.[6] The traditional patchwork of vernacular architectures was thus translated into modern terms to produce a somewhat less granular picture, in which the architectural cultures corresponded with the newly constituted republics. Nevertheless, diversity persisted, compressing a great deal of architectural phenomena—varied regionalisms, the particular articulations of certain programs, or idiosyncratic personal poetics—into a small geographical space the size of the state of Oregon. It is this complex interaction between the various particularisms and the federalist mechanisms of unity that held the country together for almost half a century—a dialectic that also determined the production of architecture.

THE IDEOLOGY OF
BROTHERHOOD AND UNITY

The origins of Yugoslavia lie in the wave of national awakening movements of the eighteenth and nineteenth centuries, when the fine-grained mosaic of cultures, which coexisted for centuries under the rule of distant imperial centers, began coalescing into modern nations. Transcending the persistent borderland condition was not easy: the process often fed the malevolent "narcissism of small differences," but it also produced a willingness to overcome the inherited divisions, manifest through the project of Yugoslavism, which sought to unite South Slavs as fundamentally kindred peoples. The project was finally realized in 1918: propelled into existence by the principle of self-determination advanced by US President Woodrow Wilson, the first Yugoslav state arose from the ashes of the Habsburg and Ottoman Empires.[7] The new state sought to emulate the example of powerful European nation-states by blending the disparate collection of ethnic groups

into a unitary nation.[8] The experiment, however, ended disastrously: as soon as the country was partitioned by the Axis in 1941, the internal tensions erupted into a bloody interethnic conflict. Communist-led partisans were the only force that fought against the occupation consistently and across ethnic lines; their success at forming a massive army by the end of the war secured their domination in the postwar state.

Socialist Yugoslavia was imagined in direct opposition to its predecessor. Rather than forging a single unitary nation, the postwar state was organized as a federation of distinct nations brought together by the ideology of brotherhood and unity. The dynamic between the particular and the common was complex and ever-changing. At the normative level, the federal state underwent persistent decentralization, increasingly shifting its prerogatives to the elites of the six constituent republics and, after the new constitution of 1974, also to Serbia's two autonomous provinces, Kosovo and Vojvodina.[9] At the same time, a certain homogenization of experience occurred, as the majority of Yugoslav citizens for the first time came to enjoy a similarly modern way of life, share a common popular culture, and meet their peers from other parts of the country through regular travel—all of which amounted to far more powerful factors for cohesion than the officially sanctioned ideological proclamations and rituals. However, by the late 1980s the balance between centrifugal and centripetal forces had spun out of control under the combined pressure of rising nationalist particularisms and the economic crisis. Plentiful, but insufficiently strong to prevent the dissolution of the common state, the bonds and networks forged over the preceding decades made the eventual collapse all the more painful.

The dialectic of diversity and unity very much conditioned the production of architecture. On the one hand, architects were tasked with constructing the national prerogatives of the individual republics, most importantly, their capitals and the attendant infrastructures of state power and culture, as well as the institutions of the architectural profession. These undertakings resulted in numerous attempts to explore and articulate the architectural identities of individual regions while also producing more or less recognizable architectural cultures equipped with their own professional organizations, schools, periodicals, leading figures, and so on. On the other hand, architects across the country shared much in their daily practice: not only similar socioeconomic conditions, but also a common federal union of architectural associations as well as the occasional opportunities to build outside of their native republic. And certain architectural programs, such as war memorials and tourism facilities, served as de facto generators of unity as well; distributed all over the country's territory, they motivated and enabled mobility, thus allowing Yugoslavs to get to know each other and to build patriotism through the shared experience of travel.

As a result, architects, architectural historians, and journalists all repeatedly engaged the question of "Yugoslav architecture,"[10] equally doubting or affirming whether there was something distinctly Yugoslav about architecture in Yugoslavia.[11] Nevertheless, common to all such discussions was the view that the very concept of Yugoslav architecture served as an umbrella

Fig. 2   Salon of the Socialist Republic of Bosnia and Herzegovina inside the Federal Executive Council Building (SIV–*Savezno izvršno veće*), Belgrade, Serbia. 1962. Zlatko Ugljen (b. 1929). Photograph: Vesna Pavlović from *Collection/Kolekcija* series (2003–2005)

Fig. 3   Salon of the Socialist Republic of Montenegro inside the Federal Executive Council Building (SIV–*Savezno izvršno veće*), Belgrade, Serbia. 1962. Vojislav Đokić (1902–1984). Photograph: Vesna Pavlović from *Collection/Kolekcija* series (2003–2005)

Fig. 4   Salon of the Socialist Republic of Croatia inside the Federal Executive Council Building (SIV–*Savezno izvršno veće*), Belgrade, Serbia. 1962. Vjenceslav Richter (1917–2002). Photograph: Vesna Pavlović from *Collection/Kolekcija* series (2003–2005)

for the collection of distinct republican architectures, just as the SIV building contained the six republican salons. With the increasing decentralization, such a view eventually evolved into a rather exclusionary reification of the republican borders. Exemplary in this sense was the 1985 volume *Architecture of the Twentieth Century,* published in the series indicatively titled *Art on the Soil of Yugoslavia,* as if to suggest that Yugoslavia was nothing more than a territorial designation, devoid of any shared identity.[12] With essays focused on each of the six republics, the book not only ignored the fine grain of the country's complex cultural composition (for example, by completely omitting any mention of Serbia's two autonomous provinces), it also made no effort whatsoever at discussing any commonalities, despite the fact that the entire book series itself was a collaborative project of three publishing houses from Serbia, Croatia, and Bosnia and Herzegovina. In contrast, the monumental 1991 chronicle *The Architecture of Yugoslavia, 1945–1990,* written by Bosnian architect Ivan Štraus (b. 1928), was a far more nuanced, sincere effort to treat the country as a whole, even if it paid its dues to individual republican scenes.[13] Published on the very eve of the war, however, the book had no time to perform its integrative role, ultimately serving instead as an appropriate coda for the disappearing country.

INFRASTRUCTURES OF FEDERALISM

Despite debate, a "Yugoslav architecture" most certainly existed, if not as a set of immediately recognizable features, then as an institution. Before there could be modern architecture, though, there had to be professional architects, but in some parts of the country there were very few of them at the end of World War II. Large cities, especially Belgrade, Zagreb, and Ljubljana, which were also the seats of the three existing schools of architecture, had already developed vibrant architectural scenes. The same, however, was not the case in the country's southeast, where the establishment of the architectural profession was directly supported by federalism. In 1945, the entire republic of Macedonia had a minuscule number of active educated architects, especially outside of Skopje; the situation was not much better in Montenegro or Bosnia and Herzegovina.[14] In order to facilitate the intended rapid modernization— similarly to the interwar period—the state dispatched professionals from the more developed to the less developed parts of the country. However, this time around, it also sought to build up local cadre by founding new institutions of higher education in the less-developed regions. Thus, in accordance with Skopje's status as the capital of the newly recognized Macedonian nation (which had been denied nationhood in the interwar kingdom), the School of Architecture was founded there in 1949, the same year as the School of Architecture in Sarajevo, the capital of Bosnia and Herzegovina. The key figure in Skopje was Croatian architect Antun Ulrich (1902–1996) (one of the original designers of the SIV building), who taught at the school for several years alongside other professors from Zagreb and Belgrade. The last architecture school created during the socialist period was founded in Pristina in 1978. By that time Kosovo was already home to numerous native architects who had been educated in other academic centers.

In some parts of the country, therefore, the very existence of the architectural profession was a result of federalist policies.

Although gathered into separate republican associations, professionals all belonged to a federal umbrella organization, which eventually assumed the name the Union of Architects of Yugoslavia. It organized congresses, symposia, and exhibitions, as well as running two consecutive architectural journals with explicitly federal ambitions: *Arhitektura,* first published in Zagreb in 1947, and *Arhitektura Urbanizam,* initiated in Belgrade in 1960.[15] However, the union's most important integrative function was arguably the organization of federal competitions, which were the chief vehicle for the mobility of architectural thinking and design across the republican borders. Even though juries sometimes conspired to favor local entries, some of the most iconic architectural achievements were the results of federal competitions won by architects from another republic. Standouts include the Macedonian Opera and Ballet in Skopje (see Deskov et al., pp. 152–55; Portfolio, XVII), the Stoteks Department Store in Novi Sad (fig. 5), and urban plans for Split 3 (see Skansi, p. 156–59), designed by Slovenian architects; the Aeronautical Museum in Belgrade (see Portfolio, VII) and the multipurpose sports centers in Pristina (fig. 6), Novi Sad, and Split, all designed by Bosnian architects; the Museum of the People's Revolution in Sarajevo, designed by Croatian architects (see Portfolio, XX; fig. 7); and the central monument and the Battle of the Sutjeska Memorial Center at Tjentište, designed by an artist and an architect from Serbia (see Portfolio, XVIII and XXXI). However, such mobility was still largely directed from the north to the south and from the west to the east, reflecting as well as reinforcing the disparities in economic and professional development across the federation.

In practice, uniting Yugoslavia in the wake of World War II had to occur both on a symbolic level and in very physical terms. On the one hand, in addition to being an occupation by Axis powers, the war was also a devastating civil conflict that pitched native populations against each other on ethnic and ideological grounds. On the other hand, Yugoslavia had almost no modern transport infrastructure, which, combined with a complicated topography, greatly impeded the ambitious modernization plans. Ethnic reconciliation and physical development thus went hand in hand, as demonstrated by one of the first large-scale postwar projects, the construction of the country's first modern road. Named the Highway of Brotherhood and Unity,

Fig. 5   Stoteks Department Store, Novi Sad, Serbia. 1968–72. Milan Mihelič (b. 1925). Southern elevation. 1:50. Ink and color marker on tracing paper, 29½ × 93⁵⁄₁₆ in. (75 × 237 cm). Personal archive of Milan Mihelič

Fig. 6   Boro and Ramiz Palace of Youth and Sport, Pristina, Kosovo. 1974–77. Živorad Janković (1924–1990) and Halid Muhasilović (b. 1934). View from the south. 2009. Photograph: Wolfgang Thaler

Fig. 7   Museum of People's Revolution, Sarajevo, Bosnia and Herzegovina. 1958–62. Boris Magaš (1930–2013), Edo Šmidihen (1930–2015), and Radovan Horvat (d. 2016). Perspective drawing. 1958. Ink on vellum, 20⅞ × 22¹³⁄₁₆ in. (53 × 58 cm). Boris Magaš Archive, Croatian Academy of Sciences and Arts

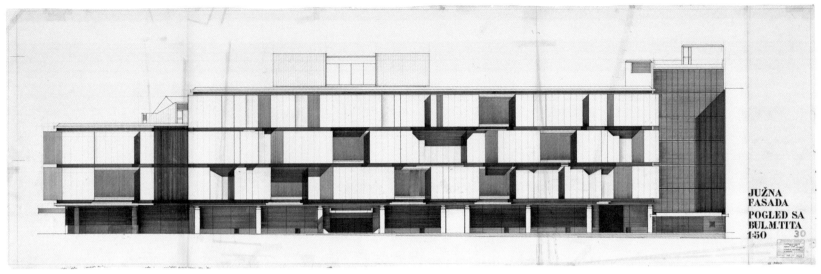

Fig. 5

Fig. 6

Fig. 7

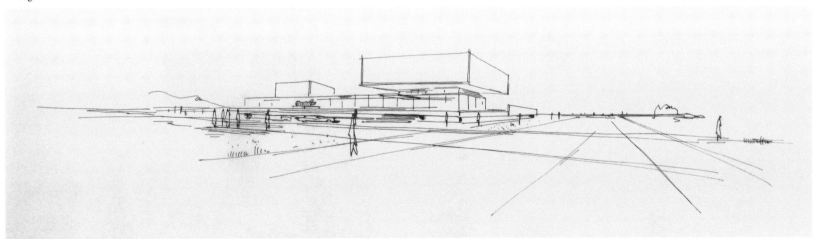

Fig. 8

Fig. 9

it connected Belgrade and Zagreb, the capitals of Serbs and Croats, the two most populous ethnicities, who had engaged in intense interethnic strife during the war. The project eventually extended further to Macedonia and Slovenia, connecting four of the six Yugoslav republics to become the country's main "spine" and facilitating not only interior mobility but also allowing the arrival of foreign tourists and connecting Central Europe with Greece and Turkey. A useful piece of physical infrastructure, the highway demonstrated unity in practice, as young Yugoslavs from all over the country took part in volunteer brigades that contributed to its construction, joined by idealistic young foreigners from the West and the East. The project's symbolic significance was such that it inspired two simultaneous exhibitions in Zagreb and Belgrade in 1950 to commemorate and publicize the completion of the first phase (figs. 8 and 9). Designed by Zagreb architects Vjenceslav Richter (1917–2002) and Zvonimir Radić (1921–1985) and painters Aleksandar Srnec (1924–2010) and Ivan Picelj (1924–2011), the exhibitions signaled the ascendance of an avant-garde visual language, which the group's members would successfully employ to represent Yugoslavia at the most important international shows, including Expo 58 in Brussels (see Kats, pp. 132–35).

In the early postwar years, mass volunteer labor was a matter of practical necessity in a war-ravaged country sorely lacking an educated cadre and modern technology. So-called youth labor campaigns (*omladinske radne akcije*) were not only a means to perform the necessary work; they also offered opportunities for ideological edification and upward social mobility, as many participants acquired various kinds of training on the construction sites, from basic literacy to professional skills. There was a great deal of genuine enthusiasm in this early period, as millions of young brigadiers built new roads, railway lines, dams, irrigation canals, factories, and cities. One of the largest early sites of volunteer labor was New Belgrade, where in the late 1940s bare-handed youths from all over the country filled in the marshlands with sand to consolidate the unstable terrain for the new federal capital. Another example was the Adriatic Highway, whose route along the coast from Slovenia, through Croatia and Bosnia and Herzegovina, to Montenegro enabled the emergence of mass tourism. As the country developed, however, the practical need for mass volunteer labor abated, and youth labor campaigns shifted to less physically taxing projects such as afforestation, the construction of youth resorts, or archaeological excavations. At the same time, the motivation to participate also shifted to travel and socialization with peers from other parts of the country, as volunteering in effect became a form of active vacationing under the banner of brotherhood and unity.[16] An entire visual culture promoting, recording, and celebrating youth campaigns emerged: posters, publications, films, vinyl record covers, uniforms, etc., were all regularly produced, sometimes by Yugoslavia's leading designers and artists.[17]

SPACES OF UNITY

As the administrative heart of socialist Yugoslavia, New Belgrade was the site where the rituals of unity were performed at the highest political level. In line with this integrative function, the city emphatically espoused the universalizing language of modern architecture. The key administration buildings, such as the SIV or the headquarters of the League of Communists of Yugoslavia, were variations of the International Style, whereas the expansive Sava Center, a conference hall built to host the 1977 meeting of the Conference for European Security and Cooperation, embraced a high-tech aesthetic (see Portfolio, XXVI and XXVII). Cultural institutions with pan-Yugoslav ambitions offered especially inspired versions of international modernism, notably the Museum of Contemporary Art (see Kulić, pp. 136–39), and Vjenceslav Richter's never-completed Museum of the Revolution. However, for most Yugoslavs, New Belgrade was a distant center that functioned predominantly on the symbolic level; in everyday life, pan-Yugoslav unity was more effectively performed through the networks of architectural programs distributed across the country.

A key example involved the commemoration of World War II (see Horvatinčić, pp. 104–11). As Yugoslavia had suffered some of the highest casualty rates in Europe, the sheer need for recognition was very real. But commemoration also had a strong ideological connotation as it conflated the memory of civilian casualties with that of the liberation struggle and the socialist revolution, producing a patriotic amalgam intended to bind the country together. Built by thousands, war memorials punctuated the entire territory, creating an invisible network spanning from the centers of the largest cities to distant uninhabited landscapes. The most important sites became destinations of patriotic tourism, visited by millions every year, with maps, guidebooks, and art-historical studies published in huge print runs in hand (fig. 10).[18] As groups of school children, veterans, workers from self-managing enterprises, or simply individual families on vacation arrived, their participation encouraged a secular communion with their fellow citizens across the country.

In aesthetic terms, however, there was nothing unitary about these sites of memory. Not only were they extremely diverse in terms of their typology—from individual sculptures to memorial cemeteries, parks, museums, and all kinds of hybrid programs that integrated commemoration with everyday life—but they also offered opportunities for a great deal of artistic experimentation. Even though realistic sculpture dominated early commemorative projects, the first experiments that departed from the conventions emerged soon after Yugoslavia's expulsion from the Soviet sphere in 1948. A veritable explosion of creativity, however,

Fig. 8   *Highway* exhibition at the Cvijeta Zuzorić Art Pavilion in Belgrade. 1950. Ivan Picelj (1924–2011), Vjenceslav Richter (1917–2002), Aleksandar Srnec (1924–2010), and Zvonimir Radić (1921–1985). Collage, ink, and tempera on paper, 19 11/16 × 27 15/16 in. (50 × 71 cm). Vjenceslav Richter Archive, Museum of Contemporary Art, Zagreb

Fig. 9   *Highway* exhibition at Zagreb Art Pavilion. 1950. Ivan Picelj (1924–2011), Vjenceslav Richter (1917–2002), Aleksandar Srnec (1924–2010), and Zvonimir Radić (1921–1985). Collage, ink, and tempera on paper, 19 11/16 × 27 15/16 in. (50 × 71 cm). Vjenceslav Richter Archive, Museum of Contemporary Art, Zagreb

began in the late 1950s; by 1961—the twentieth anniversary of the communist-led uprising—it was clear that the aesthetic terms of commemoration were radically redrawn.[19] At that time, architects and artists such as Vojin Bakić (1915–1992), Bogdan Bogdanović (1922–2010), Dušan Džamonja (1928–2009), Zdenko Kolacio (1912–1987), and Miodrag Živković (b. 1928) were already well on their way to developing their own recognizable poetics. Departing from convention, each pioneered certain strategies that soon became the new mainstream, replicated both by their professional peers and vernacular builders. With commissions scattered across the entire country, their personal oeuvres in effect embodied national unity.

Bogdan Bogdanović's career was emblematic in this respect. In thirty years as an active designer, he built memorials in all of the Yugoslav republics and autonomous provinces except for Slovenia. His idiosyncratic, Surrealist-inspired language of exuberant biomorphic shapes and abundant ornament sought to communicate the optimistic message that life overcomes death even in the face of the worst atrocities; in keeping with that message, many of his memorials were conceived as public gathering spaces, where commemoration became integrated with daily life (fig. 11).[20] Both in practice and in his writings Bogdanović adamantly contradicted the orthodoxies of high modernism, in turn deliberately dissolving architecture's supposed autonomy by merging it with landscape and sculpture into an indistinguishable whole.

A different kind of integration occurred in the 1970s, when commemorative programs became increasingly ambitious and inherently more architectural, conceived as full-fledged community centers, frequently in smaller provincial towns. Slovenian architect Marko Mušič (b. 1941) produced some of the most convincing articulations for such programs by winning a remarkable number of competitions across the country. His project for Kolašin in Montenegro is a standout achievement (see Portfolio, XVI), alongside the one for Bosanski Šamac in Bosnia and Herzegovina (fig. 12) and the never-completed project for Nikšić in Montenegro. Always based on intricate geometries, Mušič's buildings exhibited a great deal of spatial and formal complexity that also defied modernist certainties, although in a very different way from Bogdanović's organicism.

If the commemoration of the communal liberation struggle produced a special form of patriotic tourism, then actual recreational tourism in turn encouraged new forms of commonality. Just as in many other modern states, domestic tourism in Yugoslavia was bundled up with nation-building efforts as a way of learning to identify with one's own country. However, it acquired an additional ideological dimension aimed at ethnic reconciliation through direct encounter. Especially pronounced in the early postwar period, this ideology lingered on even after it was replaced by more hedonistic motivations.[21] Socialism added an additional layer: in 1946, the state introduced two weeks of annual paid leave, aiming to wrest holidaymaking from the realm of a bourgeois activity and make it available to everyone through a system of subsidies and socialized resorts. That holidays should be spent outside of one's own place of residence was far from obvious; it required

convincing and educating the population to turn "workers into tourists."[22] To further compound the matter, from the mid-1950s onward, tourism acquired an increasingly significant commercial role, as the emergent mass middle class, unsatisfied with modest standards of socialized holidaymaking, embraced tourism as a consumer activity. Even more importantly for tourism as a commercial industry, foreign visitors began arriving around the same time, adding yet another facet to an already complex situation. Popular destinations—predominantly on the Adriatic coast, which received the lion's share of foreign and domestic tourists—thus became massive social condensers of sorts, bringing together locals and visitors of varied motivations, ethnic identities, and class backgrounds.

The encounter was not always happy. As both the newly minted hosts and their guests learned how to play their respective roles, frictions arose from, among other things, ethnic animosities, a clash of cultural codes, and the failure to fulfill both the expected standards of service on the hosts' side and proper conduct on the guests'.[23] However, as tourism developed into a full-fledged industry, such conflicts abated for the most part; hosts and guests even sometimes developed long-term friendships, especially when locals started renting out rooms in their own homes as an increasingly lucrative private business.[24] Ultimately, most commercial tourism facilities themselves came to effectively function as social condensers: from the coast to the mountains, from lakeside towns to inland spas, hotels with their restaurants, bars, and open-air terraces almost invariably served not only the visitors from elsewhere, but also the local communities as their social hubs.[25] In many instances, the design encouraged such integration: for example, the permeable lobbies, restaurants, and terraces of the elegant Maestral Hotel (1965–66) in Brela invited unrestricted access, as if aiming to integrate the guests not only with the beautiful natural surroundings, but also with the small local community (p. 82, fig. 7). Even the most upscale resorts exhibited similar openness, as was the case at Haludovo Hotel (1969–72) on the island of Krk (p. 80, figs. 5 and 6), frequented by international celebrities, politicians, and gamblers. Although Yugoslav citizens were not allowed to use the property's casino, ordinary tourists and local inhabitants had free access to the resort's expansive, carefully landscaped beach, in sharp contrast with today's highly segregated forms of luxury tourism.

As with war memorials, tourism facilities proved to be fruitful grounds for architectural experimentation. Due to the sheer volume of new construction, the Adriatic coast provided the most consistent opportunities for

Fig. 10   *Selected Memorials of the People's Liberation War of Yugoslavia.* 1975. Cartographer: Ivan Gradišer (1923–1986). Illustrated map.

Fig. 11   Slobodište Memorial Park, Kruševac, Serbia. 1960–65. Bogdan Bogdanović (1922–2010). View of the "Valley of Memory." 2009. Photograph: Wolfgang Thaler.

Fig. 12   Mitar Trifunović Učo Memorial and Cultural Center, Bosanski Šamac, Bosnia and Herzegovina. 1975–78. Marko Mušič (b. 1941). Perspective drawing. Black ink on paper, 9⅜ × 7½ in. (23.8 × 18.9 cm). Personal archive of Marko Mušič

35

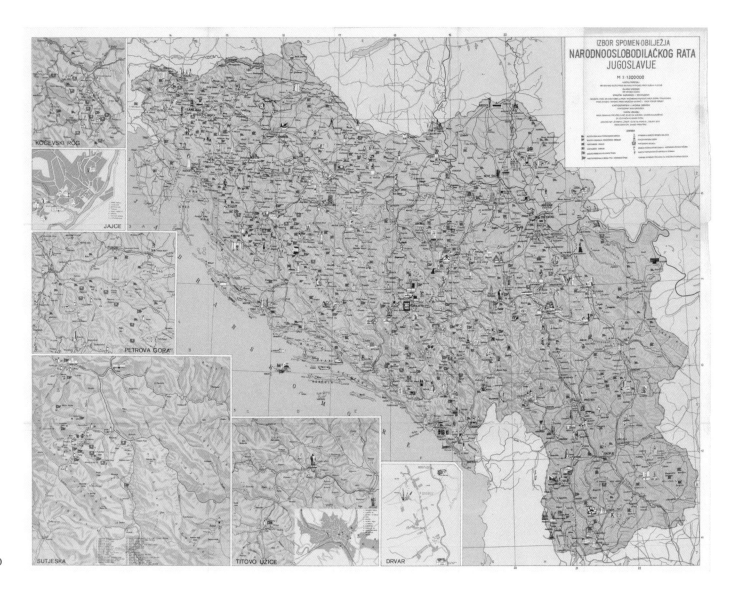

Fig. 10

Fig. 11

Fig. 12

Fig. 13

Fig. 14

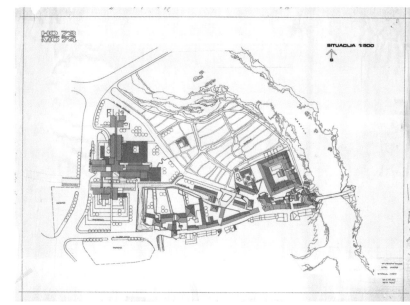

Fig. 15

Fig. 16

37

exploration, as the design of commercial hotels shifted from elegant modernist tower-and-slab typologies of the early 1960s to the increasingly complex group forms and megastructures in the following decade (see Mrduljaš, pp. 78–83). A comparable motivation to harmonize new construction with the landscape is recognizable in numerous mountain resorts through highly abstracted forms evocative of mountain peaks and ridges or monumentalized vernacular huts; such attempts only occasionally veered into explicit vernacularism. Urban hotels, in turn, produced some of the most spectacular examples of brutalism, often in their structurally expressive forms, that, for better or worse, strongly contrasted their surroundings. Even though her own hotel in Užice falls in the latter category, Svetlana Kana Radević's (1937–2000) hotel in Podgorica (see Portfolio, XXXVI) is a rare example of an urban hotel that grows out of the natural landscape, its soft sculptural forms and large pebbles built into its concrete walls blending with the banks of the nearby river Morača (see Issaias and Kats, pp. 98–100).

One of the paradoxes of Yugoslav tourism was that the vast majority of its celebrated architectural achievements belonged to the commercial realm, despite the fact that socialized holidaymaking nominally retained ideological significance until the collapse of the country. Due to their modest standards, social resorts were built with lesser architectural ambitions, but even some indisputably remarkable buildings remained largely unknown. A case in point is the Children's Sanatorium for Pulmonary Diseases in Krvavica, Croatia (1961–64), a spectacular architectural machine for healing hovering on pilotis above the surrounding pine forest and the nearby beach. Designed by architect Rikard Marasović (1913–1987) to allow maximum access to sun, air, and greenery, it reinterpreted typical Corbusian themes in a highly inspired and innovative way. Abandoned after the collapse of Yugoslavia, the structure only became widely known recently thanks to the efforts of local activists, suggesting that there may be other similarly outstanding structures that remain unknown and neglected across the former country (fig. 13).

The Krvavica sanatorium was another instance of a social condenser. It provided jobs for the local villagers as well opportunities to socialize, for example, by watching TV together at a time when TV sets were still rare in private homes.[26] In addition, the sanatorium's patients came from all over Yugoslavia, as the children's parents were employees of the largest institution in the country, the Yugoslav People's Army (YPA).

Originating in the struggle against fascism, the army was seen at once as the source, the guarantor, and the vehicle of Yugoslav unity, but it was also the country's most powerful architectural client. The YPA commissioned a number of impressive buildings, including its own headquarters (see Kulić, pp. 120–23) and the massive Military Medical Academy in Belgrade, as well as numerous tourism facilities, such as the elegant Pelegrin Hotel (1960–63) in Kupari near Dubrovnik (fig. 14). However, the army's most lasting architectural legacy was not a single building, but rather a set of building standards developed to house its own employees. Unlike most other socialist countries, Yugoslavia never standardized mass housing, which accounted for the relative diversity of the production in terms of layouts, materials, systems, and forms. The one exception were the buildings developed for the army: with tens of thousands of employees—including its own architects—the army had both the resources and the need to standardize the mass production of the apartments it financed, thus controlling the quality of their design across the entire country. However, because housing was often produced through collaboration of different investors—state institutions, self-managing enterprises, local communities, etc.—army standards often seeped into the civilian construction and came to be adopted informally by others. Thus the YPA, through housing, united the Yugoslavs in everyday life in a more profound and long-lasting way than either its coercive power or its ideological proclamations could.

CONSTRUCTING
REPUBLICAN IDENTITIES

The obverse side of the current 10 eurocent coin issued in Slovenia shows a striking building: a massive conical tower rising above a classical colonnade inscribed with the words "Cathedral of Freedom" (fig. 16). Although never executed, this design came to be widely understood as a preeminent architectural symbol of Slovenia's statehood, as the land for the first time in its modern history acquired the prerogatives of a nation-state. Produced by the celebrated architect Jože Plečnik (1872–1957)—himself an iconic national figure associated with the Slovenian identity the same way as Antoni Gaudí is associated with Catalonia—the design resulted from an actual commission for the Parliament of the People's Republic of Slovenia in 1947, thus locating the roots of Slovenia's statehood at the very beginning of the socialist period. With a height of 120 meters, the proposal was considered too gargantuan to be realized, especially at a time of extreme scarcity. Instead, Plečnik's own student Vinko Glanz (1902–1977) ultimately produced a more modest building constructed in the 1950s. In the following two decades, it was joined by the adjacent Revolution Square complex, designed by another student of Plečnik's, Edvard Ravnikar (1907–1993). This entire space became the heart of Slovenian nationhood, the same role that it continues to play today under the name of Republic Square (see Malešič, pp. 144–47; Portfolio, I and II).

Although unbuilt, Plečnik's "Cathedral of Freedom" was emblematic of the transformation that Yugoslavia's major cities underwent after the war as the federalist reorganization of the country facilitated

Fig. 13   Children's Sanatorium for Pulmonary Diseases, Krvavica, Croatia. 1961–64. Rikard Marasović (1913–1987). Exterior view. 2009. Photograph: Wolfgang Thaler
Fig. 14   Pelegrin Hotel, Cavtat, Croatia. 1960–63. David Finci (b. 1931). Exterior view. 2009. Photograph: Wolfgang Thaler
Fig. 15   Ruža Hotel, Mostar, Bosnia and Herzegovina. 1974–75, destroyed c. 1994. Zlatko Ugljen (b. 1929). Plan of the project in its urban surroundings. Ink, color marker, and letraset on tracing paper, 29⅞ × 41¼ in. (76 × 106 cm). Personal archive of Zlatko Ugljen
Fig. 16   Slovenian Parliament Building, Ljubljana. 1947–48. Jože Plečnik (1872–1957). Section. 1:200. 1947. Ink on paper, 28⅛ × 23⅝ in. (71.5 × 60 cm). Museum and Galleries of Ljubljana

the establishment of six republican capitals and two capitals of autonomous provinces. New government buildings, party headquarters, and cultural institutions—national libraries, theaters, universities, and academies of sciences and arts—were all constructed in response to these demands. Some of the capitals, such as Belgrade, Zagreb, and Ljubljana, only had to expand existing programs, established before the war; in other instances, metropolitan infrastructure had to be built from scratch. When Titograd (previously and today again known as Podgorica) became the capital of Montenegro in 1946, the small town of 13,000 inhabitants lay in ruins after massive wartime bombings. And when the similarly sized city of Pristina became the capital of the autonomous province of Kosovo the following year, it contained hardly any modern buildings. Over the following decades, both cities were not only equipped with a range of new administrative, cultural, and education buildings, but each also became the focus of urbanization and of industrial development, growing in size multifold, as did all other Yugoslav capitals. These cities also became centers of professional organizations in architecture and, with the exception of Titograd and Novi Sad (the capital of Vojvodina), of architectural education.

The architectural responses to these transformations varied as much as the six salons of the SIV building. In some instances, they followed modernism's universalizing ethos. For example, Ivan Vitić's (1917–1986) Central Committee of the League of Communists of Croatia (1961–68) in Zagreb (popularly known as the "Dice") is an exercise in high modernist abstraction that advances the self-perception of Croatia as a progressive modern nation. In other instances, architects sought to articulate more specific representations of national culture, but even then, vernacular references were rarely literal, sublimated as they were through modern technology and formal language. Petar Muličkovski's (b. 1929) Central Committee of the League of Communists of Macedonia (1970) referenced vernacular motifs through technologically advanced solutions: its deeply cantilevered floors, suspended from the load-bearing cores, evoked the overhangs of traditional Macedonian half-timber houses, whereas its facades in concrete and aluminum featured highly abstracted folk ornaments.[27] However, the most iconic example of this genre is not in Skopje but fifty miles to the north, in Pristina: the National and University Library of Kosovo (1971–82), designed by Andrija Mutnjaković (b. 1929).[28] Using high-tech materials and a "systemic" neo-avant-garde language, the building's numerous cubes and domes— the basic elements of both Byzantine and Ottoman architecture—in effect sought to reconcile Kosovo's multiethnic and multireligious composition (see Sadiki, pp. 168–71; Portfolio, XXVIII and XXIX).

Beyond formal representations, the most consistent efforts to formulate what later became known as critical regionalism occurred in Bosnia and Herzegovina. The impetus first came from Plečnik's student Dušan Grabrijan (1899–1952), who arrived in Sarajevo in the 1920s and became enchanted by the vernacular architecture of the Balkans, which he studied incessantly until his untimely death in 1952. He was joined in the 1930s by his Croatian colleague Juraj Neidhardt (1901–1979), a one-time employee of Peter Behrens and Le Corbusier, who soon came to share Grabrijan's fascination. Their collaborative tour de force, the massive volume titled *Architecture of Bosnia and the Way to Modernity* (1957), featured much of Grabrijan's ethnographic research, but what made it especially remarkable was Neidhardt's meticulous graphic layout and his many contemporary designs inspired by local vernacular architecture (see Zatrić, pp. 128–31).[29] The argument went beyond a formal reading to claim that spatial formations, material textures, and social and urban concerns of traditional Bosnian architecture constituted an ur-modernism that only needed to be technologically updated in order to serve as the basis for a new architecture of the region. Neidhardt's signature realization of these principles should have been the National Assembly (parliament) of Bosnia and Herzegovina, for which he won a competition in 1955: it was a summation of typological, spatial, and formal features of the local vernacular rendered in modern materials in a single structure. As built twenty years later, however, the project was reduced to a more generic high modernism that communicated little of the original regionalist content.

Neidhardt's built oeuvre was limited, but his teaching was formative for the generations of students at the Faculty of Architecture in Sarajevo, none more so than Zlatko Ugljen (b. 1929). In a series of projects that consistently fit the label of critical regionalism, Ugljen sought inspiration both from the immediate physical surroundings and from the broader cultural settings, producing an oeuvre as varied as Bosnia and Herzegovina's own diverse landscapes. Šerefudin White Mosque (1969–79) in the town of Visoko is certainly a masterpiece (see Zatrić, pp. 164–67, Portfolio, XIX), but so were several other projects, all tragically destroyed in the 1990s war. A case in point was the Hotel Ruža: constructed in the vicinity of the historical core of Mostar, it consisted of not a single building, but rather an intricate labirynth of small stone structures connected through internal and external passageways and interwoven with the surrounding traditional fabric (fig. 15). Unlike the nearby sixteenth-century Old Bridge, destroyed by shelling in 1993, the Ruža was never rebuilt and today exists only through surviving drawings and photographs.

CONCLUSION

Socialist Yugoslavia failed with the collapse of the delicate balance between diversity and unity that supported the country for more than forty years. In architectural terms, however, it should perhaps not be considered a failure: it produced a remarkably diverse architecture that nevertheless bespoke commonality through the many integrative functions it performed. Building on the architectural cultures developed before the war, federalism conditioned the production of architecture in multiple ways, most importantly through the organization of the profession and by defining the architectural programs to be constructed. What it did not do was prescribe how these programs should be articulated: architects were left with a great deal of agency in shaping the fledgling federal state and its constituent parts, in turn producing a vibrant architectural culture irreducible to simple ideological slogans. Among the federal and republican institutions, war memorials, resorts, and other programs, there were ample opportunities to both experiment and to develop consistent design expertise and poetics. In turn, the greatly varied natural and cultural landscapes inspired multiple regionalist explorations that complemented the accommodation of the universalizing strides of modernity. The sheer density of such diverse architectural phenomena renders Yugoslavia not only worth studying, but also rather unique in post–World War II architecture.

1   On the SIV as a realization of the synthesis of the arts, see Nikolaos Drossos, "Modernism with a Human Face: Synthesis of Art and Architecture in Eastern Europe, 1954–1958" (Ph.D. diss., CUNY, 2015). For a history of the SIV building, see Biljana Mišić, *Palata Saveznog izvršnog veća u novom Beogradu: istorija građenja* [The Palace of the Federal Executive Council: A History of the Construction] (Belgrade: Zavod za zaštitu spomenika kulture grada Beograda, 2011).

2   The building was originally designed in 1947 by a team of Croatian architects (Vladimir Potočnjak, Antun Ulrich, Zlatko Neumann, and Dragica Perak). After the death of the team leader, Potočnjak, the project was handed over to the Serbian architect Mihailo Janković, who in the second half of the 1950s brought it up to date, in accord with the standards of high modernism. The sand and gravel for New Belgrade were dug out of the Danube, but the marble for the building's facade came from the Adriatic island of Brač. Abundant artworks were produced by leading artists from all over the country.

3   For about two centuries, the site of today's New Belgrade divided the Habsburg and Ottoman empires, occasionally changing hands between them. How the changing boundaries between the Habsburg and Ottoman Empires affected the character of urban landscapes is discussed in Tanja Damljanović Conley and Emily Gunzburger Makaš, "Shaping Central and Southeastern Capital Cities in the Age of Nationalism" in *Capital Cities in the Aftermath of Empires: Planning in Central and Southeastern Europe,* ed. Conley and Makaš (New York: Routledge, 2010), 1–28.

4   The largest religious groups were Orthodox and Catholic Christians and Muslims, but there were also long-standing Jewish communities and various Protestant denominations.

5   Milan Prelog, "Yugoslavia: A Kaleidoscope of Cultures," *UNESCO Courier* 33 (November 1980): 4–18. Similar tropes were invoked at major international shows, such as Expo 58 in Brussels and the two large exhibitions of Yugoslav art in Paris held in 1950 and 1971.

6   Socialist Yugoslavia had six constituent nations (*narodi*). Ordered by population, these were Serbs, Croats, Muslims (granted national rights in the 1960s), Slovenes, Macedonians, and Montenegrins. The largest minorities (*narodnosti*) were Albanians, Hungarians, Romani, Turks, and so on. The minorities were granted rights to some cultural self-expression but not statehood.

7   Originally known as the Kingdom of Serbs, Croats, and Slovenes, the country changed its official name to Kingdom of Yugoslavia in 1929.

8   For Yugoslavism in architecture, see Aleksandar Ignjatović, *Jugoslovenstvo u arhitekturi* (Belgrade: Građevinska knjiga, 2007).

9   The process is most convincingly traced in Dejan Jović, *Yugoslavia: A State That Withered Away* (West Lafayette, Ind.: Purdue University Press, 2008).

10   For a historiography of the concepts of national architectures, see Tanja D. Conley, "Conceptualizing National Architectures: Architectural Histories and National Ideologies among the South Slavs" in *Nationalism and Architecture*, ed. Raymond Quek, Darren Deane, and Sarah Butler (London: Ashgate, 2012), 95–106.

11   How contentious the question of "Yugoslav architecture" was is perhaps best glimpsed from a collection of quotes compiled by the architectural historian Ines Tolić; see her "Impossible Interview with Some of Those Involved in the Borba Award," in *Unfinished Modernisations—Between Utopia and Pragmatism,* ed. Maroje Mrduljaš and Vladimir Kulić (Zagreb: CCA, 2012), 388–92.

12   Zoran Manević, Žarko Domljan, Nace Šumi, Ivan Štraus, Georgi Konstantinovski, and Božidar Milić, *Arhitektura XX vijeka,* series *Umjetnost na tlu Jugoslavije* (Belgrade: Prosveta; Zagreb: Spektar; Mostar: Prva književna komuna, 1985).

13   Ivan Štraus, *Arhitektura Jugoslavije, 1945–1990* (Sarajevo: Svjetlost, 1991).

14   For the situation in Macedonia, see Georgi Konstantinovski, *Graditelite vo Makedonija, XVIII–XX vek* [The Builders of Macedonia, 18th–20th Centuries] (Skopje: Tabernakul, 2001).

15   *Arhitektura* eventually narrowed its scope to Croatia in 1954, and is still published today, whereas *Arhitektura Urbanizam,* after a strong period in the 1960s, dwindled in the following decade and then eventually ceased to exist. In addition to these two publications, several locally produced journals and papers were widely read around the country, most notably *Čovjek i prostor, Arhitekt,* and *Sinteza.*

16   Dragan Popović, "Youth Labor Action (*Omladinska radna akcija, ORA*) as Ideological Holiday-Making," in *Yugoslavia's Sunny Side: A History of Tourism in Socialism (1950s–1980s),* ed. Hannes Grandits and Karin Taylor (Budapest: Central European University Press, 2010), 297–302.

17   On the visual culture of volunteer labor; see Sanja Bachrach Krištofić and Mario Krištofić, eds., *Omladinske radne akcije. dizajn ideologije* [Youth Working Campaigns: Designing Ideology], exh. cat. (Zagreb: KIC—Galerija na katu, 2017).

18   For example, the twenty-nine guidebooks in the edition *Monuments to the Revolution* were published in a total print run of more than two million copies; see Gojko Jokić, *Spomenici revolucije. Turistički vodič* [Monuments to the Recolution: A Tourist's Guide] (Belgrade: Turistička štampa, 1986).

19   On the twentieth anniversary of the uprising, the principal Yugoslav architectural journals devoted entire issues to the topic of commemoration, both of which testify to the emergent new culture of commemoration; see *Arhitektura* 15, nos. 1–2 (1961), and *Arhitektura Urbanizam* 2, no. 10 (1961).

20   Bogdan Bogdanović, *Nature and the Goddess of Remembrance,* exh. cat. (Belgrade: Museum of Modern Art, 1973).

21   Rory Yeomans, "From Comrades to Consumers: Holidays, Leisure Time, and Ideology in Socialist Yugoslavia," in Grandits and Taylor, *Yugoslavia's Sunny Side,* 69–105.

22   Igor Duda, "Workers into Tourists: Entitlements, Desires, and the Realities of Social Tourism under Yugoslav Socialism," in Grandits and Taylor, *Yugoslavia's Sunny Side,* 33–68.

23   Yeomans, "From Comrades to Consumers," 87–88, 94–96.

24   Renting rooms in private homes was allowed and regulated; due to insufficient capacities in socialized resorts, enterprises sometimes even contracted rooms from locals to accommodate their workers during the holiday season. See Karin Taylor, "Fishing for Tourists: Tourism and Household Enterprise in Biograd na Moru," in Grandits and Taylor, *Yugoslavia's Sunny Side,* 241–77.

25   This is the running subtheme of the documentary series *Betonski spavači* [Slumbering Concrete], by Saša Ban and Maroje Mrduljaš (Croatian Radio Television, 2015). Available at https://hrti.hrt.hr/search/term/betonski%20spava%C4%8Di.

26   See "Tajanstveni objekt u borovoj šumi," episode 4 of *Slumbering Concrete.*

27   Sadly, the building was recently altered beyond recognition in a misguided attempt to find the essence of Macedonian identity in the classical tradition.

28   Other libraries that articulate vernacular traditions through modern forms include the National Library of Serbia in Belgrade by Ivo Kurtović (1966–72) and the National and University Library in Skopje by Petar Muličkovski (1972).

29   Juraj Neidhardt and Dušan Grabrijan, *Arhitektura Bosne i put u suvremeno / The Architecture of Bosnia and the Way to Modernity* (Ljubljana: Državna založba Slovenije, 1957).

Fig. 1

Fig. 2

Fig. 3

Fig. 4

ARCHITECTURE FOR A SELF-MANAGING SOCIALISM

Maroje Mrduljaš

Postwar architecture in Yugoslavia was produced under a form of socialism defined by the system of self-management. A massive, continuously evolving experiment, the project of self-management attributed a great deal of agency to architects and urban planners, enabling the emergence of a range of coherent design cultures. In fact, architecture acted as an intermediary between what Max Weber defined as "value rationality" and "instrumental rationality," that is, between the pragmatic means and the ethical goals of socialist modernization. It was through such mediation that the architectural profession played an outsized role in the transformation of an unevenly developed and predominantly rural country into an industrialized and urbanized one.

One of several social systems of the "third way" developed in the second half of the twentieth century,

self-management was first instituted in 1950, in the wake of Yugoslavia's unexpected expulsion from the Soviet bloc two years earlier. It combined the native experiences of self-organization developed during the antifascist resistance with ideas from Karl Marx's early works as well as nineteenth-century utopian socialism and anarchism. In direct opposition to the highly centralized and bureaucratized system established during the country's short-lived alliance with the USSR, self-management aimed at a gradual "withering away of the state." Seen as an "alienating political force," the state apparatus was to be replaced, in theory, with direct democracy in both the economic and political life. In accordance with the slogan "factories to the workers," the management of economic resources and the accumulation of capital were gradually transferred from the central state to workers' councils. Political life similarly revolved around a complex and decentralized network of representatives, even though the Communist Party, renamed the League of Communists of Yugoslavia, continued as the only political party in the county. The system instigated unprecedented development in the region: it is often cited that, in the late 1950s, Yugoslavia had the second highest growth rate in the world. However, it also produced numerous crises and contradictions: between direct democracy and the de facto dominance of a single party, between a planned economy and a market, between the instrumental rationality of development and social idealism, and between individualism and collectivism.

Architecture often played the role of intermediary in these conflicts, with architects themselves seeking to find ways to articulate the theory's vaguely defined

Fig. 1   Kemikalija residential building, Zagreb, Croatia. 1953–56. Drago Galić (1907–1992). Detail view of the elevation. c. 1955. Tošo Dabac Archive, Museum of Contemporary Art, Zagreb. Photograph: Tošo Dabac
Fig. 2   Exhibition poster, *Family and Household*, Zagreb, Croatia. 1958. Design: Aleksandar Ljahnicky (b. 1933). Lithography, 27⅝ × 39⅜ in. (100 × 71 cm). Museum of Arts and Crafts, Zagreb
Fig. 3   Yugoslav Pavilion at the *International Exhibition of Housing*, Milan Triennial. 1957. Studio for Industrial Design (SID)/ Studio za industrijsko oblikovanje (SIO) and Niko Kralj (1920–2013). Published in *Domus* 337 (December 1957): 24.
Fig. 4   Model apartment at *Family and Household,* Zagreb, Croatia. 1958. Bernardo Bernardi (1921–1985). Croatian Museum of Architecture, Croatian Academy of Sciences and Arts

new societal forms and relations. The ideology of self-management defended such cultural autonomy and creative freedoms as specifically Yugoslav values. Cultural autonomy, however, referred not only to aesthetic and conceptual questions but also to the right of architects to self-organize and develop working conditions conducive to experimentation. Thus, the massive, centralized design institutes characteristic in many other socialist states gave way to a wide range of professional organizations in Yugoslavia. Architects most often practiced as employees of architectural offices organized as small, self-managing companies, or working at the in-house design offices of large construction companies, or in the larger urban planning institutes established in each federal republic and in major cities. They could even work as freelancers, albeit with reduced responsibilities.[1] In addition, universities and scientific institutes contained subunits licensed for design practice, which provided staff with a framework for connecting research and practice. This wide array of professional organizations produced specific niches of expertise and channels of activity, all of which allowed the profession to influence the process of urbanization with unusual freedom from market pressures or political incursions.

Moreover, the changing pace of modernization, extreme decentralization, the continuous reforms of economic and political life, and the practice of "criticism of everything existing" all played a part in preventing a standardization of typologies and codification of building norms. Instead, architects negotiated between state authorities, complicated systems of funding, expert bodies, and the construction industry. Well-organized professional organizations and a rich landscape of architectural magazines provided platforms for confronting differing views and discussing architecture within the context of the broader social concerns.

Post–World War II reconstruction triggered a wide-ranging discussion on how exactly the built forms of housing and education should be conceived in order to fit the vision of a more open and urbanized society. The advancement of a socialist market economy in the mid-1960s led toward integrated design, which applied systemic and interdisciplinary methods within a complex framework of funding systems and construction methods. This in turn enabled the mass-production of high-quality social housing. The peak of integrated design in the 1970s coincided as well with a great deal of thought devoted to the design of specialized typologies such as kindergartens. This desire to emancipate the population though lifelong education and active participation in cultural practices also introduced the evolution of multifunctional cultural centers, which became the focus of Yugoslav civic life in the 1960s and 1970s. These various typologies all resulted in part from the continuous exchange of concepts and ideas between architecture and self-managing socialism. While the relationship between architecture and the social system was not linear, architectural agency did have the power to outline the contours of a more progressive society, at the same time offering a critique of modernization.

THE WHY AND HOW OF MODERN LIVING

The political and economic priorities of self-managing socialism embraced the idea of a modern, industrial society designed for an urban working class. This vision mobilized mass migration from the countryside to the cities. In the 1950s, the "shock of modernization" was significant, and the "housing culture" became the central issue not only in architectural circles, but also in ideological debates. Intended to be available to all, a functional apartment with modern amenities became a herald for the newly emancipated citizen, especially women who were to be freed from household chores in order to become more broadly included in the workforce and public life. However, reality offered a far more complex challenge. On the one hand, some of the relatively luxurious apartment buildings constructed for lucrative companies and state institutions became architectural icons of the 1950s for their aesthetic ambitions and spatial complexity (see Bjažić Klarin, pp. 90–95) (fig. 1). In contrast, however, ordinary housing was subject to the rationalization demanded by a state bureaucracy in the early stage of urbanization. Architects and designers reacted against this situation in alliance with institutions such as trade unions and women's associations. The ensuing debate on the social role of housing addressed both "the Why" (emancipation) and "the How" (modernization) of the living, providing a direct link between self-managing socialism and architectural modernism. Furthermore, research in interior and product design became a channel to transmit emerging neo-avant-garde concepts to the widest audience.

Concerted efforts to widely disseminate ideas surrounding the housing culture began in the mid-1950s through a series of popular didactic exhibitions and symposia organized in collaboration with architects and a broad range of social organizations. Though similar to concurrent exhibitions around Europe, these were clearly geared toward building a self-managed socialist society. The pioneering event, an exhibition entitled *Housing for Our Conditions*, took place in Ljubljana in 1956. An accompanying symposium discussed broad economic, technological, and aesthetic aspects relevant to housing and stressed the functional role of the apartment within the work process: "Special attention must be devoted to the psycho-hygienic conditions of housing: a rest-period for the recreation and restitution of the working capacity of laborers."[2] The organic integration of housing into the wider currents of socialist life took on greater significance in a series of exhibitions entitled *Family and Household*, organized in 1957, 1958, and 1960 at the new Zagreb Fair (fig. 2).

Fig. 5   France Prešeren Elementary School, Kranj, Slovenia. 1960–68. Stanko Kristl (b. 1922). Interior view. 2010. Photograph: Wolfgang Thaler

Fig. 6   Catering School, Dubrovnik, Croatia. 1961–62. Vjenceslav Richter (1917–2002). Model of the second phase. Aleksandar Karolyi Archive. Photograph: Aleksandar Karolyi

Fig. 7   Mladi Rod Kindergarten, Ljubljana, Slovenia. 1969–72. Stanko Kristl (b. 1922). View of the classroom clusters. Museum of Architecture and Design, Ljubljana. Photograph: Janez Kališnik

Fig. 5

Fig. 6

Fig. 7

Fig. 8

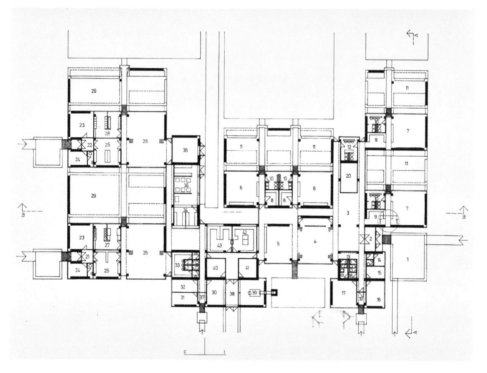

Fig. 9

Fig. 10

The second iteration was especially noteworthy in this respect, focusing on a "housing community," that is, a CIAM-style neighborhood unit equipped with all the necessary amenities: schools, kindergartens, health centers, retail shops, and community centers. These neighborhood units—meant to be developed utilizing self-management funds and with the participation of its citizens in the decisionmaking, as well as to function as self-managing communities—thus rendered architecture as the crucial mediator between the individual and society at large. An incredible 1,250,000 visitors from all over Yugoslavia saw the exhibition, making a powerful argument for architects to exert greater pressure toward improving both the building industry and standards of living.[3]

Public exhibitions on housing all included exemplary apartment settings and simple, functional modern furniture, factors militantly promoted as signs of a new era. Designs for everyday life provided a convenient link between the local rising culture of abstract art and humanistic societal goals. EXAT 51 (Experimental Studio 51), a group of Zagreb-based architects, designers, and artists, returned to the origins of historical avant-gardes, advocating creative freedom and linking the concept of synthesis of the visual arts to the total transformation of society. "Synthesis of the visual arts," a position perhaps most famously formulated by Josep Lluís Sert, Fernand Léger, and Sigfried Giedion in their 1943 paper "Nine Points on Monumentality" and later discussed in CIAM meetings, thus acquired in the Yugoslav context an ideological connotation that ascribed a more comprehensive progressive role to the idea. In 1959, Vjenceslav Richter (1917–2002), the most visible member of the group, advocated the importance of synthesis by claiming that "in the cultural sphere, the visual arts [including architecture and design] became a social factor and a democratic category of such importance, as was attributed to the workers and social self-management in the social and political spheres."[4] Putting their ideology into practice, EXAT 51's members helped create the Studio for Industrial Design (SID), which brought together twenty-eight architects, artists, and designers around the goals of "radical design for industrial objects" and "the promotion of the art of the avant-garde" in order to "raise the living standards of our people."[5] The group's most important appearance was at the Milan Triennial in 1957 (fig. 3). In competition with such design superpowers as Sweden and Italy, the SID, representing Yugoslavia, received a silver medal for its totally designed apartment equipped with modern furniture, accessories, and artworks. Though a showcase of an ideal Yugoslav apartment, the majority of items on display were only prototypes. However, EXAT 51's member Bernardo Bernardi (1921–1985), as well as Slovenian designer Niko Kralj (1920–2013), who also contributed to the Milan Triennial, eventually established successful collaborations with the furniture industry to mass-produce their designs, which became widely used in domestic and institutional settings, as well as in the hotels on the Adriatic coast (fig. 4). Furthermore, modern furniture was a successful export product, especially at East European markets.

The goal of both EXAT 51 and SID to redirect the industry toward a more comprehensive application of "synthesis" led to the establishment of the Center for Industrial Design (CID). Founded in 1963 by a group of art critics, theoreticians, and architects associated with the international artistic movement New Tendencies,[6] it was also in direct contact with Argentine designer and theorist Tomás Maldonado and the Ulm School of Design, the highly influential German school where Maldonado taught. The CID was not a design office but rather an independent institution that advocated design as the means of integration of "production and culture, culture and consumption."[7] CID was critical of instrumental modernization and the emerging Yugoslav market economy, following the argument that the key role of design is to place the entire system of material production on a value basis—that of a harmonious development of the physical environment. While the CID's vision of design's central role in development of self-management understood as "neo-humanistic version of industrial civilization"[8] proved to be utopian, in the following decades the organization collaborated with various state institutions and design and architectural offices to introduce multidisciplinary methodology in various fields, from visual communications to housing.

Discussions around housing culture were now firmly entrenched in Yugoslav society. The professional and popular press, including women's magazines, offered extensive coverage of all activities pertaining to housing. Department stores that sold furniture began to provide consultancy services on interior design, and the topic was also included in various public seminars and workshops. Inspired by such efforts, a student at a workers' university aptly summed it up in 1963: "I intend to continue to carry out reforms in my apartment."[9] Housing and interior design, too, were a battlefield for self-managed socialism.

EDUCATION REFORM MOVEMENTS

Concurrent to the debates around modern housing and its role in society, throughout the 1950s school infrastructure also received massive investments. Illiteracy rates in the country were rapidly dropping, but neither the pedagogical models nor the prevailing standardized school designs corresponded to the vision of a progressive, self-managed society. The highest levels of government engaged this "schooling explosion,"[10] responding to a reform movement that called for active, individualized, and practical education in order to produce a new crop of creative individuals suitable for self-managing socialism.[11] Educators and architects both recognized

Fig. 8   Mihaljevac Kindergarten and Nursery (today Vjeverica Kindergarten), Zagreb, Croatia. 1972–75. Boris Magaš (1930–2013). View of the roof. Personal archive of Boris Magaš. Photograph: Damir Fabijanić

Fig. 9   Grigor Vitez Kindergarten (today Izvor Kindergarten), Samobor, Croatia. 1971–74. Ivan Crnković (1941–2017). Ground floor plan. 1:200. Ink on vellum. Crnković family private collection

Fig. 10   Grigor Vitez Kindergarten (today Izvor Kindergarten), Samobor, Croatia. 1971–74. Ivan Crnković (1941–2017). Aerial view. Faculty of Architecture Archive, University of Zagreb

their mutual ambitions for reform, and thus the architecture of educational institutions became the testing grounds for new pedagogical concepts. A series of interdisciplinary symposia called for the abolishment of traditional teaching formats and rigid typological conventions, stressing instead the psychological experience of space and demanding the use of more open configurations, dynamic layouts, and flexible furniture.[12] A 1954 symposium in Ljubljana, entitled *From the Old to the New School*, was devoted specifically to educational institutions, with Swiss architect Alfred Roth, the influential CIAM delegate known for his experiments with school typologies,[13] as its keynote speaker. Despite continuing material restrictions, opportunities for experimentation were broad as the typological standards for educational institutions were defined merely as general recommendations. Public competitions served as the key instrument for research and encouraged the development of advanced solutions. An architectural competition for a new school in the small town of Stražišče pri Kranju coincided with the symposium in Ljubljana and produced a convincing result: Danilo Fürst's winning entry, realized in several phases (1959–74), envisioned a system of pavilions situated in a park, each designed according to the specificities of different age groups. The wing for younger pupils was located on a ground floor and had a flexible layout, whereas the block of classrooms for senior pupils was organized around a large common hall encouraging social interactions. Fürst's rational tectonic language also announced the tendency toward modernist aesthetics for the majority of educational buildings in Yugoslavia.

In the following years, a number of experimental schools were designed throughout Yugoslavia. The highly praised France Prešeren Elementary School in Kranj (1960–68), designed by Stanko Kristl (b. 1922), combined the architect's interest in typological innovation with attention to the perceptual effects of architecture (fig. 5). The project featured a branching system of public interior spaces interconnected with atria, which enabled a fine gradation of the school's social life. The intertwining of nature and architecture, the scale adapted to children, and a thorough attention to detail in the building, constructed in exposed concrete and wood, all contributed to the intimate atmosphere. Vjenceslav Richter's Catering School in Dubrovnik (1961–62), deconstructed the typology even more radically, introducing a structuralist approach based on the multiplication of a basic compositional unit (fig. 6). A dense fabric of smaller volumes and exterior spaces follows the slope to form a non-hierarchical agglomeration, which may be expanded according to need. The labyrinthine circulation spaces are adapted to the topography and meander between the classrooms, adding to the informal atmosphere of the institution but also echoing traditionally dense Mediterranean settlements.

The many architectural experiments conducted in the wake of the 1963 earthquake in the Macedonian capital of Skopje also included educational institutions. Significant inspiration came from Alfred Roth's own Pestalozzi Elementary School (1965–69), a Swiss donation, which included a large multipurpose hall and typological disposition that avoided long corridors in favor of more compact layout directly connected with the entrance plaza. Janko Konstantinov (1926–2010), an architect with an unusual international career who had worked for Alvar Aalto and Victor Gruen, explored a more expressive architectural language and an almost monumental approach to public spaces. His Pedagogical Academy in Skopje (1969) was organized around a multifunctional, top-lit interior courtyard and included a circular "tower" with a library accessible from the public space. Konstantinov's Nikola Karev Medical High School in Skopje (1969–73) (see Portfolio, XXXVIII) reflected a partial realization of the architect's fascination with Arata Isozaki's Cities in the Sky and included a large, linear public plaza covered by a hovering block of classrooms. Such experiments culminated in Georgi Konstantinovski's (b. 1930) Goce Delčev Student Dormitory (1969–77), an impressive complex of concrete towers linked by a continuous flying ring of various public spaces (see Deskov et al., pp. 160–63).

With the ongoing development of educational facilities, kindergartens began attracting more attention as a standard offering in the housing communities. By the beginning of the 1960s, however, construction of kindergartens was backlogged, and old-fashioned, basic care had gained precedence over the education and socialization of society's youngest citizens. This delay triggered an increased interest in typological research. For example, in 1961, Boris Magaš (1930–2013) won a competition for a typical kindergarten in Zagreb by proposing a formally elegant and compact system of atria and interior spaces; ultimately only two schools were built, and in altered versions. Following Magaš's research, several diverse and flexible modular systems that could accommodate various capacities and adapt to the local contexts were subsequently introduced. Radical, one-off experiments appeared as well. The futuristic Mladi Rod Kindergarten (1969–72) (fig. 7) designed in Ljubljana by Stanko Kristl, and the Mihaljevac Kindergarten and Nursery (today Vjeverica Kindergarten) (1972–75) by Magaš in Zagreb, both reinterpreted the theme of the shelter. Kristl applied rounded, "primordial" forms and designed clusters of classroom units that functioned as children's micro-communities, while Magaš's project generated an artificial topography of inclined roof planes over complex interior spaces (fig. 8). The Grigor Vitez Kindergarten (today Izvor Kindergarten) (1971–74) in Samobor, designed by Ivan Crnković (1941–2017), is a tightly woven network of interior spaces, roofed openspace rooms, and terraces, all connected by elongated,

Fig. 11   Prefabricated single-family house, Spačva, Croatia. 1964. Bogdan Budimirov (b. 1928), Željko Solar (b. 1924), Vladimir Robotić (b. 1930), Zlatko Žokalj (1926–1999) for Spačva (est. 1956). Exterior view. Personal archive of Bogdan Budimirov

Fig. 12   JU-61 system of prefabrication, New Zagreb, Croatia. 1961. Bogdan Budimirov (b. 1928), Željko Solar (b. 1924), and Dragutin Stilinović (b. 1927) for Jugomont (est. 1955). Detailed view of the facade. Personal archive of Bogdan Budimirov

Fig. 13   Block 23, New Belgrade, Serbia. 1968–74. Božidar Janković (b. 1931), Branislav Karadžić (1929–2007), Aleksandar Stjepanović (b. 1931), and Milutin Glavički (1930–1987). Floorplan of apartment. Published in *Katalog stanova JNA/1* [Catalogue of the Yugoslav Peoples' Army/1] (Beograd: SSNO Uprava vojnog građevinarstva, Direkcija za izgradnju i održavanje stambenog fonda JNA, 1987), 67.

Fig. 11

Fig. 12

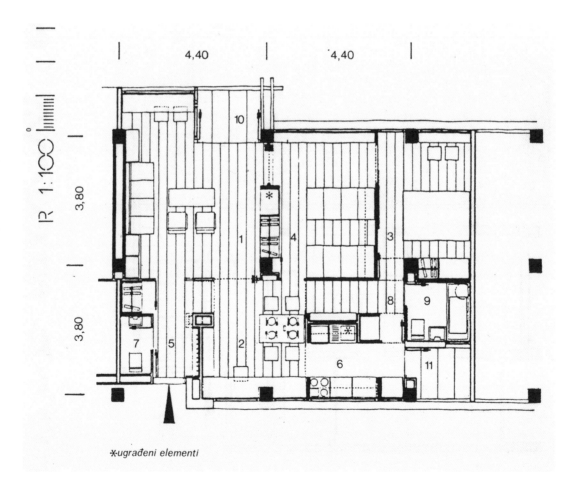

*-ugrađeni elementi

Fig. 13

narrow passages with glass roofs (fig. 9). This project paralleled the anthropological interests of Team 10 and aimed at stimulating the children to explore the logic and possibilities of abstract architectural elements. The repetition of spatial modules, the potential to expand the structure, and the thoroughly articulated "threshold spaces" testify to the influence of Aldo van Eyck and Dutch structuralism, whereas Crnković himself referred to Umberto Eco's "open work," claiming that architecture obtains its significance only through interaction with its users (fig. 10). While these kindergartens received sporadic criticism for being "monuments to the architects," they also represented major architectural breakthroughs for their time.

Throughout the entire socialist period, the dilemma of instrumental versus value rationality drove the discussion and practice of what was better for society: to accelerate the rhythm of production and build typified projects, or to continue exploring socially sensitive typologies through individual works. Both approaches, however, produced compelling results, contributed to the cultivation of typology, and resulted in a significant expansion of the country's educational network.

INTEGRATED DESIGN

After a decade of rapid economic growth in the 1950s, Yugoslavia experienced a slowdown that provoked another round of systemic reforms, instituted in 1965, which led to the significant enhancement of market mechanisms. The result was a system distinct from both capitalist market economies and socialist central planning. While a degree of planning was retained, the self-managing enterprises now competed on the domestic market as well as internationally, and powerful domestic banks managed investments rather than the state. With the liberalization of economic life, the construction of mass housing began to boom as self-managing enterprises and institutions sought to provide housing for their employees by purchasing apartments that were constructed to be sold on a socialist market.

The reforms, however, caused new tensions to emerge: increasing unemployment and growing economic emigration, the rise of a "techno-managerial elite," and the continuous problems that arose from an inefficient, bureaucratic apparatus. At the same time, the results of urbanization were viewed as alienating, and the housing crisis remained unresolved. The system compensated for these shortcomings by opening room for individual construction, supported through official loans. The construction industry responded by developing a large number of prefabricated homes that could be sold on the market (thus wood processing companies Marles and Jelovica in Slovenia, Spačva in Croatia (fig. 11), and Krivaja in Bosnia Herzegovina achieved considerable commercial success).

The modern apartment, subsidized by the state, became the most desired product of the self-managed socialism. However, the continuing housing shortages and the inflexibility of urban planning forced much of the new individual construction to occur outside of the legal system, leading to unregulated settlements on the outskirts of large cities. The architectural profession responded

to the housing crises by implementing an integrated design, which sought to increase the efficiency and economic performance of housing developments without sacrificing spatial qualities. In order to achieve such goals, architectural concepts and construction methods needed to be coordinated in all scales, from small details to the whole building to the entire urban layout.

One of the answers to achieving these goals was prefabrication. Since the late 1950s, several innovative local systems of prefabrication were already being developed, notably JU-61 for the Zagreb-based Jugomont company (fig. 12). The system's designers, architects Bogdan Budimirov, Željko Solar, and Dragutin Stilinović, considered the building not as an individual object but as part of a system that, in the spirit of Buckminster Fuller's concepts, resulted from an integrated logic of production, transportation, assembly, maintenance, and possibly demolition (see Bjažić Klarin, pp. 90–95). New Belgrade was home to especially far-reaching experiments with prefabrication. The competitions organized for the city's modernist blocks throughout the 1960s and 1970s in effect functioned as a laboratory for the perfection of housing design, typically based on prefabricated systems. The IMS-Žeželj system, designed in 1957 by engineer Branko Žeželj from Belgrade's Institute for the Testing of Materials (IMS Institute), proved particularly popular and innovative. It employed a prestressed concrete skeleton, which opened up the space to allow for more flexible floor plans and facade systems than conventional panel systems.

The IMS Institute founded the Housing Center (1970–86) to bring together research and professional practice. With a relatively small staff of about twenty, the center's architects were responsible for some of the most important housing projects in Belgrade, such as New Belgrade's Blocks 21, 23, 29, 45, and 70, as well as in many other cities (figs. 13 and 14). The Housing Center's research focused on an extremely elaborate taxonomy of functions, inspired by American psychologist Abraham Maslow's theory of the hierarchy of human needs, and resulted in apartments that would not only be efficient but also satisfy the requirements of spaciousness and flexibility. The Housing Center aspired to play an integrative role in the organization of research, design, and construction, thus initiating cooperation with other research institutions, architectural offices, and industry.

An informal "Belgrade school" of housing design, which flourished in the 1960s and 1970s, emerged from all this technological innovation and research. Its initiators were Belgrade professors Mate Baylon and Branislav Milenković, who incessantly studied the diagrams of apartment plans and arrangements and cultivated the

Fig. 14   Housing Blocks 22 and 23, New Belgrade, Serbia. 1968–74. Božidar Janković (b. 1931), Branislav Karadžić (1929–2007), Aleksandar Stjepanović (b. 1931), and Milutin Glavički (1930–1987) for IMS Institute and Osnova Atelier. Photograph of the urban model. 1968. Personal archive of Aleksandar Stjepanović

Fig. 15   *Flexible Apartment: Evolution of the System for Designing and Building the Apartments Neimar NS.* 1970–71. Milan Lojanica (b. 1939) and Radislav Marić (b. 1949). Published in *Arhitektura Urbanizam*, no. 74–77 (1975).

Fig. 14

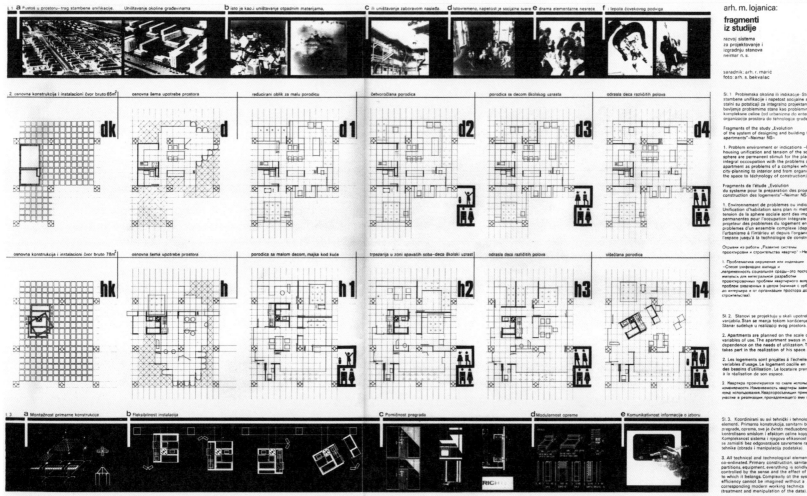

Fig. 15

methodology of designing a wide range of efficient and spatially inventive apartments with their students. The "Belgrade school" attempted to reconcile the privacy of individuals with the communal life of a family, particularly several generations living side by side, which was often the case amid unceasing housing shortages. The apartments were therefore designed as dynamic living landscapes, which could easily be transformed either for short intervals during the day by the use of partition walls, or for long-lasting transformations by changing or repositioning the non-load-bearing walls. The sophisticated floor plans, with multipurpose rooms and circular connections, were designed to allow the openness and fluidity of space (fig. 15).

Whereas much energy was spent on the meticulous design of apartments, the urban spaces in New Belgrade and New Zagreb were developed in line with rather mainstream urban planning concepts adopted from the CIAM doctrine. A prompt critical reaction, by Vjenceslav Richter, took a decidedly utopian direction: his 1964 book *Sinturbanizam* (Synthurbanism) proposed a complete vision of a self-managed socialist city, which consisted of ziggurat-like megastructures for up to ten thousand inhabitants (fig. 16). Motivated by the desire to save the time that would otherwise be spent on daily commutes, Richter's ziggurats were intended to compress all urban functions into a single structure: apartments were to be stacked at its outside slopes, while all production, institutions, and public amenities were to be housed underneath. Contemporary critics called the project dystopian, but Richter pointed out that his alternative to "functional" urban planning was not a formal solution but rather a model that sought to find a more humane and more efficient solution to the problem of the fragmentation of contemporary life. Several other unrealized experimental projects, such as the Experimental Residential Building (1968) (fig. 17) in Osijek by Andrija Mutnjaković (b. 1929) and the EVH-100 system (1973) by Savin Sever (1927–2003), tried to solve the housing crisis (as well as resolve the tension between individual initiative and collectivism) by proposing concepts in which a building's structure and early construction would be financed from the public budget, while the citizens themselves would carry out the rest of the building and participate in the final design.

From the late 1960s onward, new approaches in urban planning aimed to increase the quality of the social public space while maintaining an integrative approach. The culmination of such ambitions was certainly the construction of an entirely new town built adjacent to the coastal city of Split. Called Split 3, the project instituted close cooperation between architects and urban planners (see Skansi, pp. 156–59). The plan for Split 3 was based on pedestrian streets lined with ambitiously designed housing megastructures. Made possible through the integration and coordination of the city's financing and organization, architectural design, and construction cooperatives, the experiment proved to be incredibly successful, serving as a model for some of the last large-scale housing estates of the socialist period.

The high-quality apartment is perhaps the most advanced mass product of Yugoslav self-management. Flexible, transformable, and therefore sustainable, and

integrated into "neighborhood units" equipped with social amenities, it was designed to meet the real needs of the users. Though demand exceeded available housing and egalitarian societal promises were not entirely fulfilled, optimistic and vital "integrated design" combined with self-management housing policies proved that it was possible to harmonize progressive values and rational goals on the largest scale and significantly improve the quality of everyday life under self-managed socialism.

CULTURAL CENTERS AS INSTRUMENTS OF EMANCIPATION

If the concept of self-management was to succeed in every field of economic and political life, it required emancipated workers and citizens who could see their position, role, and interests in the broader social context. Slovenian politician Edvard Kardelj, the main theorist of the self-managing system, described this emancipation as a "profound cultural and ethical revolution…a transformation of the complete consciousness of the working man."[14] Indeed, the active involvement of citizens in cultural life and continuing education were integral parts of the project of social development.

The extensive development of cultural institutions in Yugoslavia was comparable to French Minister of Culture André Malraux's project for the decentralization of French culture in the 1960s. While the cultural life in large urban centers was mainly organized through networks of existing institutions, the development of new cultural centers occurred mainly in the smaller towns of less developed regions. It was precisely under such peripheral conditions that cultural centers initiated new forms of social life, new lifestyles, and new architectural cultures.

Cultural centers were the focus of this new landscape, where professional culture, cultural amateurism, popular culture and entertainment, education, and political activities were all intertwined.[15] As such, they were meant to create innovative forms of public space where different social groups could meet outside of the work-family pattern, and culture, free time, and political life could all benefit each other. The typology emerged simultaneously with similar developments both in the East and the West. Alvar Aalto's Cultural Center in Wolfsburg, West Germany (1959–62), for example, is comparable to many examples in Yugoslavia, but a strong accent on both the ideological and social roles elevated Yugoslav cases to crucial instruments of modernization. New hybrid typologies emerged, effectively serving as the "instruments of emancipation" to produce a new individual for self-managing socialism.

Fig. 16   *Sinturbanizam* (Synthurbanism). 1962–63. Vjenceslav Richter (1917–2002). Perspective section of Ziggurat. Exhibition copy, 43⅜ × 39⅜ in. (110 × 100 cm). Vjenceslav Richter Archive, Museum of Contemporary Art, Zagreb
Fig. 17   Experimental Residential Building. 1968. Andrija Mutnjaković (b. 1929). Model. Personal archive of Andrija Mutnjaković

Fig. 16

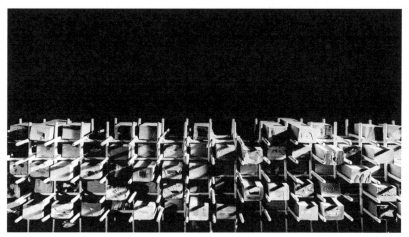

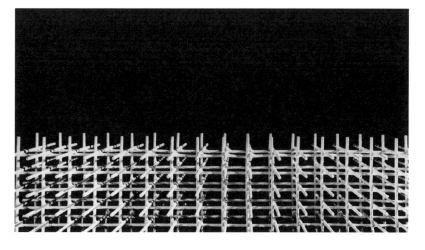

Fig. 17

Fig. 18

Fig. 19

53

One of the first and certainly most outstanding examples of this type was Josip Jože Osojnik's (1923–1999) Cultural Center (1957) in the Bosnian town of Konjic (fig. 18). Organized along a sweeping line of the local road, the complex consists of an open system of terraces, staircases, and galleries that function as an open-air lobby. This formally rich public space hosted a comprehensive program, including a fully equipped, open-air amphitheater, a theater, and a library, but also included an ample café and dancing terrace, thus combining urban everyday life with various cultural activities.

Another ubiquitous format for cultural centers, the many Yugoslav People's Army (YPA) Clubs were intended not only to serve the cultural and entertainment needs of the military, but also to bring together officers and recruits with local inhabitants. As the most powerful institution in Yugoslavia, the army was also a resourceful client willing to invest in advanced architecture, as was the case with Ivan Vitić's (1917–1986) works on the Adriatic coast. Vitić's YPA Clubs in Komiža on the island of Vis (1961–67), Šibenik (1960–61), and Split (1962–66) combined formal precision reminiscent of Neo-Plasticism with a subtle regionalist attitude toward the Mediterranean context. Common to these projects were innovative folding-plate roofs that produced characteristic building contours and enabled large spans and flexible open-plan interiors capable of accommodating various programs. Particularly radical was the YPA Club in Šibenik, located within a sensitive historical area (fig. 19). Vitić displayed an extraordinary degree of self-confidence when he placed an elegant, oblong, crystal-like glass volume on a Renaissance fortification wall, a provocative element in the urban landscape.

Important contributions also came from Marko Mušič (b. 1941), a Slovenian architect who had worked with Louis Kahn and who won numerous competitions across Yugoslavia. Mušič's Memorial and Cultural Center, and Town Hall, in Kolašin (1969–75) (see Portfolio, XVI) was a hybrid between a memorial museum, a cultural center, and an administrative municipal building, thus satisfying a range of ideological, political, and cultural needs of the small Montenegrin town. Designed as an imposing sculpture, the geomorphic agglomeration of tetrahedral volumes occupies the center of the main town square (fig. 20). Its exterior is brutalist, but the interiors are designed as a colorful "house within a house," with their own interior shells (fig. 21). The result of such formal expressiveness is an introverted building, detached from the town's main square and surrounding park, which emphasizes its representative role. Not only a reinterpretation of the building type, the center was also a design experiment that demonstrated the formal ambitions of Yugoslav architects when conceiving key public buildings.

An extensive cultural-educational infrastructure was thus developed over time, followed by a rich offering of programs. The majority of citizens participated in some form of cultural activity and continuing education. By the early 1980s, one third of the financing for cultural centers came from their own profits, created through popular programs or entertainment, indicating a strong tie between the informal practices of everyday life and institutional culture. The original intention of a self-managed cultural center was best suited for open projects, capable of embracing change and adapting to the needs of the community. They challenged the divisions between high and popular culture and, at least in theory, between politics and the everyday, making them hubs of socialist modernity and a means of social integration.

BETWEEN PRAGMATIC MEANS AND ETHICAL GOALS

The political and economic crisis impacting the Yugoslav socialist system escalated in the 1980s, thwarting further development of self-management. As a result, the close ties between progressive social goals and architectural experimentation loosened, and architects withdrew into "paper projects," as practiced by the MEČ Group in Belgrade, or into subtle regionalist interventions on the periphery, as was the case for the Kras Group in Slovenia.[16] At the same time, already existing concepts were perpetuated in a rather demagogic manner and in some cases beyond reasonable scale. Indicative in this respect is another cultural center by Marko Mušič, the enormous Revolution Center for the industrial town of Nikšić in Montenegro (fig. 22). Designed in 1979, the project envisioned an ambitious assembly of programs, from a multipurpose hall to a number of different workshops, as well as a youth center, a workers' club, and even a television studio. The project kept growing with the insatiable appetite of the various stakeholders, resulting in a near doubling of the original square footage. The Revolution Center exposed the inherent contradictions of Yugoslav socialist modernization. The unrestrained growth of the building, legitimized by its nominal purpose of commemorating the revolution, led to a project with many social uses but at a scale designed without any thought for the facility's sustainability. Partially built with considerable delays and interruptions, construction was finally halted with the fall of socialism. It remains uncompleted to this day, posing a serious problem for the town of Nikšić.[17]

It would certainly be difficult to identify a unique form of "self-managing architecture" in socialist Yugoslavia. It is beyond doubt, however, that architecture as a discipline played a significant role in the construction of Yugoslav self-managing socialism by servicing the social project of modernizing the country. The architects' expanded agency enabled the manifestation of important breakthroughs, thus overcoming bureaucratic barriers, the logic of the emerging socialist market, and the inertia of the construction industry. As a result, segments of the built environment became fields of experimentation and research. Broad public discussions and didactic campaigns redefined the relationship between "high culture," expert knowledge, and everyday life. The impact of research-based architectural knowledge in large technocratic organizations and state institutions allowed for a more complex application of

Fig. 18   Cultural Center, Konjic, Bosnia and Herzegovina. 1957.
Josip Jože Osojnik (1923–1999). Exterior view.
Museum of Architecture and Design, Ljubljana

Fig. 19   YPA Club, Šibenik, Croatia. 1960–61. Ivan Vitić
(1917–1986). Exterior view. Private collection

modernization efforts, as was the case with mass housing. Experiments with educational institutions and cultural centers allowed new forms of socialization in which institutionalized and informal modes of life were intertwined. Indeed, the architectural urbanization of socialist Yugoslavia produced a complex patchwork that combined the generic and the experimental and demonstrated how a self-managing socialism in its idealized state could look and function.

Translated from Croatian by Helena Biffio Zorko.

1   Freelance artists were limited to performing tasks related to interior design, stage sets, and exhibition and stand design, which fell under the domain of "applied art."
2   "Zaključci 1. Jugoslavenskog savjetovanja o stambenoj izgradnji i stanovanju u gradovima" [Conclusions of the First Yugoslav Symposium on Housing Construction and Apartments in the Cities], *Čovjek i prostor*, no. 8.
3   Andrija Mutnjaković, "Stambena problematika u okviru 2. Međunarodne izložbe Porodica i domaćinstvo" [Housing Problematics within the 2nd International Exhibition Family and Household], *Čovjek i prostor*, no. 79 (1958): 4.
4   "Likovni regulator industrijske proizvodnje" [Art Regulator of Industrial Production], *Čovjek i prostor*, no. 86 (1959): 1.
5   "Stan za naše prilike" [Housing for Our Conditions], *Arhitektura*, nos. 1–6 (1956): 46.
6   For a discussion of New Tendencies, see Armin Medosch, *New Tendencies: Art at the Treshold of the Information Revolution (1961–1978)* (Cambridge, Mass.: MIT Press, 2016).
7   "Uputa za industrijski dizajn" [Instructions for Industrial Design], CID, Zagreb, n. p.
8   Josip Županov, Fedor Kritovac: "Odakle otpori industrijskom dizjanu?" [Where Does Resistance to Industrial Design Stem From?], in Eugen Canki, ed., *Industrijski dizajn i privredno-društvena kretanja u Jugoslaviji* [Industrial Design and Economic-societal Movements in Yugoslavia] (Zagreb: Radničko sveučilište Moša Pijade, 1969), 258.
9   Radovan Ivančević, "Kultura svakodnevnog života" [Culture of Everyday Life], *15 Dana*, no. 20/21.3 (1963): 6.
10 Term coined by Stipe Šuvar, influential Croatian sociologist and politician, leader of schooling reforms of 1970s.
11 "Savjetovanje arhitekata Jugoslavije o izgradnji osmogodišnjih škola" [Symposium of the Architects of Yugoslavia on the Building of Elementary Schools 1957], in *Arhitektura*, nos. 1–6 (1958): 1–2; 19–20.
12 See *Arhitekt*, nos. 12–13 (1954).
13 Alfred Roth, *The New School / Das Neue Schulhaus / La Nouvelle École* (Zurich: Girsberger, 1950).
14 Edvard Kardelj, *Pravci razvoja političkog sistema samoupravljanja* [Developmental Orientations for the Political System of Self-management], 2nd rev. ed. (Belgrade: Komunist, 1978), 115.
15 In Yugoslav socialism, the notion of "culture" was understood and applied in very broad terms. Along with the conventional forms, the notion also implied the "technical culture," for instance photography and amateur radio; "physical culture," which was related to sport and recreation; and a number of other fields.
16 The members of the MEČ group were Marjan Čehovin, Dejan Ećimović, Slobodan Maldini, Mustafa Musić, and Stevan Žutić. The core members of the Kras Group were Vojteh Ravnikar, Matjaž Garzarolli, Marko Dekleva, and Egon Vatovec. Increasing interest in introspective research and a shift away from conventional practice is clearly demonstrated by the success of younger Yugoslav architects at the influential international Shinkenchiku competitions in Japan. In 1983, Ivan Crnković and Emil Šverko won with the project New Croatian Manor: House with Six Identical Rooms, and in 1984 Vinko Penezić and Krešimir Rogina did the same with the project Style for the Year 2001.
17 The Revolution Center in Nikšić is not the only case of unfinished large-scale cultural centers from late socialism: with the Dubrava Cultural Center in Zagreb and the Youth Center in Split, only rough works were executed, while others, such as the Cultural Center in Bosanski Šamac, were only partially completed.

Fig. 20   Memorial and Cultural Center, and Town Hall, Kolašin, Montenegro. 1969–75. Marko Mušič (b. 1941). Exterior view. 2009. Photograph: Wolfgang Thaler

Fig. 21   Memorial and Cultural Center, and Town Hall, Kolašin, Montenegro. 1969–75. Marko Mušič (b. 1941). Interior view. Personal archive of Marko Mušič

Fig. 22   Revolution Center, Nikšić, Montenegro. 1979–89 (incomplete). Marko Mušič (b. 1941). Exterior view. 2016. Photograph: Valentin Jeck

Fig. 20

Fig. 21

Fig. 22

FOCAL POINTS

Fig. 1

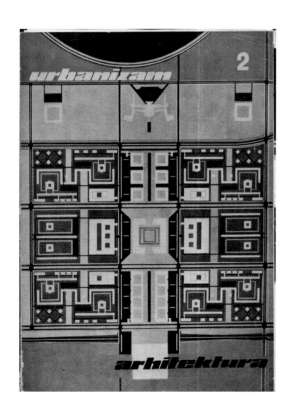

Fig. 2

Fig. 1   Belgrade master plan, Serbia. 1949–51. Urban Planning
Institute of Belgrade. Plan. 1:10000. 1951. Ink and
tempera on diazotype, 64⁹/₁₆ × 91¾ in. (164 × 233 cm).
Urban Planning Institute of Belgrade

Fig. 2   Cover of *Arhitektura Urbanizam*, no. 2 (1960), showing
plan for the central zone of New Belgrade, Serbia.
1960–61. Uroš Martinović (1918–2004), Milutin Glavički
(1930–1987), Leonid Lenarčić (b. 1932), Dušan Milenković
(b. 1925), and Milosav Mitić (1932–1970)

CITY BUILDING
IN YUGOSLAVIA

In 1911, on his journey to the East, the young Le Corbusier arrived in Belgrade via the Danube. Although disappointed with the "ridiculous capital" (noting, however, the site's "excellent [geographical] position"), the many folk artifacts at the city's ethnographic museum fascinated him,[1] and he marked Belgrade with an F for "folklore" on his travel map, as he also did for most of the sites he visited in the Balkans. Fifty years later, however, the rustic capital had become the site of a Corbusian endeavor on a grand scale: New Belgrade.[2] This vast building project was vested with symbolic meaning: the country chose to drain a swamp along the former border between the Ottoman and Habsburg Empires to erect the only new capital in postwar Europe. New Belgrade was but the most visible of the many manifestations of Yugoslavia's specific form of urban development, the ambitious pursuance of which transformed the formerly rural, underdeveloped country into a predominantly urbanized and industrialized state in less than fifty years.

The postwar urbanization of Yugoslavia paralleled the process in much of Europe, with one significant distinction: the combination of socialist self-management and modernist principles, developed in close interaction with international movements in city planning. In the early 1950s, while the rest of Eastern Europe was building socialist cities filled with classicist boulevards and monumental, symmetric squares in the Stalinist vein, Yugoslavia looked instead to the modernist doctrine of the Congrès Internationaux d'Architecture Moderne (CIAM) and Le Corbusier's Athens Charter to guide its most significant urban development endeavors, such as New Belgrade, the southward expansion of Zagreb, and the new towns of Nova Gorica, Titovo Velenje, and Majdanpek.[3] Alternative approaches appeared at the 1950 Symposium of Architects and Urban Planners in Dubrovnik, which acknowledged that the life of a city was much more complex than the "four functions" (housing, recreation, work, and transportation) of CIAM's formula. Professionals were invited to develop and implement knowledge about cultural heritage, to consider architecture in conjunction with urban planning, and to shift the focus from cities to regions and their urban networks.[4] Thus the foundations were laid for a complex system of city building, one that combined a growing degree of decentralization with the integration of urban planning, design, and construction.

In the immediate aftermath of World War II, the country's situation was grim, as a consequence of extensive material damage as well as irreparable loss of life. The First Five-Year Plan for the 1947–1951 period responded by introducing urbanization as both the goal and the tool of socialist modernization.[5] In addition to renovation projects, the plan also called for an ambitious construction program—from infrastructure to industry and institutions—presenting an extraordinary challenge for a little-urbanized country with weak industrial capacities and limited urban planning experience. The transition to a system of self-management in the early 1950s facilitated decentralization, which granted significant autonomy to all the stakeholders and enabled urban development to be considered on different scales. The resulting experiments placed a pronounced emphasis on local needs and circumstances.

During the early 1950s, the architectural profession adhered closely to CIAM principles, as a result of the strong ties established with the organization before the war. Yugoslav cities became laboratories of modernist urban planning based on CIAM's aforementioned urban functions, with

Fig. 3

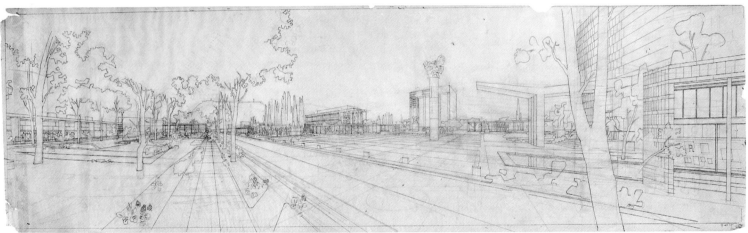

Fig. 4

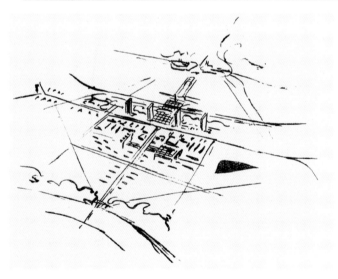

Fig. 5

Fig. 3   Project for the central zone of New Belgrade, Serbia.
1960–61. Uroš Martinović (1918–2004), Milutin Glavički
(1930–1987), Leonid Lenarčić (b. 1932), Dušan Milenković
(b. 1925), and Milosav Mitić (1932–1970). Perspective.
Published in *Novi Beograd 1961* (Belgrade: Direkcija za
izgradnju Novog Beograda, 1961)

Fig. 4   Regulation of Nova Gorica, Slovenia. 1948–50. Edvard
Ravnikar (1907–1993). Perspective of the main road. 1948.
Ink and graphite on tracing paper, 14 3/16 × 40 15/16 in.
(36 × 104 cm). Private collection

Fig. 5   Regulation of Zagreb, Croatia. 1949. Vlado Antolić
(1903–1981). Preliminary sketch. Published in *Arhitektura*,
nos. 3–4 (1949)

the basic typology consisting of freestanding towers and slabs surrounded by abundant green spaces. The most important new cities, such as New Belgrade, New Zagreb, and the new industrial town of Titovo Velenje, were all laid out according to such principles.

Alternatives to this model, however, occurred relatively early. For example, the ancient core of Zadar on the Croatian Adriatic coast, badly damaged during the war, was reconstructed after 1953 following a somewhat regularized version of the historic urban layout. Developed by the architect Bruno Milić, the plan sought to preserve the traditional character of Mediterranean cities, retaining the narrow profiles and stone paving of pedestrian streets. The space within the surviving urban fabric, which included several medieval and Renaissance monuments, was filled with buildings that left no doubt as to their modern origins, though their materials and general contours conformed to the local idiom. Here, the traditional and modern were almost seamlessly intertwined through a syncretic approach that layers one over the other. Concurrently, the city of Titovo Užice in central Serbia embraced a rather different approach: designer Stanko Mandić's plan replaced the former modest half-timber buildings and Ottoman-type market places with a new monumental Partisan Square, which commemorated the city's historic status as the first liberated territory in occupied Europe during World War II. However, just as in Zadar, modernist architecture encloses a compact urban space: towers and slabs suspended on pilotis tightly frame the intricately cascading square, thus forming a clearly defined urban "room," rather than the amorphous open space advocated by CIAM.

Yugoslav architects were only observers at CIAM's penultimate congress in Dubrovnik in 1956; nevertheless, they witnessed during the proceedings the rise of a generation of revisionist modernists known as Team 10, who considered urbanism to be a complex problem of the human "habitat" rather than an assemblage of discrete functions, as the orthodox modernists saw it. One of the links with Team 10 was established through the Belgrade-based architect Aljoša Josić, who became a member of the Candilis-Josic-Woods office; several Yugoslav architects also joined the Dutch firm Van den Broek and Bakema. By the mid-1960s, the country commenced numerous discussions about urban identity and traditional urban form, while the application of historic preservation strategies began transforming whole urban neighborhoods, not just individual structures.

In the aftermath of the devastating earthquake in Skopje in 1963, global attention turned to urban planning in Yugoslavia, with reconstruction efforts being coordinated under the auspices of United Nations. The project included leading planners and architects from both sides of the Cold War divide, such as Konstantinos Doxiadis, Adolf Ciborowski, and Kenzō Tange, and eventually led to another collaborative endeavor with the United Nations, which focused on regional plans for the Adriatic coast. Aimed at regulating a harmonious development for the booming tourist industry, the Adriatic projects brought together offices from several European countries as well as urban institutes from all four Yugoslav republics with access to the sea (Slovenia, Croatia, Bosnia and Herzegovina, and Montenegro). The group considered the scale of space for the entire region down to the specific micro-locations of individual resorts.[6]

Slovenian architect Vladimir Braco Mušič was a key figure in the paradigmatic shift in Yugoslav planning, both for his international connectedness and for his practical contributions. Part of a generation schooled in modernist curricula, Mušič took part in CIAM IX and CIAM X as a student at the Faculty of Architecture in Ljubljana. In the early 1960s, he was awarded a Ford Foundation fellowship to study at Harvard, where he obtained his master's degree under Josep Lluís Sert and Jaqueline Tyrwhitt. From the mid-1960s onward, Mušič initiated and headed, in cooperation with the American urban planner Jack Fisher, the American-Yugoslav Project in Urban and Regional Planning (under the auspices of the Ford Foundation, the US Department of State, and the Yugoslav government), which served as a training ground for new interdisciplinary techniques of quantitative analysis and the use of computers in planning. The program's lessons, applied widely across Yugoslavia, were also disseminated to neighboring countries in both the Eastern and Western blocs. Mušič's greatest practical contribution was to initiate a "return to the street," a hybrid approach that introduced intimate pedestrian streets into large-scale urban projects.

Employed to greatest acclaim in Split 3, the massive expansion of the coastal city of Split (in present-day Croatia), the model served as inspiration for numerous other projects across Yugoslavia through the 1970s and early 1980s.

As elsewhere in the developing world, rapid urbanization in Yugoslavia also included "rogue construction" on the outskirts of large cities, built by those unable to acquire housing by legal means.[7] Tacitly tolerated in a permanently extralegal state, unofficial building lay bare the system's inability to deliver on its promise of a just modernization for all. Even as the collapse of the federal Yugoslav state in the early 1990s brought radical deregulation and massive privatization of urban space, large portions of existing cities across the region still date back to the socialist period. That these cities have retained their character even under altered social conditions is a testament to their resilience.

Jelica Jovanović and Vladimir Kulić

Translated from Serbian by Helena Biffio Zorko.

1   Le Corbusier, *Journey to the East*, trans. Ivan Žaknić (Cambridge, Mass.: MIT Press, 2007).
2   For a history of the planning of New Belgrade, see Ljiljana Blagojević, *Novi Beograd—osporeni modernizam* [New Belgrade—Contested Modernism] (Belgrade: Zavod za udžbenike i nastavna sredstva, Arhitektonski fakultet Univerziteta u Beogradu, Zavod za zaštitu spomenika kulture grada Beograda, 2007).
3   The Congrès Internationaux d'Architecture Moderne was an important organization of modernist architects and urban planners, founded in Switzerland in 1928. The Athens Charter, which proposed that cities be planned according to strictly segregated functional zones, was its most influential document. The charter's principles were partly based on the conclusions of CIAM's fourth congress held in 1933 aboard a ship sailing from Marseilles to Athens, but the final document was published by Le Corbusier only in 1943. The Athens Charter had significant impact on postwar urban planning around the world.

4   See Branislav Krstić, ed., *Atinska povelja i misao arhitekata i urbanista FNRJ 1950-ih* [Athens Charter and the Thought of Architects and Urban Planners in the Federal People's Republic of Yugoslavia of the 1950s] (Belgrade: B. Krstić, 2014).
5   *Petogodišnji plan razvitka narodne privrede FNRJ 1947–1951* [Five-Year National Economy Development Plan of the Federal People's Republic of Yugoslavia, 1947–1951] (Belgrade: Savezna planska komisija, 1947).
6   Vladimir Mattioni, *Jadranski projekti. Projekti južnog i gornjeg Jadrana 1967–1972* [Adriatic Projects: Projects of the South and Upper Adriatic, 1967–1972] (Zagreb: Urbanistički institut Hrvatske, 2003).
7   "Rogue construction" refers to illegal or extralegal construction, as introduced by the historian Brigitte Le Normand in her book *Designing Tito's Capital: Urban Planning, Modernism, and Socialism in Belgrade* (Pittsburgh: University of Pittsburgh Press, 2014).

63

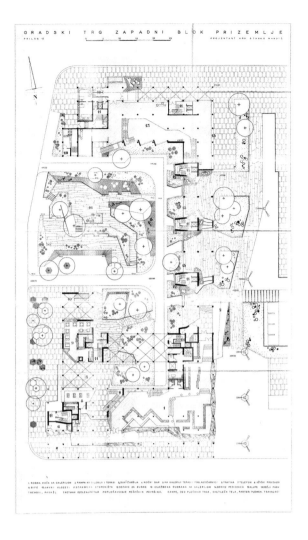

Fig. 6

Fig. 7

Fig. 6   Partisan Square, Užice, Serbia. 1958–62. Stanko
          Mandić (1915–1987). Plan. Diazotype, 55⁷⁄₈ × 14¹⁵⁄₁₆ in.
          (142 × 38 cm). Museum of Science and Technology,
          Belgrade
Fig. 7   Archaeological Museum, Zadar, Croatia. (1964–72).
          Mladen Kauzlarić (1896–1971). c. 1974. Exterior view.
          Museum of the City of Zagreb

Fig. 1

Fig. 2

Fig. 1   Hall 1, Belgrade Fair, Belgrade, Serbia. 1954–57.
Milorad Pantović (1910–1986). Engineers: Branko Žeželj
(1910–1995) and Milan Krstić (1914–1974). Model
of the dome under strain. Historical Archives of Belgrade

Fig. 2   Mašinogradnja Pavilion, Zagreb Fair, Zagreb, Croatia.
1957. Božidar Rašica (1912–1992). Exterior view.
1957. Croatian Academy of Sciences and Arts, Zagreb.
Photograph: Ante Roca

UNITY IN HETEROGENEITY:

BUILDING WITH A TASTE FOR STRUCTURE

As Yugoslavia emerged from the devastation of World War II, its level of technological development was exceptionally low. By the late 1950s, however, a gifted generation of architects and engineers would compensate for the lag, taking advantage of substantial investments in research and in the construction industry. Using the challenge of low-level technology as their starting point, they produced a series of projects, heterogeneous in language and structure, but whose architectural forms all derived directly from material conditions—laws of statics, construction techniques, building procedures, and the nature of the materials at hand—rather than from aspirations to create a distinct stylistic expression or personalized artifact.

Trade fair pavilions—facilitated through fruitful encounters between architectural and engineering cultures—represent some of the more spectacular early highlights of postwar Yugoslav architecture. Key in that respect was the year 1957, when both the Belgrade and Zagreb fairgrounds were inaugurated.[1] The Belgrade complex is home to three monumental exhibition halls with large-span reinforced-concrete domes built using varied structural systems by architect Milorad Pantović and engineers Branko Žeželj and Milan Krstić. The two smaller domes are doubly curved shells, whereas the largest dome, called Hall 1, features eighty prestressed radial semiarches. The semiarches rest with their lower ends on a prestressed girder ring raised on eight elegant V-shaped pilasters. With a span of 106 meters, Hall 1 boasted the largest concrete dome in the world until the Astrodome was built in Houston in 1965. The design of this great, prefabricated dome, conceived by Žeželj, is of particular interest: such technically innovative architecture was unprecedented in the country and had few parallels anywhere. Pier Luigi Nervi's dome for the Palazzo dello Sport in Rome, a similar but much better-known structural solution, wouldn't be completed until three years later, in 1960.

Within a couple of years, additional Yugoslav trade fairs allowed for the realization of other visually and structurally significant designs: For the 1957 Zagreb Fair, Božidar Rašica completed the Mašinogradnja, or Pavilion of Heavy Industry, a glass box with a light skeletal steel structure, while Ivan Vitić, together with engineer Krunoslav Tonković, built the Pavilion of West Germany (see Portfolio, xxx), with slanted, ribbed-concrete walls that support a suspended roof with prestressed steel cables. At the Ljubljana Fair, Branko Simčič covered Hall A (1958) with a thin reinforced concrete shell; Marko Šlajmer realized one of the first mushroom structures in the country with his design for the Jurček Pavilion (1960). Architect Milorad Cvetić and engineer Edmond Balgač applied prestressed steel cables for the suspended roof of the main hall of the Leskovac Fair (1960), whose hyperbolic, paraboloid geometry directly quotes Polish architect Maciej Nowicky's design for the J. S. Dorton Arena in Raleigh, North Carolina (1952). Each of these pavilions—derived from advanced structural principles, the specific application of materials, and diverse tectonic solutions—testifies to a culture of experimentation in engineering and architecture in postwar Yugoslavia.

The excellence manifested in the exhibition pavilions of the late 1950s, however, was not yet mirrored in the country's average level of construction. Residential architecture, produced in high volume during the 1950s, relied predominantly on conventional technologies and some rudimentary prefabrication. But intense research was conducted during this decade across the country, yielding two exceptional prefab construction methods. The first was conceived by experts at the IMS Institute, the leading Serbian engineering and technology institute specializing in research and development of construction techniques and materials, under the guidance of engineer Branko Žeželj. It was closely associated with the construction of New Belgrade, especially with its neighborhood units, known as "blocks" (p. 90, fig. 1). Žeželj was one of the pioneers of prestressed concrete, a technology that became relatively common during the postwar reconstruction of Europe. Characteristic of this system, and relatively uncommon in postwar architectural practice, though, was the use of prestressed prefabricated elements—columns and floor slabs—in mass housing, which enabled the designers to conceive light structures and unusually thin components (the pretensioning and assembly of which were done at the construction site). This skeletal system gave architects great flexibility in organizing housing units and near total freedom in designing the facades. It was widely used around the country and exported as far as Angola and Cuba.

The second exceptional system was conceived during the 1950s and 1960s at the Zagreb-based Jugomont company. Under the technical leadership of architect Bogdan Budimirov, Jugomont developed its systems JU-60 (designed by Bogdan Budimirov and Željko Solar) and JU-61 (designed by Budimirov, Solar, and Dragutin Stilinović) (p. 90, figs. 2 and 3), which perfected the industrial production of concrete elements that could be assembled at the construction site.[2] The simplicity of the production processes, transport, and assembly of the prefabricated components enabled construction in record time (five-story buildings with fifty-some apartments could be delivered within a hundred days), and the prefabricated elements accommodated a wide range of applications (from multistory civic buildings and housing structures to schools and tourist facilities). Jugomont's concrete structures were not always found to be aesthetically pleasing, but the huge number of housing complexes built using these systems in Yugoslavia and abroad until the 1980s is affirmation of the efficiencies, and consequent market competitiveness, that prefabrication technology engenders.

Alongside international brutalist currents, the 1960s boom years of Yugoslav contemporary architecture brought a taste for structurally advanced design with a pervasive focus on honesty of materials and of structure. Many Yugoslav architects intensively explored the interactions between structure and space, considering the relationships between structural and formal components as well as between prefabricated elements and decoration. In this context it is interesting to single out the Slovenian school of architecture, which, under the intellectual and professional influence of Edvard Ravnikar, realized a large number of high-quality structures of this kind.[3] Projects by architect Savin Sever—the Merkur store (1970), the Technical Center of the Slovenian Automobile Association (AMZS; 1968), and the Mladinska Knjiga Printing House (1966), for example—were based on the assemblage of load-carrying elements and their repetition in space. Conversely, Milan Mihelič always established straightforward, transitive relations between the structural core and the architectural expression in his works (the gas station Petrol [1968], Pavilion C [1967], S2 Office Tower [1972–1978] [see Portfolio, v], and housing blocks in Ljubljana [1971]).[4] He never treated his structures as purely functional, however, instead producing complex and suggestive sculptural forms. The skyscraper S2 in Ljubljana is an instructive, exceptional example of Mihelič's distinct sensibility. The building is composed of two structurally and functionally different segments: a concrete tower with vertical circulation, and an office volume with a skeletal steel structure and an open-space concept. Simple formal gestures —two cuts along the entire concrete core and two thin pillars supporting the office volume—completely transform the structural system and relieve the architectural mass.

The characteristic themes of structural architecture met with the contemporaneous experimentation with open forms and abstract art in the 1960s, especially in the Croatian context. The result was formally varied works by Vjenceslav Richter, Zdravko Bregovac, Boris Magaš, and Boris Krstulović. Their designs for hotels, pavilions, public buildings, and museums (whether realized and unrealized) all relied on clear and powerful structural concepts. However, specific articulation varied greatly: at times it was abstracted in the spirit of contemporary avant-garde tastes (Richter's Yugoslav Pavilion at Expo 58 in Brussels [see Kats, pp. 132–35]), at other times it was concealed (Bregovac's Hotel Ambassador in Opatija

Fig. 3

Fig. 4

Fig. 3   Main hall, Leskovac Fair, Leskovac, Serbia. 1960.
          Architect: Milorad Cvetić (b. 1932).
          Engineer: Edmund Balgač. Exterior view. Published
          in *Arhitektura Urbanizam*, no. 14 (1962)
Fig. 4   Gas station Petrol, Ljubljana, Slovenia. 1967–68.
          Milan Mihelič (b. 1925). View of the canopy. c. 1969.
          Milan Mihelič Archive. Photograph: Janez Kališnik

Fig. 5

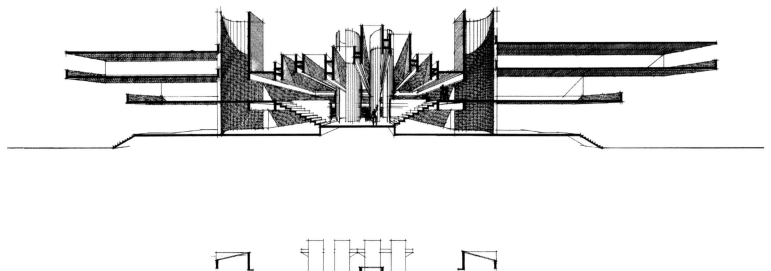

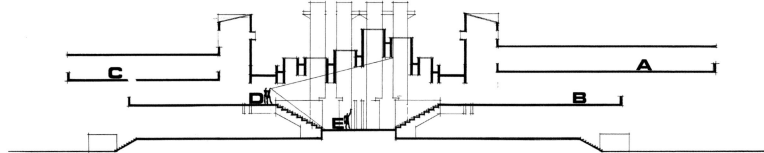

Fig. 6

Fig. 7

Fig. 8

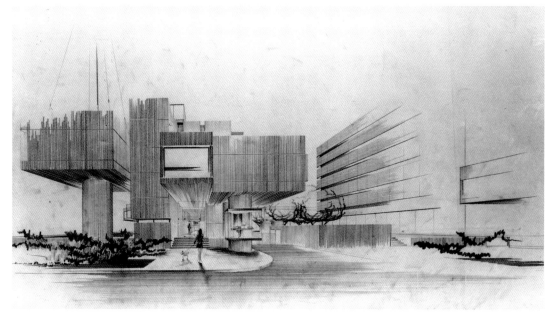

Fig. 9

Fig. 8   Elektroslavonija Headquarters, Osijek, Croatia. 1967–71.
           Boris Krstulović (1932–2014). Exterior view. 2010.
           Photograph: Wolfgang Thaler
Fig. 9   Elektroslavonija Headquaters, Slavonski Brod, Croatia.
           1969–71. Boris Krstulović (1932–2014). Perspective.
           c. 1969. Pencil on vellum, 24$^{7}/_{16}$ × 46$^{7}/_{16}$ in. (62 × 118 cm).
           Personal archive of Boris Krstulović

71 [1966]), or it was put to the service of creating clear spaces (Magaš's Museum of the People's Revolution in Sarajevo [1958–62] [see Portfolio, xx]), structural figures (Boris Krstulović's Elektroslavonija Headquarters in Osijek [1967–71]), or special contextual relations (Magaš's Hotel Solaris [1967–68] and Haludovo Hotel [1969–72] [see Mrduljaš, pp. 78–83]).[5]

This structural sensibility persisted in the region throughout the 1970s: Magaš's City Stadium Poljud in Split (1976–79) (see Worsnick, pp. 172–75) and Ivan Štraus's Aeronautical Museum near Belgrade (designed 1969, built 1989) (see Portfolio, vii) represent the two last masterpieces of Yugoslav structural architecture. A sensitivity to landscape informed Magaš's intervention in Split—an exceptionally suggestive figure situated in the delicate coastal topography. Cantilevered stands that rise from the ground are held together by an almost 700-meter-long prestressed belt; a light reticular roof structure, which cantilevers across the stadium seating, suggests the metaphor of an opening shell.[6] Štraus's Aeronautical Museum has a similar figurative intensity, but its shape is a result of its inner organization, namely the museum's display concept. The airplanes in the collection float inside a gridded, rotund, cloudlike volume, offering the sky as a natural backdrop for topical exhibitions.[7]

In Yugoslavia, as elsewhere, the taste for structure gradually lost its appeal with the onset of the 1980s. Long before postmodernist tendencies emerged in the country during the 1970s, professional interest began to shift away from structural honesty toward symbolic representation. Buildings by Marko Mušič (University Center in Skopje [1967–74] [see Portfolio, x]; Memorial and Cultural Center, and Town Hall, in Kolašin [1969–75] [see Portfolio, xvi]), Mihajlo Mitrović (Genex Tower [1977] [see Portfolio, x]; residential building in Belgrade [1979]), Georgi Konstantinovski (City Archive in Skopje [1966–68]), and Janko Konstantinov (Telecommunications Center in Skopje [1968–81] [see Portfolio, xxxvi and xxxvii]) embody this transition.[8] The rough poetry of the materials along with the use of symbolic forms prevailed in these projects.

Structural components, structural figures, honesty of materials—these themes marked much of the postwar history of architecture in Yugoslavia. The architects adopted structural thinking from the engineers and experimented with a large repertoire of forms. Regardless of whether they worked on housing projects, monuments, or museums, whether building with prefabricated reinforced concrete or steel structures, these architects often rejected stylistic expression and achieved the desired degree of impersonality in their works through an emphasis on engineering logic and functionalist concerns in the design process. By the early 1980s, Yugoslav architects, like their international counterparts, once again began to distinguish their career paths from those of their engineering colleagues. In so doing, they brought an end to one of the most prolific phases of architectural production in the twentieth century, and even today this "structural turn" is rarely acknowledged to have been a concerted tendency in modern architectural history.

Luka Skansi

Translated from Croatian by Irena Šentevska.

1   *Arhitektura urbanizam*, no. 14 (1962), special issue dedicated to the fair pavilions.
2   See the monthly journal *Jugomont. List za probleme industrijalizacije građevinarstva*, Zagreb, 1961–.
3   Stane Bernik, *Slovenska arhitektura dvajsetega stoletja/ Slovene Architecture of the Twentieth Century* (Ljubljana: Mestna galerija, 2004).
4   Stane Bernik, *Arhitekt Milan Mihelič* (Ljubljana: Arhitekturni muzej, 1980).
5   See "Arhitektura u Hrvatskoj 1945–1985" [Architecture in Croatia, 1945–1985], special issue, *Arhitektura* 39, no. 196–99 (1986): 31–101; Vladimir Kulić, "An Avant-Garde Architecture for an Avant-Garde Socialism: Yugoslavia at Expo '58," special issue, *Journal of Contemporary History* 47, no. 1: "Sites of Convergence —

The USSR and Communist Eastern Europe at International Fairs Abroad and at Home," (January 2012): 161–84; Vladimir Kulić, Maroje Mrduljaš, and Wolfgang Thaler, *Modernism In-Between: The Mediatory Architectures of Socialist Yugoslavia* (Berlin: Jovis, 2012), passim.
6   Boris Magaš, "Gradski stadion Split" [City Stadium Split], *Čovjek i prostor* 321 (1979): 5–13.
7   Biljana Mišić, "Muzej vazduhoplovstva u Beogradu" [The Aeronautical Museum in Belgrade], *Naslede* 13 (2012): 127–51.
8   See Ivica Mlađenović, *11 istaknutih arhitekata Jugoslavije* [11 Outstanding Yugoslav Architects] (Belgrade: Udruženje likovnih umetnika primenjenih umetnosti i dizajnera Srbij, 1986).

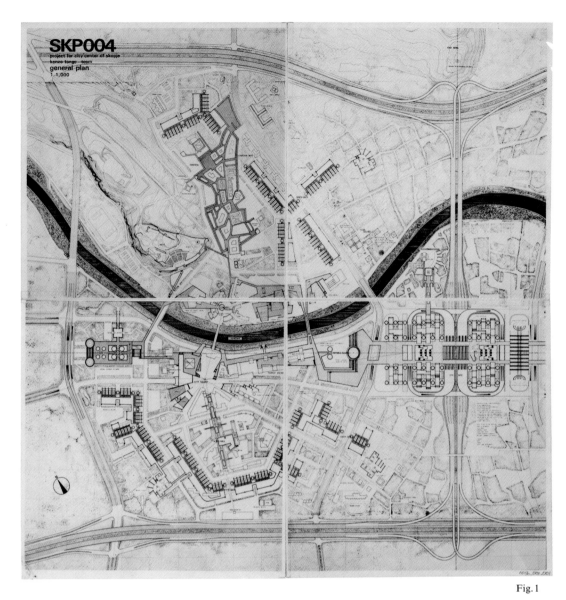

SKP004
project for city center of skopje
kenzo tange team
general plan
1:1,000

Fig. 1

Fig. 2

Fig. 3

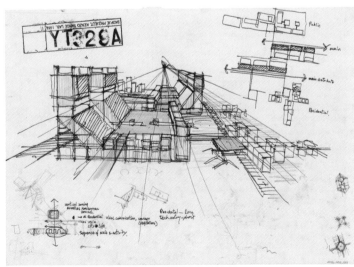

Fig. 4

Fig. 1   Skopje Master Plan. 1965. Kenzō Tange (1913–2005).
General plan. 1965. Ink, on tracing paper. 1:1000.
Kenzō Tange Archive, Frances Loeb Library, Harvard
University Graduate School of Design

Fig. 2   Photograph of Kenzō Tange with the competition team
and Skopje Master Plan model. c. 1965. Published in
*Skopje Resurgent: The Story of a United Nations Special
Fund Town Planning Project*. (New York: United Nations,
1970), 327.

Fig. 3   Skopje Master Plan. 1965. Kenzō Tange (1913–2005).
Competition model. 1965. Wood, 88 9/16 × 88 9/16 × 6 11/16 in.
(225 × 225 × 17 cm). Museum of the City of Skopje

Fig. 4   Skopje Master Plan. 1965. Kenzō Tange (1913–2005).
Perspective studies of City Gate interchange. 1965.
Ink, colored pencil, pencil, and marker on tracing paper,
17 × 24 in. (43.2 × 61 cm). Kenzō Tange Archive,
Frances Loeb Library, Harvard University Graduate
School of Design

THE RECONSTRUCTION OF SKOPJE

The world now expects that the New Skopje will
become a model city, built not for the present but for
the future. Any less eloquent result of the work done
by the leadership of the United Nations . . . will tell that
a great opportunity has been wasted. For the world's
sake, Skopje has to be not just a city to live in but also
a monument to the hope in a better world.[1]
—Maurice Rotival, UN expert on urban planning
and participant in the international competition
for rebuilding Skopje's city center, 1963

On July 26, 1963, Skopje suffered a catastrophic earthquake that killed more than one thousand people and destroyed up to 80 percent of the existing buildings. Just one day later, the Yugoslav government met in the flattened Macedonian capital and committed to reconstructing the city with resources derived from both the nation's internal ideology of "brotherhood and unity" and international solidarity. Yugoslavia's particular type of socialism as well as its independent position within the Cold War dichotomy of East and West determined the highly internationalized redevelopment of the previously provincial town. The earthquake provoked immediate response on an unprecedented scale; in various forms, and over a period of more than a decade, the city received help from more than eighty countries worldwide.

Aware of the scope and complexity of the rebuilding endeavor, Yugoslav officials approached the United Nations for assistance in recruiting international experts to join the reconstruction process. Under UN auspices, Skopje became a forum for global cooperation and exchange for planners, architects, and other experts.[2] One of the driving forces behind such efforts was Ernest Weissmann, an official in the UN Secretariat's Economic and Social Council. Weissmann became Chair of the International Consulting Team, a group appointed by the UN in 1964 to coordinate the city's reconstruction. Originally from Zagreb, he had been a founding member of the Yugoslav national group in the Congrès Internationaux d'Architecture Moderne (CIAM) in the early 1930s, and he cultivated a lifelong commitment to architecture as a social project to improve living conditions for the masses. At the UN, he was instrumental in disseminating modern urban planning expertise across the developing world.[3]

Adolph Ciborowsky, the chief planner of the postwar reconstruction of Warsaw, and Doxiadis Associates from Greece, who had worked across the developing world, led efforts to advance the Skopje Master Plan. The choice of leadership reflected a clear intention to balance the influence of the two rival Cold War blocs, an approach that underlay the entire reconstruction.[4] The resulting Master Plan became a strategic tool for the city's transformation into a cosmopolitan metropolis, one based on a new methodology that considered not only spatial and physical dimensions but also took economic, social, and environmental issues into account.

In 1965, the UN and the Yugoslav government jointly organized an international design competition for the city center. Eight teams were invited—four Yugoslav and four international—including Edvard Ravnikar from Ljubljana, Van den Broek and Bakema from the Netherlands, and Kenzō Tange from Japan. Though first prize was split 60/40 between Tange and the Yugoslav architects Radovan Miščević and Fedor Wenzler from

Zagreb, Tange ultimately ended up as the chief designer of the final plan, which bore a clear stamp of Japanese Metabolism. The first major project by a Japanese architect for a non-Japanese context presented a radically progressive scheme—one that questioned the inherited functionalist model of city organization. Instead, Tange proposed two megastructural urban areas symbolically named City Gate and City Wall, which referenced the forms of Medieval European cities and the local urban history.[5]

The spectacular City Gate proposal, in many aspects resembling Tange's 1961 Tokyo Bay project, attracted immense popular attention. Envisioned as a symbolic entrance to the city, it provided a multimodal hub for regional transportation, including Skopje's central train station. Additionally, the main axis contained offices, commercial areas, hotels, housing, and other programs. The horseshoe-shaped City Wall, on the other hand, contained the new city center, while at the same time following the historical, pre-earthquake urban geometry. Predominantly residential in character, the City Wall introduced housing as an important social project, significantly increasing the density of the city center. Interestingly, the concept of a symbolic wall around the city core was also present in Van den Broek and Bakema's competition proposal, which, in this case, had Team 10 origins.

Tange intended these new urban forms, with their size and symbolism, to transcend the scale of the pre-earthquake city. His optimistic proposal expressed an abiding faith in technology, mass production, and systemic urban infrastructure and growth. Even though it faced criticism for its outsize scale, questionable feasibility, and vulnerability to seismic and climatic conditions, the plan was greeted with enthusiasm. It delivered what everyone expected: an urban-scale monument that demonstrated the full potential of international cooperation.

The globalized ethos of the planning project was also replicated on the architectural scale. Skopje became an arena of transnational exchange, juxtaposing competing architectural ideologies and transforming the former backwater into a veritable laboratory of formal and technological experimentation, which wrought an idiosyncratic architectural identity.

Various countries donated notable buildings, including the Pestalozzi Elementary School (1967–69), funded by Switzerland and designed by the Swiss CIAM luminary Alfred Roth, and the Museum of Contemporary Art (1969–70), paid for by Poland and designed by the Warsaw architects Jerzy Mokrzyński, Eugeniusz Wierzbicki, and Wacław Kłyszewski. Other projects were designed by renowned architects from fellow Yugoslav republics: the Military Hospital (1969–71), by Josip Osojnik and Slobodan Nikolić; the highly conceptual University Center (1970–74) by Marko Mušič; and the Cultural Center (1968–81; unfinished) by Biro 71 (see Portfolio, xxx). However, most of the buildings were designed by Macedonian architects, some of whom worked abroad—several in the United States—and then returned to Skopje alert to the latest architectural paradigms.

The reconstruction produced a number of conceptually and aesthetically exceptional buildings that engage a multitude of architectural languages—from High Modernism and the International Style (e.g., the Museum of Modern Art and the Military Hospital), to various attempts to critically reinterpret local vernacular traditions (Boris Čipan's Macedonian Academy of Sciences and Arts [1973–76]), often only loosely fitting within the available stylistic nomenclature.[6] For example, the City Commercial Center (1969–73) attests to architect Živko Popovski's reinterpretation of a traditional bazaar through contemporary ideas acquired during his stint at Van den Broek and Bakema's office in Rotterdam. Organized around a system of pedestrian decks, the Commercial Center was planned as the final point of Tange's footpath, which started at the City Gate.

Much of the post-earthquake architecture in Skopje is loosely brutalist, especially as civic-scale sculptural forms rendered in exposed reinforced concrete.[7] Notably, Georgi Konstantinovski, Janko Konstantinov, and Marko Mušič designed public buildings that privileged concrete's expressive formal capacity. A standout in this group, the University Center by the Slovenian Mušič, consists of four separate buildings gathered around a central public agora. Konstantinov designed the Telecommunications Center (1972–81) (see Portfolio, xxxvi and xxxvii), another outstanding example of a highly sculptural concrete structure, in several phases that reconciled modern idioms with archaic, transhistorical motifs reminiscent of the nearby fortress.[8] Finally, the fragmented, angular topography of

ЈАНКО КОНСТАНТИНОВ
АРХИТЕКТ

Fig. 5

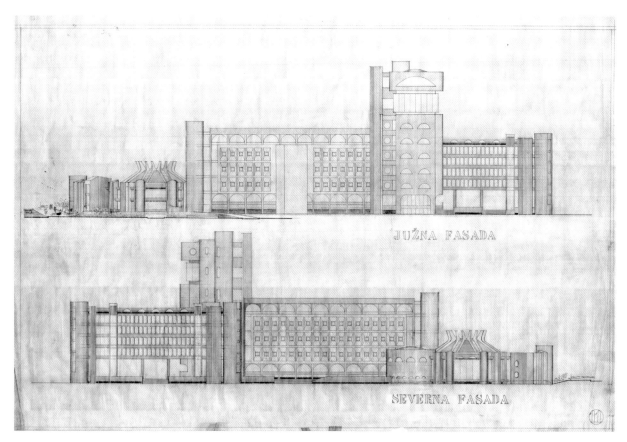

JUŽNA FASADA

SEVERNA FASADA

Fig. 6

Fig. 5   Exhibition poster for the retrospective of architect
         Janko Konstantinov. 1984. Janko Konstantinov (1926–2010).
         Collage diazotype and tracing paper, 29¹⁵⁄₁₆ × 51³⁄₁₆ in.
         (76 × 130 cm). Personal archive of Jovan Ivanovski

Fig. 6   Telecommunications Center, Skopje, Macedonia. 1968–81.
         Janko Konstantinov (1926–2010). South and north
         elevations. Pencil on tracing paper, 30⅞ × 42¹⁵⁄₁₆ in.
         (78.5 × 109 cm). Personal archive of Jovan Ivanovski

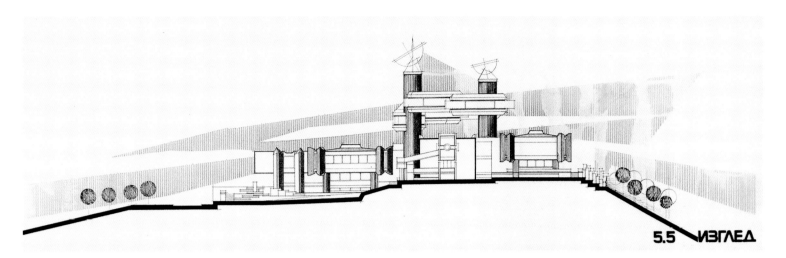

Fig. 7

Fig. 8

Fig. 9

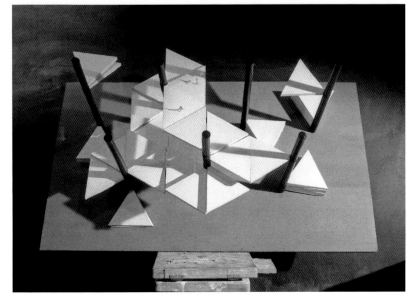

Fig. 7   State Hydrometeorological Institute, Skopje, Macedonia.
         1972–75. Krsto Todorovski (1936–2016). Section. 1:200.
         Ink on paper, 19⅛ × 27 in. (48.5 × 68.5 cm). Personal
         archive of Ana Ivanovska Deskova
Fig. 8   State Hydrometeorological Institute, Skopje, Macedonia.
         1972–75. Krsto Todorovski (1936–2016). Exterior view.
         2008. Archive Damjan Momirovski/Mitko Donovski.
         Photograph: Damjan Momirovski
Fig. 9   Museum of Modern Art, Skopje, Macedonia. 1966.
         Oskar Hansen (1922–2005). Model. Zofia and Oskar
         Hansen Foundation

Biro 71's Macedonian Opera and Ballet, anticipated themes that would become mainstream only decades later (see Deskov et al., pp. 152–55).

Skopje's post-earthquake renewal resulted from an exceptional commitment that transcended local borders. Though the project remains unfinished, the city now showcases landmark feats of architectural experimentation as the products of unprecedented international cooperation. Unfortunately, these achievements are currently under attack: in a recent attempt to reimagine national identity, the government of Macedonia has defaced the capital with figurative sculptures and historicist facades deliberately designed to reshape, conceal, or simply demolish the cosmopolitan city erected in the wake of the earthquake.

Vladimir Deskov, Ana Ivanovska Deskova, and Jovan Ivanovski

1   Maurice Rotival, "Notes at Random", October 1963, box 143, Maurice E. H. Rotival Papers, Manuscripts and Archives, Yale University Library, New Haven, Conn., p. 3., as quoted in Ines Tolić, "Japan Looks West: The Reconstruction of Skopje in the Light of Global Ambitions and Local Needs," in *Unfinished Modernisations: Between Utopia and Pragmatism*, ed. Maroje Mrduljaš and Vladimir Kulić (Zagreb: Croatian Architects' Association, 2012), 218–31.

2   On one hand, the Skopje planning process was a UN experimental model, exemplary for future interventions of this kind. On the other hand, it established a base for future cooperation between Yugoslavia and the UN, which continued throughout the 1960s with the regional planning of the Adriatic coast. See Derek Senior, *Skopje Resurgent: Story of a United Nations Special Fund Town Planning Project* (New York: United Nations, 1970).

3   Tamara Bjažić Klarin, *Ernest Weissmann: društveno angažirana arhitektura 1926–1939/Ernest Weissmann: Socially Engaged Architecture, 1926–1939* (Zagreb: Hrvatska akademija znanosti i umjetnosti, 2015).

4   For more on the political dimensions of the reconstruction, see Ines Tolic, *Dopo il terremoto. La politica della ricostruzione negli anni della Guerra Fredda a Skopje* [After the Earthquake: The Politics of Reconstruction in Skopje in the Cold War Era] (Reggio Emilia, Italy: Edizioni Diabasis, 2011).

5   Kenzō Tange, "Skopje Urban Plan," *Japan Architect*, no. 130 (1967): 30–69.

6   See Ana Ivanovska Deskova, "Arhitekturata od periodot na postzemjotresnata obnova na Skopje—vrednosti i sostojba vo ramki na sovremeniot kontekst" [Architecture of the Post-Earthquake Reconstruction of Skopje—Values and Conditions in the Contemporaneous Context] (Ph. D. diss., University Ss. Cyril and Methodius, Skopje 2015).

7   Maroje Mrduljaš and Ana Ivanovska Deskova, "Skopje: The Japanese-Yugoslav Experiment After the Earthquake," in *SOS Brutalism: A Global Survey*, ed. Oliver Elser, Philip Kurz, and Peter Cachola Schmal (Zurich: Park Books, 2017), 58–63.

8   Jovan Ivanovski, Ana Ivanovska Deskova, and Vladimir Deskov, *Biography of an Architectural Work: Telecommunications Center Skopje, Architect Janko Konstantinov* (Skopje: Museum of the City of Skopje, 2017).

Fig. 1

Fig. 2

Fig. 4

Fig. 3

Fig. 1	Prototype for the Sljeme Motels. 1964–66. Ivan Vitić (1917–1986). Perspective of unrealized project. 1964. Ink on vellum. Croatian Museum of Architecture, Croatian Academy of Sciences and Arts
Fig. 2	Hotel Plat, Mlini, Croatia. 1969–71. Petar Kušan (1932–2008). Exterior view. Personal archive of Petar Kušan
Fig. 3	Libertas Hotel, Dubrovnik, Croatia. 1968–74. Andrija Čičin-Šain (1920–2009) and Žarko Vincek (1918–2001). Exterior view during construction. Croatian Museum of Architecture, Croatian Academy of Sciences and Arts
Fig. 4	Hotel Excelsior, Dubrovnik, Croatia. 1958–65. Neven Šegvić (1917–1992). Exterior view. CCN-Images

TOWARD AN AFFORDABLE ARCADIA:

THE EVOLUTION OF HOTEL TYPOLOGIES IN YUGOSLAVIA, 1960–1974

Encouraged and subsidized by the state, mass tourism became the main driving force behind the modernization of the economically deprived coastal region of Yugoslavia, with architects and urban planners successfully operating as critical mediators between economic demands and social responsibility.[1] The Yugoslav model of coastal urban transformation was remarkable in several respects, chiefly in its establishment of a sensible interaction between tourist development and sensitive urban environments while fostering the preservation of nature. Simultaneously, hotel design became a field of experimentation. The resulting tourist architecture and infrastructure addressed some of the central cultural dilemmas of the second half of the twentieth century: "high" culture versus the "banal" or "popular" social practices of leisure, accommodation of the masses versus individual comfort and privacy, and mobility versus sense of place.[2]

The tourism industry developed gradually until the mid-1960s. Hotels, modern in design, were of modest size, and their planning concepts of dispersed pavilions carefully set in the landscape established a dialogue with the Mediterranean environment and lifestyles. Advanced projects, like the Helios Hotel in Lošinj (Zdravko Bregovac, 1960) and the series of Sljeme Motels in the towns of Preluk, Biograd, and Trogir (Ivan Vitić, 1964–66), introduced networks of elaborated exterior spaces: covered terraces, walkways, and atria that mediated between public, semipublic, and private realms and encouraged living in nature. The master plan for the Brela tourist region (Ante Rožić, Matija Salaj and Julije De Luca, 1961) represents the pinnacle of these concepts, which favored lower densities and organic setting of individual buildings in the landscape. The refined, elongated prism of Brela's flagship Maestral Hotel (Rožić, Salaj, and De Luca, 1965–66) was suspended between two hilltops, which enabled the flow of terraces and staircases descending the slope to enter the building and shape the sequence of exterior and interior public spaces. A close collaboration between the project architects and the product designer and architect Bernardo Bernardi (a proponent of the synthesis of the visual arts and a member of the neo-avant-garde group EXAT 51) resulted in an airy interior with a meticulous coordination of custom-designed furniture, artistic interventions, and architectural details. In this way, hotels emerged as important venues for the exploration of a "total design" approach, and they were often equipped with impressive collections of modernist design and site-specific artworks, thus effectively operating as galleries for the dissemination of modern culture to tourists and locals alike.

The early 1960s also saw the emergence of luxury hotels conceived as sculptural landmarks in Dubrovnik, Split, Opatija, and elsewhere, confidently complementing the historic urban fabric. This is especially true for the Marjan Hotel in Split (Lovro Perković, 1962–63), interpolated into the waterfront in the vicinity of Diocletian's Palace; Nikolaus Pevsner lauded the resort as "exceptional in terms of composition of mass and detail" and emphasized its subtle distancing from the historical urban core.[3] Thanks to an extensive offering of public programs, these urban hotels became popular gathering places as well as modern architectural icons of Mediterranean cities.

Completion of Adriatic Highway in 1966 and the reforms of 1964 and 1965, which introduced some elements of a free-market economy, propelled coastal development. Urban planners and the Yugoslav government acknowledged tourism as the most promising source of foreign hard

Fig. 5

Fig. 6

Fig. 5   Haludovo Hotel complex, Malinska, Krk, Croatia.
1969–72. Boris Magaš (1930–2013). Exterior view.
CCN-Images

Fig. 6   Haludovo Hotel complex, Malinska, Krk, Croatia.
1969–72. Boris Magaš (1930–2013). Interior view.
CCN-Images

currency but also recognized the environmental impact of the tourist industry and the potential danger of overbuilding on the coast. Significant interdisciplinary research was undertaken to devise strategies to control this growth, which culminated in a collaboration between the Yugoslav planning institutions, headed by the Croatian Urban Planning Institute, and the United Nations Development Program (UNDP).[4] Between 1967 and 1972, local experts joined consultants from both Eastern and Western bloc countries to develop regional plans for the Southern Adriatic, the Split region, and the Upper Adriatic. Planning on both macro and micro scales focused on keeping the majority of the coastline free from construction through the use of concentrated developments, built at least one hundred meters from the shore, which was envisioned as public space accessible to all. Plans also determined the appropriate distance between historic settlements and the tourist developments to encourage interactions while maintaining the integrity of both entities. Within defined constraints, plans set the accommodation capacity of the Yugoslav coast at 2.25 million visitors per day.

Such planned high capacity triggered further topological research while the architectural language turned toward brutalism. Two fundamentally different typologies evolved. On the one hand, large-scale tourist complexes were envisioned as amalgams of several hotels situated in parks with supporting sports and entertainment facilities. On the other hand, hotel megaforms[5] included all programmatic elements within a single building, bringing density to the extreme. These projects attempted to reconcile massive developments with the need for individualized spatial experience. Southern Dalmatia's steep topography offered an opportunity to explore megaforms by blending the structures naturally into the landscape. The buildings evolved into complex aggregations of accommodation units with green exterior spaces. The twelve-story Hotel Plat in Mlini (Petar Kušan, 1969–71), for example, is a high-density structure perforated with deep courtyards and connected by an intricate, three-dimensional web of staircases, walkways, and bridges, spaces that encouraged random social encounters on routes from one's accommodation to the variety of public programs distributed throughout the building. In a manner of organic architecture, the underlying rock formations were left visible in the courtyards, clearly demonstrating that the hotel was built with minimal interventions in the landscape. This city-like building corresponded to the urban tradition of densely built, variable, and porous Mediterranean settlements. Conversely, the Libertas Hotel in Dubrovnik (Andrija Čičin-Šain and Žarko Vincek, 1968–74) rejected the notion of an autonomous structure in favor of a "landform building,"[6] a megaform that subtly responded to the topographical reality of the bay's exposed steep cliffs. Curved, amphitheater-like terraces planted with lavish greenery gradually descend toward the sea, offering unobstructed views of the Mediterranean. Fully integrated with the terrain, Hotel Libertas blurred the delineation between figure and ground, between the natural and the artificial landscape. These types of megaform hotels came closest to the ideal of the affordable, individual "Mediterranean Arcadia" within the framework of high-density, collective structures, which in turn affected developments in Yugoslav housing architecture.

In areas with less pronounced topographical features and more available land for the development, tourist complexes were deployed. These extensive tourist territories, which included various accommodations and elaborate supporting infrastructure, are comparable to the works of Team 10 members Candilis, Josic, and Woods in the Languedoc-Roussillon region from 1969 onward. While most of the complexes featured compilations of individual buildings designed by different architects, Boris Magaš conceived both the urban layout and the buildings of the Solaris Hotel complex near Šibenik (1967–68) as well as of the Haludovo Hotel complex near Malinska on the island of Krk (1969–72) (see Portfolio, XXI and XXII).[7] Whereas Solaris encompassed a system of multifunctional clusters, Haludovo was formulated as a collage of different typologies. The central hotel, located on the hilltop, claimed the position of the city's "castle," the linear sequences of apartments and hotels alluded to the city walls, and the inner complex was composed of clusters of atrium villas. The project introduced "design surpluses" such as extravagant flying concrete beams covering the pool. Moreover, unlike the lobbies with sea views, and rather than disperse public facilities as in other typologies, the monumental and inward-looking lobby in Haludovo was spectacular and hosted the majority of the hotel's

Fig. 7

Fig. 8

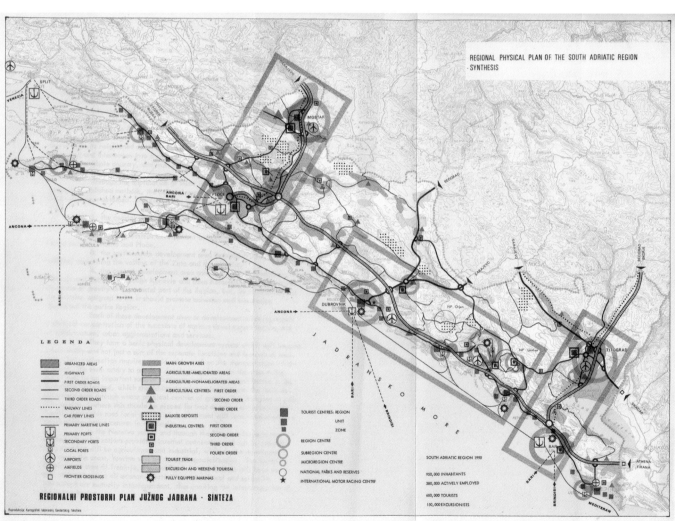

Fig. 9

Fig. 7   Maestral Hotel, Brela, Croatia. 1965–66. Ante Rožić
(b. 1934), Matija Salaj (1932–2014), and Julije De Luca
(1929–2005). Interior view. 2009. Photograph:
Wolfgang Thaler
Fig. 8   Solaris Hotel complex, Šibenik, Croatia. 1967–68.
Boris Magaš (1930–2013). Exterior view. 2011.
Photograph: Wolfgang Thaler
Fig. 9   Physical Plan of South Adriatic Region—Synthesis.
1967–69. Croatian State Archives

public programs.[8] Haludovo marked a shift from purist "Mediterranean modernism" toward a more eclectic approach to both architecture and the tourist experience, announcing postmodern tendencies. After this time, developments were directed toward more picturesque tourist settlements composed of smaller-scale, single- and multiunit houses intended for rent or sale on the domestic market, reflecting the increasing global (and Yugoslav) taste for the private realm.

   The Yugoslav model of modernization managed to channel the development of mass tourism toward the creation of a new urban layer, one that was both culturally compelling and competitive on the international market. Thanks to the policy of free access to all types of interior and exterior public spaces, locals were able to appropriate tourism infrastructure for everyday use. Supported by reasonable planning strategies that managed to reconcile growth and preservation, the architects in Yugoslavia merged modernist concepts with lessons of the Mediterranean and utilized the hotel typology for research in cultural and, to some extent, social authenticity. Yugoslav hotel architecture coaxed spatially diverse structures out of the highly standardized and commodified typology, proving that unique spaces are not necessarily a privilege of the few but can be designed for the greatest number.

Maroje Mrduljaš

Translated from Croatian by Irena Šentevska.

1 For a history of tourism in socialist Yugoslavia, see Hannes Grandits and Karin Taylor, eds., *Yugoslavia's Sunny Side: A History of Tourism in Socialism (1950s–1980s)* (Budapest: CEU Press, 2010).

2 For experiments with typology of tourism facilities, see Michael Zinganel, Elke Beyer, Anke Hagemann, eds., *Holidays After the Fall: Seaside Architecture and Urbanism in Bulgaria and Croatia* (Berlin: Jovis, 2013); and Dafne Berc, Luciano Basauri, Maroje Mrduljaš, Dinko Peračić, and Miranda Veljačić, "Constructing an Affordable Arcadia," in *Unfinished Modernisations: Between Utopia and Pragmatism*, ed. Maroje Mrduljaš and Vladimir Kulić (Zagreb: Udruženje hrvatskih arhitekata, 2012).

3 Nikolaus Pevsner, "U povodu diskusije historičara umjetnosti i arhitekata u Splitu" [À propos the discussion between art historians and architects in Split], *Savez arhitekata Hrvatske, Čovjek i prostor*, nos. 160–61 (1966): 10–11.

4 Vladimir Mattioni, *Jadranski projekti* [Adriatic Projects] (Zagreb: Urbanistički institut Hrvatske, 2003).

5 Kenneth Frampton describes megaforms as "the place-creating [strategy] ... a one-off urban intervention capable of affording a programmatically different experience ... which is integrated as much as possible with the site." See Frampton, *Megaform as Urban Landscape* (Urbana: University of Illinois, 2010), 45–48.

6 For comparative modern and contemporary cases, see Stan Allen and Marc McQuade, eds., *Landform Building: Architecture's New Terrain* (Zurich: Lars Müller, 2011).

7 Boris Magaš, "Hotelski kompleks, Solaris kraj Šibenika" [Solaris Hotel Complex near Šibenik], *Arhitektura*, no. 101 (1969): 23–30.

8 The impressive architectural features of Haludovo attracted Bob Guccione, the late publisher of *Penthouse* magazine, who established a joint venture with the local company Brodokomerc, which built the complex, and ran a casino popular among international charter-flight gamblers in early 1970s.

NIGERIAN INTERNATIONAL TRADE FAIR – LAGOS 7

external trafic connections and
internal circulation

- external trafic – buses, cars
- mini rail
- pedestrains
- yachting

N

FEDERAL GOVERNMENT OF NIGERIA   ENERGOPROJEKT ENGINEERING & CONSULTING CO. YUGOSLAVIA

Fig. 1

Fig. 2

Fig. 3

Fig. 1   International Trade Fair, Lagos. 1973–77. Zoran Bojović
(1936–2018) for Energoprojekt (est. 1951). Plan of external
traffic connections and internal circulation. 1973.
Felt-tipped pen on tracing paper mounted on cardboard,
27 9/16 × 39 3/8 in. (70 × 100 cm). Personal archive of
Zoran Bojović

Fig. 2   International Trade Fair, Lagos. 1973–77. Zoran Bojović
(1936–2018) for Energoprojekt (est. 1951). Exterior
view of Hall of Nigerian Organizations under construction.
c. 1977. Personal archive of Zoran Bojović. Photograph:
Zoran Bojović

Fig. 3   International Trade Fair, Lagos. 1973–77. Zoran Bojović
(1936–2018) for Energoprojekt (est. 1951). Interior
view of ITF building under construction. c. 1977. Personal
archive of Zoran Bojović. Photograph: Zoran Bojović

YUGOSLAV ARCHITECTURE ACROSS THREE WORLDS:

LAGOS AND BEYOND

Reporting on the 1977 Lagos International Trade Fair, the journal *Africa* noted the presence of Yugoslav firms, and concluded, "The greatest export ... [they] have brought to Nigeria and other parts of Africa is in the field of industrial architecture, design and construction."[1] The fair itself was a case in point. The Belgrade-based state firm Energoprojekt was charged with the fair's construction, while the firm's architect Zoran Bojović created the project's design. Since its founding in 1951, Energoprojekt had applied its expertise in industrial engineering to realize an impressive range of buildings. By the time of the fair's opening, Energoprojekt had already gained extensive experience with architecture and urban planning in Africa, including design and construction of conference centers in Zambia, Uganda, and Gabon in the early 1970s. And in Nigeria itself, the firm had previously produced master plans for seven towns in Kano State (in 1973, with the Yugoslav Institute for Urbanism and Housing) and had designed and built the State Secretariat in Kano (1973–78).[2]

The Lagos Trade Fair—and Energoprojekt's international operations writ large—exemplified the mechanisms by which Yugoslav design and construction companies capitalized on the country's multiple global affiliations beyond the geopolitical dichotomies of the Cold War. The very presence of Energoprojekt in Nigeria, a country that was hardly a Soviet ally, confirmed to *Africa*'s correspondent that "the Cold War no longer has a crippling hold on people's minds."[3] More generally, in the course of the 1970s, design and construction companies from socialist Europe received numerous commissions in Nigeria, funded by the country's newfound oil wealth. Eschewing the dominant historical narratives focused on Western Europe and the United States as centers of architectural diffusion, examples include a Hungarian state company that delivered a development plan for the city of Calabar; East German engineers who produced designs for prefabricated housing and sport facilities; Polish designers and educators working in Nigerian architectural offices and universities; Romanian planners who drafted the entire country's housing program; and Bulgarian architects who designed venues for the Second World Black and African Festival of Arts and Culture (known as Festac '77), including the National Theatre in Lagos (1977).[4] In contrast to the previous decade's promise of a distinct socialist modernity conveyed by translating Soviet typologies and technologies to the tropical conditions in Guinea, Ghana, and Mali, projects in the 1970s instead focused more generally on overcoming underdevelopment. Hence, when questioned about his qualifications for working in Nigeria, Hungarian architect Charles Polónyi pointed not only to his contributions to the modernization of postwar Hungary but also to longstanding traditions in Central Europe of architectural responses to economic and cultural subordination to external powers—an experience that he compared to the colonization of Africa.[5]

These traditions of adaptation and resistance included the practice of combining impulses from competing external centers within programs of national emancipation, and no country seemed better suited for such an operation than Yugoslavia. Integrated with the capitalist world market since the mid-1960s, Yugoslavia was both an associated member of the Council for Mutual Economic Assistance (Comecon), the economic organization of the Soviet bloc, and among the founders of the Non-Aligned Movement. These multiple affinities placed the country within overlapping global networks, and Yugoslav construction companies such as

Energoprojekt capitalized on these syncretic relationships to gain access to foreign commissions. Accordingly, the firm's first commission in Nigeria, a land reclamation scheme in Kano State (1966), can be traced back to earlier visits from Nigerian delegations to the Yugoslav government in Belgrade.[6] Development projects by Yugoslav design and construction firms were often financed through loans offered by the Yugoslav government to Non-Aligned countries, as well as by West German, British, Italian, and French credits, which Energoprojekt sometimes brokered. Cooperation with Comecon was also used to gain footholds in Africa and the Middle East, with Yugoslav companies acting as specialized subcontractors for state firms from socialist Europe.

Much of Energoprojekt's work in Lagos consisted of assembling resources from places linked by Yugoslavia's global networks. At the Trade Fair construction site, Energoprojekt's architects, engineers, managers, and foremen worked with Nigerian workers and administrators while consulting British quantity surveyors and scholars, the latter recruited by Energoprojekt's London branch. Similarly, the limited supply of construction materials produced in Nigeria was complemented by steel structures, facade elements, and furniture imported from Serbia, Croatia, and Slovenia; equipment provided by French, British, and American firms; and machinery occasionally borrowed from the nearby Bulgarian construction site of the National Theatre.[7]

Energoprojekt deployed these resources in response to the acute urban crisis of 1970s Lagos. Construction of the trade fair supported the Nigerian government's efforts to decentralize the city by developing the territory west of Lagos Island, the traditional center. Equally, the city's traffic congestion, unreliable infrastructure, and environmental hazards were to be resolved by the application of modern planning principles: functional zoning, cross-ventilation by an overarching sequence of green spaces, and a nested system of transportation networks.[8] The fair's array of circular layouts delineated a territory both protected from frequent blackouts and interruptions in water supply and conceived as a kernel of the city's hypothetical expansion. The social and technical infrastructure of the fair was designed to service neighboring settlements, with an eye to alleviating severe deficiencies in educational, health, and cultural facilities in the area. This vision of an expandable compound was supported by the architecture, with its pavilions envisaged as an open-ended sequence of walls and decks in reinforced concrete and steel, all based on a limited number of components to minimize costs and simplify logistics.[9]

Yet if the construction of the trade fair benefited from Yugoslavia's multiple affinities, the process of working across competing worlds also resulted in contradictions that undermined some of the project's intentions. This situation was readily evident in the operations of one of the fair's subcontractors, a joint venture called the Nigerian Engineering & Construction Company Ltd (NECCO), established in 1974 by Energoprojekt and the Nigerian government. NECCO's hybrid ownership structure was reflected in a "mutual benefit" that combined commercial profit for Yugoslavia and technical assistance for Nigeria.[10] In both countries, the government permitted and encouraged such joint ventures with foreign companies as a way of modernizing their respective national economies while maintaining control over them. Accordingly, Nigeria's Federal Commissioner for Works, O. E. Obada, promised government commissions to NECCO while urging the joint venture to, among other things, fill shortages in the construction services in the country, introduce modern technologies and building standards, and train local workers and design professionals.[11] Few of these objectives came to fruition; NECCO's Nigerian workers repeatedly went on strike in protest against the use of training programs as an excuse for low salaries,[12] and the importation of building materials conflicted with the goal of developing the domestic construction industry. Announcing the increasing participation of economic actors from socialist countries in Western-dominated globalization, NECCO's operations in Lagos closely resembled those of Western multinational corporations—leading to accusations by Nigerian Marxist critics of "developing underdevelopment."[13]

While the public quickly came to appreciate the trade fair, its visitors voiced concerns about the fair's future uses—qualms reiterated a few years later by planners who, by then, found the buildings of the compound largely empty.[14] More than a decade after the opening, however,

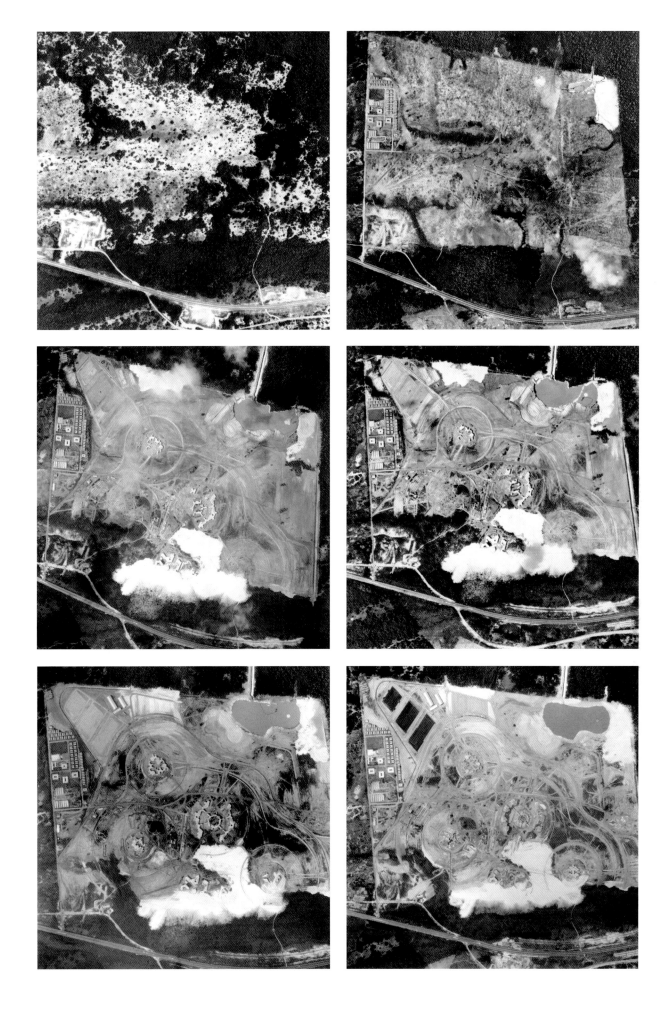

Fig. 4

Fig. 4   International Trade Fair, Lagos. 1973–77. Zoran Bojović
(1936–2018) for Energoprojekt (est. 1951). Sequence of six
aerial photographs showing the site at different moments
during construction. Personal archive of Zoran Bojović

Fig. 5

Fig. 6

Fig. 7

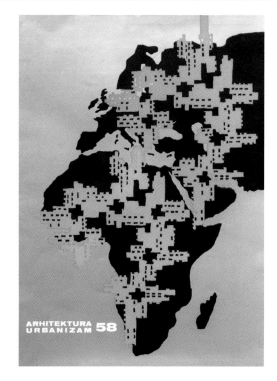

Fig. 5   Ministry Complex, Kano, Nigeria. 1978. Milica Šterić
          (1914–1998) and Zoran Bojović (1936–2018) for
          Energoprojekt (est. 1951). Exterior view. c. 1978.
          Personal archive of Zoran Bojović
Fig. 6   National Theatre, Lagos, Nigeria. 1972–77. Stefan
          Kolchev (b. 1931) for Technoexportstroy (est. 1964).
          Exterior view. 2015. Photograph: Łukasz Stanek
Fig. 7   Cover of *Arhitektura Urbanizam*, no. 58 (1969). Sketch of
          Fort Lamy Project. 1962. Candilis–Josic–Woods
          (est. 1955)

a new purpose was given to the area when the plots that had previously been assigned to temporary pavilions were taken over by stores and workshops relocated from the Lagos mainland. Today, forty years after its construction, the fair functions as a commercial hub for the metropolis, and its circular layout serves as an infrastructural framework and a system of scale and visibility for later additions. Launched as a hypothesis of Lagos's urban future, the trade fair continues to produce new ones.

Łukasz Stanek

1   Rex Owusu, "Nigeria's First International Market Place," *Africa* 78 (February 1978): 110.

2   "35 godina arhitekture Energoprojekta" [35 Years of Architecture at Energoprojekt] (Belgrade: Energoprojekt, 1987).

3   Owusu, "Nigeria's First International Market Place," 111.

4   Łukasz Stanek, "Second World's Architecture and Planning in the Third World," *Journal of Architecture* 17, no. 3 (2012): 299–307.

5   Charles Polónyi, *An Architect-Planner on the Peripheries: The Retrospective Diary of Charles K. Polónyi* (Budapest: Műszaki Könyvkiadó, 2000); Łukasz Stanek, "Architects from Socialist Countries in Ghana (1957–67): Modern Architecture and Mondialisation," *Journal of the Society of Architectural Historians* 74, no. 4 (2015): 416–42.

6   "Veliki broj poseta u decembru" [Numerous Visits in December], *Energoprojekt*, December 1965, 7.

7   Zoran Bojović, interview with the author, October 2015; Andrej Dolinka, Katarina Krstić, and Dubravka Sekulić, eds., *Tri tačke oslonca / Three Points of Support: Zoran Bojović*, exh. cat. (Belgrade: Museum of Contemporary Art, 2013); Dubravka Sekulić, "Energoprojekt in Nigeria: Yugoslav Construction Companies in the Developing World," *Southeastern Europe* 41 (2017): 200–29.

8   Energoprojekt—Yugoslavia/Federal Government of Nigeria, "Nigerian International Trade Fair Lagos," tender documentation, Lagos, June 1973; Doxiadis Associates International, "Regional Plan for Lagos State. Existing Conditions. Report No. 2" (1976), vol. 1–2, DOX-NIG-A 88, Constantinos Doxiadis Archives, Athens; Wilbur Smith and Associates, "Master Plan for Metropolitan Lagos. Executive Summary" (July 1980).

9   "Nigerian International Trade Fair Lagos."

10 "Parafiran ugovor sa federalnom vladom Nigerije" [Contract with the Federal Government of Nigeria Signed], *Energoprojekt*, November 1973, 3.

11 "Commissioner Urges the Board to Guide the Coy," *West African Pilot*, October 26, 1976, 1.

12 "Sa sajma ukratko" [A Brief Note from the Fair], *Energoprojekt*, August 1977, 4.

13 Bade Onimode, John Ohiorhenuan, and Tunde Adeniran, *MNC's in Nigeria: Multinational Corporations in Nigeria* (Ibadan: Les Shyraden Nigeria, 1983).

14 Wilbur Smith and Associates, "Master Plan for Metropolitan Lagos. Vol. 1. Existing Conditions and Needs," August 1980, 50–51.

Fig. 1

Fig. 2

Fig. 3

Fig. 1   JU-61 system of prefabrication, Novi Zagreb, Croatia.
         1961. Bogdan Budimirov (b. 1928), Željko Solar (b. 1924),
         and Dragutin Stilinović (b. 1927) for Jugomont (est. 1955).
         View of the construction site. c. 1962. Personal archive
         of Bogdan Budimirov. Photograph: Branko Brnce

Fig. 2   JU-61 system of prefabrication, Novi Zagreb, Croatia.
         1961. Bogdan Budimirov (b. 1928), Željko Solar (b. 1924),
         and Dragutin Stilinović (b. 1927) for Jugomont (est. 1955).
         Aerial view of the neighborhood. Personal archive of
         Bogdan Budimirov. Photograph: Branko Brnce

Fig. 3   Building B9, Block 21, New Belgrade, Serbia. 1959–66.
         Mihailo Čanak (b. 1932), Leonid Lenarčič (1932–2011),
         Ivan Petrović (1932–2000), and Milosav Mitić (1932–1970).
         View of the building under construction. Personal archive
         of Ivan Petrović

HOUSING IN SOCIALIST YUGOSLAVIA

In 1957, the Zagreb Fair presented two opposing visions of contemporary life. The American pavilion featured symbols of capitalist consumer society: a supermarket and a model single-family home, designed as a part of soft-power efforts to win the "hearts and minds" of Europeans in the Cold War era. At the same time, the Zagreb Fair also hosted the *Family and Household* exhibition, which offered a rather different vision of everyday life, one based on collective housing and social programs. Shown again at the 1958 and 1960 fairs, the exhibition marked the peak of efforts to raise awareness of the culture of contemporary dwelling in Yugoslavia. Architects played a pivotal role, especially by helping establish the discipline of modern design in Yugoslavia. At the same moment, consumerism was rapidly becoming part of quotidian life in the socialist state.

To build everyday living environments within the system of socialist self-management and to educate the newly arrived urban population about contemporary lifestyles—these were among the most comprehensive architectural tasks in socialist Yugoslavia. Although the existing housing stock was greatly insufficient, the new political system guaranteed the right to housing—a right enshrined in the constitution itself. By necessity, therefore, all new social development plans included collective housing from the very beginning of the state's establishment. From the mid-1950s onward, a rich and diverse housing architecture emerged, often exceeding the standards typical of the socialist world. Housing typologies, apartment organization, and furniture designs were constantly upgraded to reflect not only current housing policies but also international trends. Development pursued a modernist, "towers in the park" urbanism, followed by criticism of modernist models, which grew more frequent in the early 1960s. Common to both trends were attempts to reconcile the scale of socialist mass housing with that of consumerist individualism.[1]

Facing the need to build enormous numbers of apartments with only limited design experience in collective housing and technical resources, architects in the 1950s relied on Western European references obtained from professional journals and exhibitions, but also gained on study trips to Scandinavia, the Netherlands, and France. A frequent source of inspiration was Le Corbusier's Unité d'Habitation, most consistently exemplified by Drago Galić's buildings on Vukovarska Street in Zagreb (1953–57). Immediately after, Ivan Vitić's apartment block on Laginjina Street (1957–62) integrated a fragment of the functional city into the historic fabric of Zagreb, introducing a playful Neo-Plasticist facade composed of multicolor slabs and sliding panels. Both constructions, intended for intellectuals and the staff of important state institutions, considerably exceeded the standard production of the time.

In Yugoslavia, Slovenian architects were the first to disseminate Scandinavian experiences with standardization, modular coordination, expressive forms, and natural materials, especially through the journal *Arhitekt*. For example, Stanko Kristl's apartment blocks in Velenje (1960–63), redramatized concrete structure by hinting at classical capitals, architraves, and triglyphs. His apartments integrated corridors and living and dining rooms to produce a sense of spaciousness that defied their minimal plans. A few years before, Ivan Antić had designed similar apartments for his skyscrapers at Zvezdara in Belgrade (1957–58); their straightforward outside appearance, however, was defined by structural elements—load-bearing walls and infill—thus anticipating 1960s structuralism.

Abstract art and the industrial aesthetics of the Bauhaus and the Ulm School of Design provided further sources. Designers conceived a wide range of items for industrial production, including simple and affordable yet aesthetically refined furniture and household appliances. A working model for industrial designers was created by the architect Niko Kralj, in-house designer at the Stol Kamnik furniture factory, where he established the first specialized design department in an industrial enterprise in Yugoslavia. Kralj's most iconic design, the Rex folding chair (1956), was produced in hundreds of thousands copies and exported both to Western and Eastern Europe. International recognition for these new designs came first with the Zagreb Studio of Industrial Design's award at the Milan Triennial in 1957 (p. 84, fig. 3) and, later, through industrial products such as Jugokeramika dishware and Iskra household appliances.

FROM MASS PREFABRICATION TO SINGLE-FAMILY HOMES

The prefabrication of apartments on a massive scale envisioned by Yugoslavia's first five-year plan in 1947 materialized only in the early 1960s. Among the many construction systems, two exceptional ones stand out: the JU-60 (Bogdan Budimirov and Željko Solar) and JU-61 (Budimirov, Solar, and Dragutin Stilinović) panel systems (1960–61) produced by the Zagreb company Jugomont, and the IMS-Žeželj system of prestressed columns and slabs developed by the Institute for Testing of Materials from Belgrade (Branko Žeželj, 1957). Both were exported extensively, as they provided greater flexibility than the large-panel systems typical of both Western and Eastern Europe at that time (see Skansi, pp. 64–71).[2]

Crucial to further developments in residential architecture was the opportunity to freely sell apartments, enabled in 1965 through economic reforms. At the same time, a reaction against the ubiquitous presence of the tower-in-the-park typology led to a new imperative of urban identity, resulting in more diverse and humane environments and new typologies, including megastructures, cascading buildings, and single-family homes. Urban-planning and architectural competitions, which were regularly organized for large-scale projects, became key vehicles for design innovation. Groundbreaking in this respect was the massive development known as Split 3 in Split (Vladimir Braco Mušič, Marjan Bežan, and Nives Starc, 1968–80), which rearticulated urban space through elevated pedestrian platforms, streets, squares, and parks. A number of other projects built further on such ideas, including Belgrade residential complex Block 19A (Milan Lojanica, Borivoje Jovanović, Predrag Cagić, Radisav Marić, 1975–81) and the Cerak Vinogradi housing development (Darko and Milenija Marušić, and Nedeljko Borovnica, 1977–87).

Throughout this period, the private construction of single-family homes continued, often with the financial support of companies and banks, mitigating the housing system's incapacity to fully satisfy the universal "right to housing."[3] Production was significant and accelerated even more in the 1960s with the construction of weekend homes, and both types of house often existed on the edge of legality (having been constructed without building permits). One of the rare, integrally designed single-family housing developments was the Murgle settlement in Ljubljana (Marta and France Ivanšek, 1965–80) (p. 23, fig. 16), where the Scandinavian typology of the serial, atrium house brought to life the ideal of individual housing in greenery.[4]

Within the systems of mass construction, formal and tectonic expression were given an unusual degree of attention and variety. Dinko Kovačić designed the dynamic, expressive, primary white forms of the Brače Borozan building in Split 3 (1970–79) (see Portfolio, xv) by relying on the Zagreb Neo-Plasticist tradition. In contrast, the New Belgrade neighborhood known as Block 23 (Aleksandar Stjepanović, Branislav Karadžić, Milutin Glavički, and Božidar Janković, 1968–76) (see Portfolio, viii and ix) achieved its expressive quality by weaving together a large number of small, intricately connected, prefabricated elements. Between these two extremes, the most emulated model in the 1970s was Edvard Ravnikar's Ferantov vrt in Ljubljana (1964–73), a set of buildings with fragmented forms, emphasizing the tectonic expression of exposed concrete and intricate brickwork.

Fig. 4

Fig. 5

Fig. 6

Fig. 4   Apartment building on Laginjina Street, Zagreb, Croatia.
          1957–62. Ivan Vitić (1917–1986). Perspective drawing.
          1960. Tempera, pencil, and ink on paper, 27 15/16 × 39 3/8 in.
          (71 × 100 cm). Ivan Vitić Archive, Croatian Academy of
          Sciences and Arts
Fig. 5   Apartment blocks, Velenje, Slovenia. 1960–63. Stanko
          Kristl (b. 1922). Exterior view. Museum of Architecture
          and Design, Ljubljana. Photograph: Janez Kališnik
Fig. 6   Buildings on Vukovarska Street, Zagreb, Croatia. 1953–57.
          Drago Galić (1907–1992). Exterior view. Croatian
          Museum of Architecture, Croatian Academy of Sciences
          and Arts

Fig. 7

Fig. 8

Fig. 7   Exhibition, *Housing for Our Conditions*, Ljubljana,
         Slovenia. 1956. Model living room. Museum of
         Architecture and Design, Ljubljana. Photograph: Janez
         Kališnik
Fig. 8   Ferantov vrt Residential and Commercial Complex,
         Ljubljana, Slovenia. 1964–73. Edvard Ravnikar (1907–1993).
         Exterior view. 2010. Photograph: Damjan Gale

The complex also includes a protruding apsidal volume, evoking the remains of a Roman Basilica found in situ.

By the 1970s, apartment design evolved considerably, allowing for larger units that almost always included balconies and terraces. Future residents were sometimes included in the decision making, allowing them a degree of participation in the articulation of their own spaces. Innovations included an opening up of the plan and continuous circulation through the apartment, negating the traditional understanding of an apartment as a collection of separate boxes. New Belgrade was one of the hubs of research, with the Housing Center of the IMS Institute taking a particularly prominent role.[5]

Today, a quarter of a century after the fall of socialism, socialist housing construction has held up remarkably well. Once criticized as mass dormitories in the suburbs, many of the socialist housing neighborhoods, rich with greenery and public programs, have now become desirable living spaces, thus forcing us to question the prevalent myth of the failure of modernist housing production within welfare states.

Tamara Bjažić Klarin

Translated from Croatian by Helena Biffio Zorko.

1 For housing in Yugoslavia, see *Arhitektura Urbanizam* 14, nos. 74–77 (1975), and Grozdan Knežević, *Višestambene zgrade* [Multifamily Buildings] (Zagreb: Tehnička knjiga, 1989).

2 For prefabrication in housing, see *Arhitektura Urbanizam* 6, nos. 35–36 (1965).

3 The "right to housing" was guaranteed by the constitution. An article titled "Right to Housing" was published on the cover page of the first edition of the journal *Čovjek i prostor* in 1954.

4 There were several companies that specialized in producing single-family and weekend homes, such as Krivaja and Marles. In addition, several design studios presented typical designs in catalogues.

5 One of the novelties introduced in New Belgrade was flexibility within and among apartments, which could be configured according to family size. Spaces could be easily divided or expanded. One unexpected consequence of this flexibility within a housing program designed principally for its functionality was that it allowed for the emergence of spaces that didn't necessarily serve a particular function and could be adapted freely to the needs of occupants.

Fig. 1

Fig. 2

Fig. 1   Museum of Macedonia, Skopje, Macedonia. 1963–72.
         Mimoza Nestorova-Tomić (b. 1929) and Kiril Muratovski
         (b. 1930). Exterior view. 2009. Photograph:
         Wolfgang Thaler
Fig. 2   Museum of Macedonia, Skopje, Macedonia. 1963–72.
         Mimoza Nestorova-Tomić (b. 1929) and Kiril Muratovski
         (b. 1930). Model. 1:200. Mixed media. Museum of
         Macedonia

GENDER AND THE PRODUCTION OF SPACE IN POSTWAR YUGOSLAVIA

In socialist Yugoslavia's founding narrative, the woman partisan had won her emancipation with the rifle.[1] The activities of the Women's Antifascist Front (AFŽ) during World War II, which extended from the armed fight to grassroots political organization, advanced feminist causes and solidified women's position in the creation of the socialist federation. With the transition to civilian life, Yugoslavia's first postwar constitution of 1946 unequivocally granted Yugoslav women full citizenship, both by guaranteeing voting rights to all citizens regardless of sex and by providing special protection for women's place in the production process.[2] It also adhered to one of the fundamental tenets of the socialist-Marxist ideology; that is, women's emancipation depended on the egalitarian distribution of wealth and vice versa. Nevertheless, this promise of equality was more rhetoric than action. Systemic and structural gender disparities persisted, hindering women's participation in the labor force and advancement in leadership positions.

The architectural profession was no exception. The few women architects who ultimately commanded public profiles did so in spite of, not through the dismantling of, both the region's and the profession's male-dominated cultures. Therefore, the contributions of women architects —who have so often been omitted from the histories of socialist Yugoslavia's architecture—are examined here in relation to the successes and failures of this constitutional promise of equality.[3]

The modernization and industrialization of postwar Yugoslavia set off an exodus from the rural areas to the cities, not only creating a new urban working class but also shifting women's roles in the production process. The official political discourse optimistically assumed—or rather proclaimed—that all social injustices and alienating conditions could be eradicated with the establishment of the socialist self-management system.[4] As such, gender inequality was not recognized as an autonomous issue but was rather subsumed under the general discourse of class struggle and self-management. Vida Tomšič, Minister for Social Policy of Slovenia and a Yugoslav representative to the United Nations, explained that "the struggle for profound social changes is a part of the struggle of the working class.... This is why there can be no question of a struggle between women and men, between the sexes."[5] Feminist organizations in Yugoslavia were abolished, as they were considered bourgeois and unnecessary until the late 1970s.[6]

Nonetheless, women made some remarkable breakthroughs in the decades after World War II. By 1961, illiteracy among Yugoslav females had fallen to 28.8 percent from a high of 54.4 percent in the early 1930s.[7] Similarly, enrollment in higher education steadily increased for the first three decades after the war, with female students accounting for 40.3 percent of the total student body in the 1973–74 academic year. Schools of architecture and art academies followed a parallel upward trend; for example, between 1962 and 1982, 45 percent of graduates from the Faculty of Architecture in Zagreb were female.[8] The percentage of actively employed women increased from 24.5 percent in 1948 to 32.8 percent in 1971,[9] and by 1978, women accounted for one third of the Yugoslav labor force. Despite these advances in the social and economic standing of women in Yugoslavia, however, reactionary presuppositions about gender roles both within the household and the labor market endured. Women were concentrated in primarily low-income and labor-intensive professions, such as textiles and nursing.[10] And as late as 1971, women held less than 10 percent of management positions, an underrepresentation that endured across the hierarchies of

Fig. 3

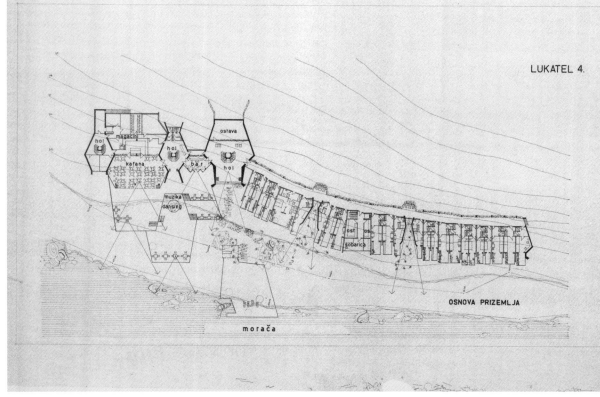

LUKATEL 4.

Fig. 4

Fig. 5

Fig. 3   Podgorica Hotel, Podgorica, Montenegro. 1964–67.
         Svetlana Kana Radević (1937–2000). Floor plan. 1:200.
         Ink on tracing paper. Personal archive of Svetlana
         Kana Radević
Fig. 4   Cover of *Arhitektura Urbanizam*, nos. 45–46 (1967),
         showing sketch of Podgorica Hotel, Podgorica, Montenegro.
         1964–67. Svetlana Kana Radević (1937–2000)
Fig. 5   Zlatibor Hotel, Užice, Serbia. 1975–81. Svetlana Kana
         Radević (1937–2000). Exterior view. c. 1982. Svetlana
         Kana Radević Legacy Collection, Faculty of Architecture,
         University of Podgorica

the one-party system and the self-management councils.[11] At the same time, the nuclear family in which both parents were employed became the fundamental economic unit in socialist Yugoslavia. Institutional support through legal provisions like paid maternity leave as well as social services and amenities like daycare centers and kindergartens were meant to ease some of the family burden. Nevertheless, unpaid labor within the household remained almost entirely a woman's task.

The comprehensive restructuring of the domestic environment, encompassing all scales from the individual apartment to the neighborhood preoccupied the postwar generation of architects. It was that very effort to reform housing and the domestic sphere through design research, publications, and didactic exhibitions where women practitioners often took the lead, building on the legacy of the previous generation of women who had entered the architectural profession by way of interior design and the applied arts. Architects such as Branka Tancig Novak (1927–2013), who pioneered the design of prefabricated kitchens, for example, thus focused their attention on the modernization of the household.

Marta (née Ravnikar) Ivanšek's (1920–2009) professional trajectory is also paradigmatic of this effort. After graduating from Jože Plečnik's seminar at the University of Ljubljana, she joined the large furniture design companies Slovenijaprojekt and Dom.[12] From 1954 to 1959 Ivanšek and her husband, France, moved to Sweden and experienced firsthand the flourishing of welfare-state architectural experimentation in Scandinavia. Upon her return to Yugoslavia, she worked at the newly established Urban Planning Institute before forming, in collaboration with her husband, the architectural and design practice Ambient. Their work introduced design methodologies such as resident surveys and user participation in the design process, and spanned multiple scales from product design to the planning of large housing developments, most notably the Murgle estate, a residential neighborhood in Ljubljana (1965–80) (p. 23, fig. 16). Though highly successful, Marta Ivanšek, whose career developed in close collaboration with her husband and co-author, did not receive equal recognition for their shared work.[13] This was likewise true for numerous other practitioners who worked in collaboration with their life partners or other male architects, including Ivanka Raspopović (1930–2015), who codesigned with Ivan Antić the Museum of Contemporary Art in Belgrade (1959–65) (see Kulić, pp. 136–39) and the 21st October Memorial Museum in Kragujevac (1971–76).

Indeed, individual studio practice, and the degree of authorial credit that it bestowed, often proved an untenable professional model for women, and they often entered the profession as employees in research institutes or in design departments embedded in large-scale construction companies. Mimoza Nestorova-Tomić (b. 1929), for example, assisted at the Institute for Planning and Architecture in Skopje in the aftermath of the 1963 earthquake, working closely with Kenzō Tange's team on the reconstruction scheme for the Macedonian capital. A prolific architect—she designed the celebrated Museum of Macedonia (1963–72) with Kiril Muratovski (b. 1930)—she became the Institute's director two decades later.[14]

Milica Šterić (1914–1998) represents the apogee of this trajectory for women. After graduating from the Faculty of Architecture in Belgrade in 1937, Šterić joined Elektroistok, a predecessor to the Belgrade-based construction giant Energoprojekt. In 1947, after working briefly at the Ministry of Construction, she went on to lead Energoprojekt's Department of Architecture and Urbanism.[15] Her adroit management steered the company's complex geopolitical relations across Africa, the Middle East, and domestically, enabling her ascent up the corporate hierarchy to occupy an executive seat on the Energoprojekt managing board.[16] She eventually became the Assistant Director General of the entire company and designed the first Energoprojekt Headquarters (1956–60). The commanding presence of the complex's thirteen-story tower and advanced installation of curtain-wall facade systems announced the company's technological ambitions and served as a branding tool.[17]

As the prolific principal designer and proprietor of her own studio, Montenegrin-born architect Svetlana Kana Radević (1937–2000) was the rare exception to the norm of these women designers who often remained anonymous collaborators. Raised in Cetinje and Podgorica, Radević graduated from both the Faculty of Architecture and the Art History department of the University of Belgrade, and won the competition to design the Hotel Podgorica (1964–67) (see Portfolio, xxxv) in the Montenegrin capital shortly thereafter. She rose to national prominence in 1967 when she won the federal Borba Prize for Architecture for the project.[18] The building follows the undulating bank of the Morača River along which it stands, enabling a symbiotic relationship between plan and site. Truncated three-story walls, impregnated with local river pebbles, frame the residential quarters and the common facilities, and their materiality further reconciles landscape and building. Oblique walls separate individual hotel rooms, each with a balcony that faces the river, in turn providing waterfront views for each unit. The project underscores how Radević not only absorbed formal tendencies from contemporary brutalism but invented an idiosyncratic formal lexicon, which she continued to develop after she won a Fulbright scholarship to study with Louis Kahn at the University of Pennsylvania in the 1972–73 academic year. After her return to Yugoslavia, she designed a great number of projects, most notably the Hotel Zlatibor (1975–81), a mono-lithic concrete tower in the western Serbian city of Užice. An active agent in global architectural networks, she worked with Kishō Kurokawa in Tokyo and was elected a foreign member of the Russian Academy of Architecture and Construction in 1994.

Today, Radević's Hotel Podgorica and Šterić's Energoprojekt Headquarters are under threat: the contextual integrity of the former is endangered by the construction of an adjacent twelve-story tower,[19] and Šterić's building, stripped of its original facade, exists only as a concrete skeleton. A new historiography of Yugoslav postwar architecture cannot alone salvage these architects' built work, but it stands to reassess their respective legacies. Radević's hotels, Tancig's prefabricated kitchen, Ivanšek's research surveys, Šterić's managerial legacy, Raspopović's museums, Nestorova-Tomić's urban plans and museums, Nives Kalin Vehovar's (1932–2007) furniture, Seta Mušič's (1930–2017) set designs, Milenija Marušić's (b. 1940) housing projects, Srebrenka Sekulić-Gvozdanović's (1916–2002) pedagogical methods and deanship, Zoja Dumengjić's (1904–2000) hospitals, Tatjana Vanjifatov-Savić's (1929–2002) schools, Majda Dobravec-Lajovic's (b. 1931) graphic and exhibition design, Atelje LIK's (est. 1957) airports—among other contributions—all testify to the multitude and diversity of these architects' achievements in socialist Yugoslavia. Those practitioners who claimed agency and shifted professional paradigms did so even as the state's constitutional promise of gender equality remained unfulfilled and the architectural profession itself failed to cultivate parity.

Theodossis Issaias and Anna Kats

We would like to thank Marta Vukotić Lazar for her preliminary research toward this text in her unpublished essay "Women in Yugoslav Architecture."

Fig. 6

Fig. 7

Fig. 6   Energoprojekt Headquarters, Belgrade, Serbia. 1956–60.
         Milica Šterić (1914–1998). View of the tower. c. 1960.
         Energoprojekt Archive
Fig. 7   Working at the Department of Architecture and Urbanism
         at the Energoprojekt Headquarters. Belgrade, Serbia.
         1956–60. Milica Šterić (1914–1998). Energoprojekt Archive

Fig. 8

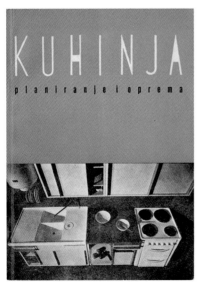

Fig. 9

Fig. 8   Belgrade Airport, Serbia. 1957–62. Atelje LIK (est. 1957).
Exterior view. c. 1962. Miloš Jurišić Archive. Photograph:
Dušan Jovanović

Fig. 9   Cover of Branka Tancig Novak, *Kuhinja: Načrtovanje
in oprema* [Kitchen: Design and Equipment] (Ljubljana:
Center za napredek gospodinjstva, 1958)

103

1 Adriana Zaharijević, "Being an Activist: Feminist Citizenship through Transformations of Yugoslav and Post-Yugoslav Citizenship Regimes," *CITSEE*, no. 28 (2013): 3.

2 "Women were also proclaimed equal with men in all spheres of economic, state and social life, and their place in the production process was supposed to be especially protected (Art. 24)." Ibid., 5.

3 The growing body of scholarship includes Ana María Fernández García et al., eds., *MoMoWo: 100 Works in 100 Years* (Ljubljana: Založba ZRC, 2016); Sara Levi Sacerdotti et al., eds., *MoMoWo Women. Architecture & Design Itineraries across Europe* (Ljubljana: Založba ZRC, 2016); and Mary Pepchinski and Mariann Simon, eds., *Ideological Equals: Women Architects in Socialist Europe 1945–1989* (New York: Routledge, 2016), as well as exhibitions such as *To the Fore: Female Pioneers in Slovenian Architecture and Design* by the Center arhitekture Slovenije and Helena Seražin in collaboration with DESSA Gallery, Ljubljana, 2016.

4 Sabrina P. Ramet, "In Tito's Time," in *Gender Politics in the Western Balkans: Women and Society in Yugoslavia and the Yugoslav Successor States*, ed. Ramet (University Park: Pennsylvania State University Press, 1999), 94.

5 Vida Tomšič, *Women, Development, and the Non-Aligned Movement* (New Delhi: Centre for Women's Development Studies, 1988), 9.

6 Francisca de Haan, Krasimira Daskalova, and Anna Loutfi, eds., *Biographical Dictionary of Women's Movements and Feminisms in Central, Eastern, and South Eastern Europe: 19th and 20th Centuries* (Budapest: Central European University Press, 2006), 8.

7 Vida Tomšič, *Žena u razvoju socijalističke samoupravne Jugoslavije* [Women in the Development of Socialist Self-Managing Yugoslavia] (Belgrade: Jugoslovenska stvarnost, 1980), 20.

8 Sena Sekulić Gvozdanović, *Žena u arhitekturi: tragom žene kreatora i žene teoretičara u povjesti arhitekture* [Women in Architecture: In the Footsteps of Women Practitioners and Theorists in the History of Architecture] (Zagreb: Nakladništvo Udruženja hrvatskih arhitekata, 1998), 310.

9 Vesna Barilar, Željka Jelavić, and Sandra Prlenda, "Women in Croatia: Continuity and Change," in *Female Well-Being: Toward a Global Theory of Social Change*, ed. Carolyn Fluehr-Lobban and Janet Mancini Billson (London: Zed Books, 2013), 166.

10 Ramet, "In Tito's Time," 97.

11 Barilar, Jelavić, and Prlenda, "Women in Croatia," 166.

12 Tina Potočnik, "Female Students of Jože Plečnik Between Tradition and Modernism," in Pepchinski and Simon, *Ideological Equals*, 28–29.

13 Martina Malešič, "Ob slovesu od arhitektke Marta Ivanšek" [On the Reputation of the Architect Marta Ivanšek], *Trajekt. Zavod za prostorsko kulturo*, March 2009; Potočnik, "Female Students of Jože Plečnik," 29.

14 For further information on Nestorova's work, see Mirjana Lozanovska, "Performing Equality: The Exceptional Story of Mimoza Nestorova-Tomić in the Post-1963 Earthquake Reconstruction of Skopje," in Pepchinski and Simon, *Ideological Equals*, 123–38.

15 Milica Šterić worked for six months in 1957 at the office of Van den Broek and Bakema in the Netherlands. Slavica Bradarić, "Milica Šterić, in Memoriam," Academy of Architecture of Serbia, available at http://aas.org.rs/225.

16 Dubravka Sekulić, "Energoprojekt in Nigeria: Yugoslav Construction Companies in the Developing World," *Southeastern Europe* 41, no. 2 (2017): 200–9.

17 In 1961, she was awarded the July 7th Grand Prize, a government-granted accolade for cultural achievement, for this early example of the office tower typology in Belgrade, and in 1984, the Grand Prix in Architecture, awarded by the Union of Architects of Serbia in recognition of her career.

18 Zoran Petrović, "Hotel 'Podgorica' u Titogradu," *Arhitektura Urbanizam*, no. 45–46 (1967): 56–58.

19 See protest letter by Docomomo chair Ana Tostões, "Heritage in Danger—Hotel Podgorica, Montenegro," February 29, 2016 (Documentation and Conservation of Buildings, Sites and Neighbourhoods of the Modern Movement).

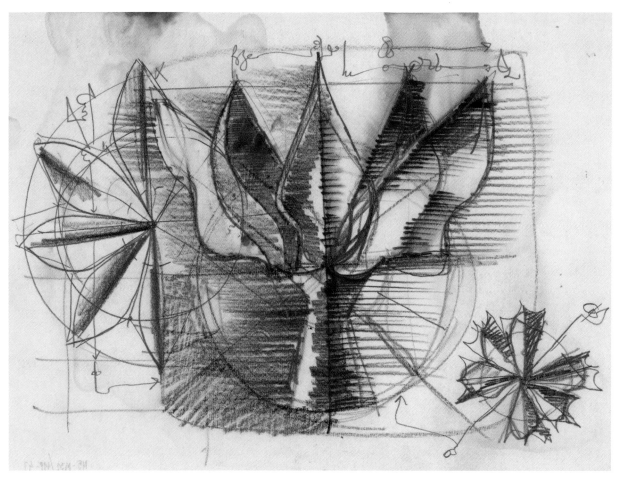

Fig. 1

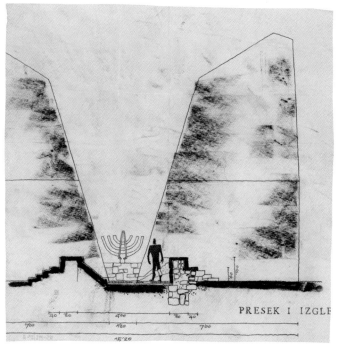

Fig. 3

Fig. 2

Fig. 1   Jasenovac Memorial Site, Jasenovac, Croatia. 1959–66.
         Bogdan Bogdanović (1922–2010). Study: elevation, plan,
         and cross section superimposed. Pencil, colored pencil,
         and charcoal on paper, 8 ¼ × 11 ⅝ in. (21 × 29.5 cm).
         Architekturzentrum Wien

Fig. 2   Monument to the Jewish Victims of Fascism, Belgrade,
         Serbia. 1951–52. Bogdan Bogdanović (1922–2010).
         Construction plans. c. 1951. Ink and pencil on tracing paper,
         11 ³/₁₆ × 11 in. (28.4 × 28 cm). Architekturzentrum Wien

Fig. 3   Monument to the Revolution, Mrakovica, Mount Kozara,
         Bosnia and Herzegovina. 1970–72. Architect: Marijana
         Hanžeković. Sculptor: Dušan Džamonja (1928–2009).
         Engineer: Miro Rak. Exterior view. Dušan Džamonja
         Archive. Photograph: Aleksandar Karolyi

MEMORIAL SCULPTURE
AND ARCHITECTURE
IN SOCIALIST YUGOSLAVIA

Upon receiving the prestigious Rembrandt Prize in 1977, sculptor Dušan Džamonja suggested that such international recognition for his art, and especially for his monument projects, was the result of auspicious circumstances in Yugoslavia, which, in his opinion, did not exist on either side of the Iron Curtain.[1] Namely, the country's sculptors and architects had been afforded a unique opportunity to cultivate and construct a culture of remembrance, as that ambition closely aligned with their fledgling nation's sociopolitical interests in the postwar era. The sheer number of resulting monuments—and their unusual, often remote locations—may be explained both by the specificity of the Yugoslav war experience and by a demand that came, in large measure, directly from the people. A democratic system of anonymous public competitions bolstered the advancement of the memorials' aesthetic quality. From the mid-1950s until the early 1980s, federal competitions were a hotbed of artistic networking and experimentation. As a consequence, contemporary sculptural and architectural thinking flowed into the field of monumental sculpture and resulted in innovative, interdisciplinary amalgamations of ideas.[2]

Strengthening the official narratives of the Yugoslav People's Liberation Struggle and the Yugoslav socialist revolution (the first successful socialist revolution since the October Revolution of 1917) served not only to legitimate the now-dominant ideology but also to create a unifying symbolic order for the new society. Yugoslavia's exit from the sphere of Soviet influence after 1948 further reinforced the need for collective consciousness about the massive—and largely self-reliant—antifascist resistance of all Yugoslav peoples. Yugoslavia had one of Europe's highest casualty rates in World War II, and the tens of thousands of memorials strewn around the country were as much an expression of a grassroots need for sites of collective remembrance as they were the result of an organized politics of memory.[3]

Key innovative breakthroughs were generally tied to the highest level of production—that is, to the monuments that surpassed local significance and commemorated events that contributed to the construction of a common Yugoslav identity. The push to elevate these memorials' aesthetic criteria was a reaction to the prior large-scale academic-realist production of the late 1940s and early 1950s, a short period that reflected the influence of Socialist Realist tendencies and an adaptation of local vernacular traditions. Numerous critical debates of this period directed young sculptors to search for their own, authentic artistic expressions and espouse the lessons of mainstream European postwar modernism. Simultaneously, architects experimented with new commemorative practices in line with the modernist idea of a synthesis of the arts. Three architectural projects of the early 1950s served as reference points for future explorations. Bogdan Bogdanović's Memorial to the Jewish Victims of Fascism (1951–52) in Belgrade and Zdenko Kolacio and Zdenko Sila's Monument to Vladimir Gortan (1953) in Beram, Croatia, were both bold modernist interpretations of the region's traditional funerary typology, which incorporated folk or religious iconography. Meanwhile, Edvard Ravnikar's Memorial Complex Kampor (1952–53), built on the site of the Kampor concentration camp on the Croatian island of Rab, stands out for its multifaceted, axial organization along an architectural promenade that links several functionally diverse elements (entry court, burial grounds, vaulted "museum"). This exceptional project reconciled iconographic and tectonic precedents of Ravnikar's mentor Jože Plečnik with Le Corbusier's principles of spatial organization into a new, synthetic expression, producing an early manifestation of regionalist modernism.[4]

Although new commissions to commemorate sites of mass killings or guerrilla warfare often focused on a central sculptural object, architects frequently played an important role in the monuments' final resolution. This interdisciplinary cross-fertilization between architecture and sculpture led to the development of new typologies, most clearly evident in hybrid designs that brought a pronounced sculptural quality to functional architectural objects, such as the Monument to the Ilinden Uprising in Kruševo, Macedonia (Iskra and Jordan Grabul, 1970–73) (see Portfolio, XXXIII), or both the first (Igor Toš, 1970) and the realized project for the Monument to the Uprising of the People of Kordun and Banija on Petrova Gora, a mountain in Croatia (Vojin Bakić and Berislav Šerbetić, 1979–81), which included a conference and exhibition space, a library, and a lookout.[5]

Memorial construction culminated in the 1960s and 1970s. Ambitious designs were realized with financial support from not only the state but also the system—self-managed enterprises and citizens who regularly participated with individual contributions and donations. Such hybrid patronage characterized the multiyear fundraising campaign for Vojin Bakić's Monument to the Revolutionary Victory of the People of Slavonija in Kamenska, Croatia (1958–68), the largest abstract sculpture in Europe at the time.[6] By inserting a thirty-meter-tall, curvilinear form sheathed in reflective stainless steel plates into a natural landscape, Bakić produced an expressive, almost surreal effect.[7] Both the monument's hilltop location and the technical requirements of its steel skeleton entailed close collaborations with architect Josip Seissel, landscape architects Silvana Seissel and Anđela Rotkvić, and a team of engineers. This type of memorial design —an abstract form of imposing dimensions constructed using cutting-edge technologies—stemmed not from individual artistic exhibitionism but rather reflected the refined joint effort of experts to respond to thematic and contextual conditions. Most such monuments, built in remote locations, corresponded to the expansiveness of the surrounding landscape by means of oversized dimensions, new typologies, or the expressive use of form and material.[8]

Some of the large-scale interventions of this kind preceded similar land art projects in the United States. Bogdan Bogdanović's Jasenovac Memorial Site (1959–66) (see Portfolio, III), built on the grounds of a fascist concentration camp in Croatia, emerges from the natural setting of the swampland. The architect's intervention into the topography of the site of the Yugoslav territory's greatest mass atrocity relies on the symbolism of natural elements (earth, water). Earth mounds mark the positions of the destroyed camp barracks, while a symbolic concrete flower establishes the central place of memory, contemplation, and redemption. Zdenko Kolacio's Partisan Hospital Memorial Complex (1980–81) marks the locations of a secret wartime hospital and barracks on Mount Javornica near Drežnica, Croatia. Here, instead of creating a space of mourning, the sculptural elements open up a space for dialogue with a new generation of visitors, who must attempt their own reconstruction of the historical events that once took place at this site.

Džamonja, for his part, activated a similarly dialogic experience by creating works intended to induce a psychosomatic effect. Examples include his Memorial Ossuary in Barletta, Italy (collaborating architect Hildegard Auf Franić, 1970); his Monument to the Revolution on Mount Kozara in Bosnia and Herzegovina (collaborating architect Marijana Hanžeković and construction engineer Miro Rak, 1970–72); and his unrealized Monument to the Victory and the Fallen Fighters at the Syrmian Front (collaborating architect Krešo Kasanić and construction engineer Miro Rak, 1974). The dark interior space inside the Kozara monument's vertical cylinder causes discomfort, simulating to some degree the anxiety suffered by the besieged local population at the time of the 1942 Axis offensive. The horizontal, radially placed concrete blocks around the central vertical evoke the drama of the siege, thus enacting a sculptural allegory. In his designs for the Syrmian Front monument, Džamonja pushed this tendency even further: an expansive field of vertical concrete blocks forms a grid of narrow slated corridors meant to viscerally evoke the trenches in which the Partisans fought one of the last battles for the liberation of Yugoslavia.[9]

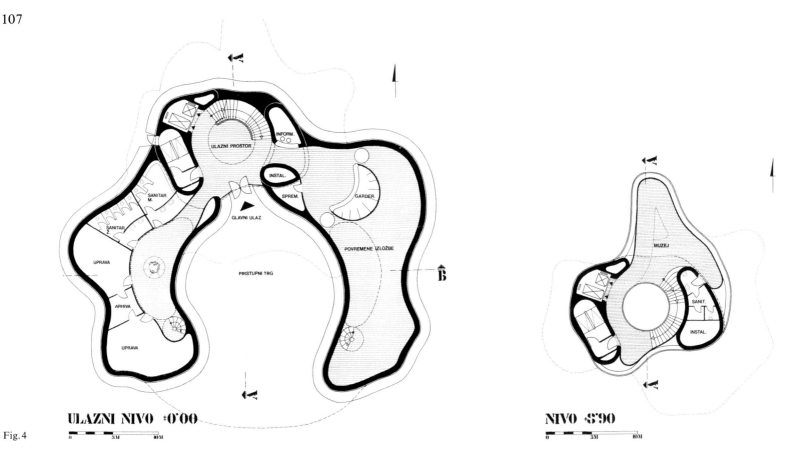

ULAZNI NIVO ±0'00

NIVO +8'90

Fig. 4
0   5M   10M

Fig. 5

Fig. 4   Monument to the Uprising of the People of Kordun
           and Banija, Petrova Gora, Croatia. 1979–81.
           Architect: Berislav Šerbetić (1935–2017) and Zoran Bakić
           (1942–1992). Sculptor: Vojin Bakić (1915–1992).
           Floor plans. 1:20. Diazotype, 35 7/16 × 42 1/8 in.
           (90 × 107 cm). Personal archive of Vojin Bakić
Fig. 5   Monument to the Uprising of the People of Kordun
           and Banija, Petrova Gora, Croatia. 1979–81.
           Architect: Berislav Šerbetić (1935–2017).
           Sculptor: Vojin Bakić (1915–1992). Interior view. 2010.
           Photograph: Wolfgang Thaler

Fig. 6

Fig. 7

109

Fig. 8

Fig. 9

Fig. 6   Memorial Complex Kampor, Rab, Croatia. 1952–53.
         Edvard Ravnikar (1907–1993). 1953. Photograph:
         Vladimir Braco Mušič
Fig. 7   Memorial Complex Kampor, Rab, Croatia. 1952–53.
         Edvard Ravnikar (1907–1993). View of the vaulted
         structure. 2012. Photograph: Matthew Worsnick
Fig. 8   Monument to the Battle of the Sutjeska, Tjentište, Bosnia
         and Herzegovina. 1964–72. Sculptor: Miodrag Živković
         (b. 1928). Engineer: Đorđe Zloković (1927–2017).
         The memorial during construction. c. 1971. Photograph:
         Miodrag Živković
Fig. 9   "Partisan Hospital," Partisan Hospital Memorial Complex,
         Mount Javornica, Drežnica, Croatia. 1980–81.
         Zdenko Kolacio (1912–1987). View of the architectural
         markings. 1984. Aleksandar Karolyi Archive.
         Photograph: Aleksandar Karolyi

Fig. 1

Fig. 1   Lebbeus Woods (1940–2012). Untitled, *War and
         Architecture*. Altered photograph, electrostatic print on
         vellum with scratching and colored pencil, 9½ × 10 in.
         (24.1 × 25.4 cm). Photograph: Željko Puljić. Estate of
         Lebbeus Woods. Published in Lebbeus Woods, *Radical
         Reconstruction* (New York: Princeton Architectural Press,
         1997), 72.

ARCHITECTURE, DESTRUCTION, AND THE DESTRUCTION OF YUGOSLAVIA

In some measure, socialist Yugoslavia—as a state, society, territory, and political project—was constructed by architecture. Building, in the form of mass housing, public institutions, monuments, and other typologies, did not simply accommodate the political, social, economic, and spatial dimensions of socialist Yugoslavia so much as it materialized those categories and, in so doing, made manifest their potentials, limits, and contradictions.

The architecture of Yugoslavia's socialist modernity, as with other modes of modernity, emerged through the conjoined practices of construction and destruction; as one of the slogans of Popular Front work brigades put it, "Destroy the old, build the new!" Destruction was often directed at buildings associated with the Ottoman Empire or religious buildings, many of which stood in the place of proposed new buildings.[1] Across Yugoslavia this "counter-heritage" formed a counterpart to historical buildings that were protected and preserved as part of a national heritage; like other modernizing projects, socialist Yugoslavia emerged from a complicated engagement with the forms of premodernity that its modernity presumably overcame.

Architectural destruction also contributed to the demise of socialist Yugoslavia, a consequence of violent, ultimately successful, attempts to supplant the federation of socialist Yugoslavia with ethnically defined nation-states occupying the territory of Yugoslavia's six republics (Bosnia and Herzegovina, Croatia, Macedonia, Montenegro, Serbia, and Slovenia) and Kosovo, one of Serbia's two former autonomous provinces. The destruction that accompanied this mass violence extended and transformed a trajectory of socialist spatial politics while annihilating socialist space itself.

The political violence of the 1990s heavily impacted the socialist state's architectural heritage. Many commercial, institutional, and residential buildings by some of Yugoslavia's leading architects were destroyed during sieges waged by Serb forces against the Bosnian city of Sarajevo (for example, Ivan Štraus's Elektroprivreda B & H), Serb and Croatian forces against the Bosnian city of Mostar (Zlatko Ugljen's Hotel Ruža), and by Serb forces against Croatian cities such as Vukovar and Osijek.[2] In the Bosnian, Croatian, and Kosovar countryside, antifascist and Partisan monuments were denounced as "Serb" and obliterated; the monument at Petrova Gora designed by Vojin Bakić was vandalized, for example, and his monuments in Bačkovica, Bjelovar, Gudovčan, and Kamenska were destroyed.[3] In attacks on Dubrovnik's Old Town, as well as on Mostar, Osijek, Sarajevo, Vukovar, and many smaller towns in Bosnia and Croatia, Serb forces demolished many historic monuments listed on the state registry.[4] Finally, NATO's aerial bombardment of Serbia also destroyed important buildings deemed "military targets," such as Nikola Dobrović's Generalštab (see Kulić, pp. 120–23) and the Avala TV Tower, designed by Uglješa Bogunović and Slobodan Janjić.[5]

The primary architectural destinations of political violence in the 1990s, however, were in rural villages and urban neighborhoods—houses occupied by members of targeted ethnic communities, historic architecture associated with these targeted communities, and religious buildings such as mosques and churches. The destruction of this architecture is often understood as part of "ethnic cleansing"—a term that has served to reify political violence as fundamentally determined by ethnic conflict as well as, in certain instances, euphemize genocide.[6] More precisely, such acts served to ethnicize political violence that was aimed against, and accomplished the abolition of, the socialist Yugoslav state. Architectural destruction rendered political violence in ethnic terms that, in the context of postsocialist nationalisms, had deep historical legacies, wide social legitimizations, and powerful political effects. This suggests that postsocialist ethnicity, then, might be a social construction partly materialized by transformations of architecture into ethnic artifacts through violent destruction.[7]

Some of this destruction occurred during the course of warfare. In Kosovo, for example, the destruction of religious and historic buildings was a component of both a state-sponsored counterinsurgency and parastate, postwar violence. During the Serb counterinsurgency campaign against the Kosovo Liberation Army in 1998 and 1999, approximately 225 mosques were vandalized, damaged, or destroyed; the Ottoman-era centers of the predominately Kosovar Albanian cities of Pëja/Peć and Gjakova/Djakovica were demolished; and other buildings associated with Kosovar Albanian history and culture were burned or shelled.[8] Accompanying the mass expulsion of Kosovar Albanians from their homes and from Kosovo itself, these actions both asserted and legitimized Serb sovereignty in Kosovo by removing architectural signs of the communities that contested it. After the conclusion of formal hostilities in Kosovo in 1999, Kosovar Albanians reciprocally destroyed approximately 155 Serbian Orthodox churches, monasteries, and other sites, in imitation of the preceding violence—a manifestation of spatial violence as a cross-cultural necropolitics.[9]

Much of this destruction, however, occurred at a distance from military conflict. For example, the Bosnian city of Banja Luka, administered by a Bosnian Serb–led municipal government, saw no military action. Nevertheless, between 1991 and 1995, all of the city's fifteen mosques (including twelve Ottoman-era buildings listed as historic monuments in Yugoslavia) were demolished, while in the Roman Catholic Diocese of Banja Luka, forty-five of the diocese's ninety-one churches were destroyed and all but six of the remainder were vandalized or damaged.[10] This violence accompanied efforts to define the city's population in ethno-religious terms—Muslim Bosniaks, Catholic Bosnian Croats, and Orthodox Bosnian Serbs—and displace abjected Bosniak and Bosnian Croat communities from the city.

The political efficacy of architectural destruction during the break-up of Yugoslavia is testified to by, among other things, the reports and surveys that documented this destruction. Yet this documentation was itself politically effective, especially for the European institutions that authored it. The Council of Europe railed against "cultural destruction" in Yugoslavia, calling it "a major cultural catastrophe" to "our European heritage" in "the heart of Europe."[11] And yet, just as the council was framing destroyed Bosnian and Croatian monuments in terms of a "European heritage," the European Union and its member states chose to create a Europe with highly restrictive borders, tightening immigration and asylum policies in response to the rising exodus of post-Yugoslav refugees. As Europe's cultural space was expanded to encompass architectural heritage in the former Yugoslavia, this expansion both compensated for and repressed the defense of Europe's political space against former Yugoslav citizens.

Attention to architectural destruction within the postsocialist political violence that dismantled Yugoslavia refracts on often-assumed or argued claims that the political project of socialist Yugoslavia in some way "failed." Rather, it emphatically reveals that socialist Yugoslavia was destroyed, from both within and without. To register the difference between the *failure* of a political project and the *destruction* of a political project is to solicit attention to both the narration of that project's past and assays of its potential futures.

Andrew Herscher

Fig. 2

Fig. 3

Fig. 4

Fig. 2   Postwar condition of a mosque in Reti e Poshtme, Kosovo.
            1999. Photograph: Andrew Herscher
Fig. 3   Postwar condition of the Church of Holy Trinity, Petrić,
            Kosovo. 1999. Serbian Orthodox Eparchy of Raška-Prizren
Fig. 4   Shelling of the National Assembly of Bosnia and
            Herzegovina (today Parliament), Sarajevo, Bosnia and
            Herzegovina. 1992. Architect: Juraj Neidhardt (1901–79).
            Project built 1965–79. Getty Images. Photograph:
            Mikhail Evstafiev

Fig. 5

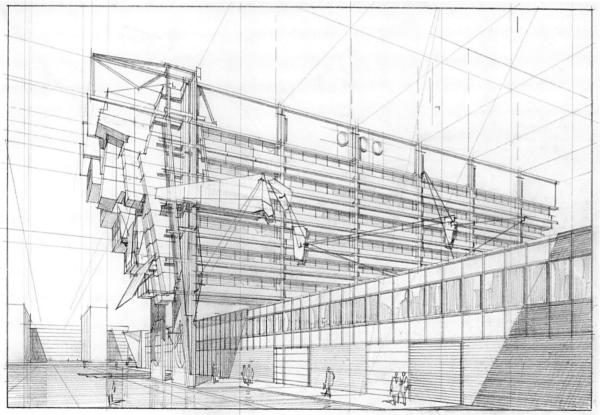

Fig. 6

Fig. 5   Lebbeus Woods (1940–2012). Elektroprivreda Building,
         War and Architecture. Altered photograph, electrostatic
         print on paper with scratching and colored pencil,
         10½ × 15½ in. (26.7 × 39.4 cm). Photograph: Ekkehard
         Rehfeld. Estate of Lebbeus Woods. Published in Lebbeus
         Woods, *Radical Reconstruction* (New York: Princeton
         Architectural Press, 1997), 76.

Fig. 6   Lebbeus Woods (1940–2012). Untitled (Elektroprivreda
         Building Sketch), *War and Architecture*. 1993–94.
         Graphite on vellum, 12⅞ × 19⅞ in. (32.7 × 50.5 cm).
         Estate of Lebbeus Woods

117

1   On the destruction of the Baščaršija in Sarajevo, see Dijana Alić and Marjam Gusheh, "Reconciling National Narratives in Socialist Bosnia and Herzegovina: The Baščaršija Project, 1948–1953," *Journal of the Society of Architectural Historians* 58, no. 1 (March 1999); on the destruction of the Čaršija in Pristina, see Andrew Herscher, "A Relic of the Past, Fast Disappearing," in Herscher, *Violence Taking Place: The Architecture of the Kosovo Conflict* (Stanford, Calif.: Stanford University Press, 2010); on the destruction of religious buildings in Yugoslavia, see Vjekoslav Perica, *Balkan Idols: Religion and Nationalism in Yugoslav States* (Oxford, U.K.: Oxford University Press, 2002).

2   On destruction in Sarajevo, see *Urbicid—Sarajevo* (Paris: Centre Georges Pompidou, 1994), and *Bosnia and the Destruction of Cultural Heritage,* ed. Helen Walasek (New York: Routledge, 2015); on destruction in Vukovar, see *Plan i program obnove i razvitka grada Vukovara 1.1.2004–21.12.2008* [Plan and Program for the Restoration and Development of the City of Vukovar, January 1, 2004–December 21, 2008] (Vukovar, Croatia: Vlada Republike Hrvatske, 2003); on destruction in Mostar, see *Mostar: Urbicid,* ed. Safet Oručević (Mostar, Bosnia and Herzegovina: Centar za mir, 2004).

3   On the destruction of antifascist and Partisan monuments in Croatia, see *Rušenje antifašističkih spomenika u Hrvatskoj, 1990–2000* [Destruction of Antifascist Monuments in Croatia, 1990–2000], ed. Juraj Hrženjak (Zagreb: Savez antifašističkih boraca Hrvatske, 2002).

4   On the destruction of architectural heritage in Dubrovnik, see Ivica Žile, "War Damage to Cultural Monuments in Dubrovnik and Its Surroundings," *Radovi Instituta za Povijest Umjetnosti* 17, no. 1 (1993), and Ferdinand Meder, ed., *Dubrovnik 1991–1992* (Paris: UNESCO, 1993); on the destruction of architectural heritage in Bosnia, see Walasek, *Bosnia and the Destruction of Cultural Heritage*; on the destruction of architectural heritage in Croatia, see Vlado Ukrainčik and Božidar Urišič, "Ratne štete na spomenicima kulture" [War Damage to Cultural Monuments], *Godišnjak Zaštite Spomenika Kulture Hrvatske*, 24/25 (1998), and Igor Fisković, ed., *Cultural Heritage of Croatia in the War 1991/1992* (Zagreb: Hrvatske Sveučilišna Naklada, 1993).

5   On the architectural consequences of NATO's bombardment, see Srdjan Jovanović Weiss, "NATO as Architectural Critic," *Cabinet* 1 (2000–2001), and Herscher, "The Right Place: A Supplement on the Architecture of Humanitarian War," in Herscher, *Violence Taking Place.*

6   On ethnicity and political violence in Yugoslavia, see V. P. Gagnon Jr., *The Myth of Ethnic War: Serbia and Croatia in the 1990s* (Ithaca, N.Y.: Cornell University Press, 2004).

7   See Herscher, *Violence Taking Place*, and Andrew Herscher, "In Ruins: Architecture, Memory, Countermemory," *Journal of the Society of Architectural Historians* 73, no. 4 (2014).

8   See Sabri Bajgora, ed., *Barbaria Serbe ndaj monumenteve Islame në Kosovë* [Serbian Barbarities Against Islamic Monuments in Kosovo] (Pristina: Dituria Islame, 2000).

9   Zoran Stefanović, ed., *Raspeto Kosovo* [Kosovo Crucified], vols. 1–3 (Belgrade: Glas Kosova i Metohije, 1999, 2000, 2001).

10   On the destruction of mosques in Banja Luka, see Sabira Husedzinović, "Zločinačko unistavanje: spomenika islamske arhitekture u Banjoj Luci" [Criminal Destruction: Monuments of Islamic Architecture in Banja Luka], BH Media, 2002, http://bhmedia.se/banjaluka/tekstovi/unistavanje.htm; on the destruction of churches in Banja Luka, see Human Rights Watch, *War Crimes in Bosnia-Hercegovina: UN Cease-Fire Won't Help Banja Luka*, D 608, June 1, 1994.

11   Parliamentary Assembly of the Council of Europe, "Information Report on the Destruction by War of the Cultural Heritage in Croatia and Bosnia-Herzegovina," February 2, 1993, 3. On the activities of the Council of Europe in Bosnia during the war, see Walasek, *Bosnia and the Destruction of Cultural Heritage.*

CASE STUDIES

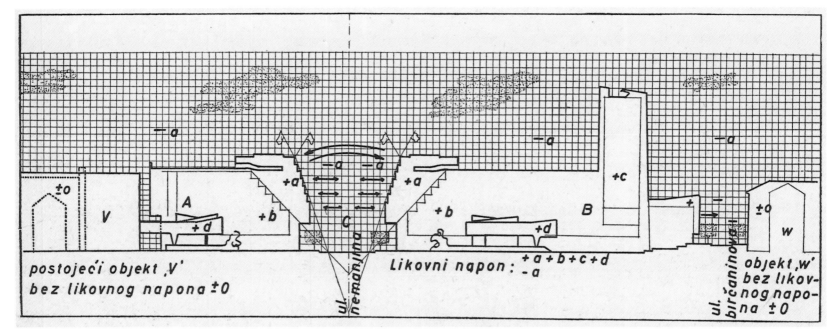

Fig. 1

Fig. 1   Generalštab (Secretariat of People's Defense and the
Headquarters of the Yugoslav People's Army), Belgrade,
Serbia. 1954–63. Nikola Dobrović (1897–1967).
Diagram of "visual tensions." 1960. *Čovjek i prostor* 7,
no. 100 (1960). Association of Croatian Architects

GENERALŠTAB

Secretariat of People's Defense and the
Headquarters of the Yugoslav People's Army

Architect	Nikola Dobrović (1897–1967)
Built	1954–63
Location	Belgrade, Serbia

This sprawling building is the magnum opus of Nikola Dobrović, one
of Yugoslavia's most prominent modernists. Dobrović was a typical Central
European cosmopolitan: born to a Serbian family in Hungary, he studied
architecture at the Czech Technical University in Prague, one of the hotbeds
of interwar functionalism, before moving to Dubrovnik in 1934, where
he built a series of exquisite modernist villas. Despite his success at architectural competitions across Yugoslavia, he was unable to penetrate the
conservative circles of the capital until the end of World War II, when in
October 1944 he arrived in the newly liberated city with the victorious
Partisans. Dobrović was immediately put in charge of postwar reconstruction, but despite his enthusiastic efforts, he realized only one project in
Belgrade, the dual structure colloquially known as the Generalštab (General
Staff), the headquarters of the national defense system of new socialist
Yugoslavia.

Straddling an important intersection in downtown Belgrade, the
Generalštab engages the urban fabric in heightened spatial dynamism and
numerous visual contrasts: a cascading, wedge-shaped void over Nemanjina
Street balances a tall tower at the opposite end; rough, red stone walls are
joined by smooth white spandrels; and various horizontal, vertical, and
diagonal lines organize the form. These tightly knit relationships reflected
Dobrović's ideas about the socialist city as an organic whole, marking an
explicit counterpoint to the chaotic development accumulated during the
decades of capitalist speculation. These ideas culminated in his influential
theory of "space in motion," based in part on the writings of the French
philosopher Henri Bergson. Dobrović argued that the whole city should be
tied into an unbroken chain of dramatic spatial scenes by engaging its
buildings in carefully thought-out dynamic relationships rather than leaving
them to sit inertly like "randomly fallen dust."[1] The architect, however,
also offered an alternative explanation for the project when he described the
symmetrical cascades on either side of Nemanjina Street as "an urban
symbol of the Sutjeska," referring to a canyon in Bosnia and Herzegovina
where one of the key battles of the Yugoslav liberation war had taken place
in 1943. The seat of the Yugoslav army thus also became a monument
to that army's victorious war effort.

It is ironic that a building designed to unify a fragmented, chaotic
city ended up being its most famous ruin: the Generalštab was bombed
in NATO's 1999 campaign against the truncated Yugoslavia, and its future
remains uncertain.

Vladimir Kulić

---

1   See Nikola Dobrović, "Pokrenutost prostora–Bergsonove
    'Dinamičke sheme'–nova likovna sredina" [Space in
    Motion—Bergson's "Dynamic Schemes"—A new Visual
    Environment], *Čovjek i prostor* 7, no. 100 (1960): 10–11.

Fig. 2

Fig. 3

Fig. 1

Fig. 1   Moša Pijade Workers' University, Zagreb, Croatia.
1955–61. Radovan Nikšić (1920–1987) and Ninoslav
Kučan (1927–1994). Exterior view. c. 1961. Tošo Dabac
Archive, Museum of Contemporary Art, Zagreb.
Photograph: Tošo Dabac

MOŠA PIJADE
WORKERS' UNIVERSITY

Architect	Radovan Nikšić (1920–1987) and Ninoslav Kučan (1927–1994)
Built	1955–61
Location	Zagreb, Croatia

The Moša Pijade Workers' University (RANS) is a doubly coded edifice—a monument to the tenth anniversary of the Partisan liberation of Yugoslavia and home to a new socialist institution dedicated to the workers of Zagreb.[1] Starting from the premise that the state's progress depended on the education of all social classes, the university provided adult education to workers, training them, among other things, to take on the responsibilities demanded of citizens within the Yugoslav system of socialist self-management. Immediately after its opening, RANS was recognized as a model for the possibilities and aspirations of this system.

Radovan Nikšić and Ninoslav Kučan won the 1956 competition for a new building with a proposal that updated the fundamental principles of interwar functionalism: free plan, skeletal structure, and non-load-bearing facade. In these young architects' design, open spaces became important organizing devices: all educational, social, cultural, and administrative spaces were gathered around two courtyards under a single roof, and a long porch at the front entrance entered into a dialogue with the surrounding city. However, during the six years of construction, the building's concept underwent an evolution under the influence of the revisionist theories of Team 10. In 1956, Nikšić had spent six months in the Netherlands as part of a program that provided technical aid to Yugoslavia. The resulting contact with Jacob Bakema, a Dutch architect who was a key member of Team 10, informed an increasing emphasis on social interaction in the design for RANS. Endowed with generous dimensions and abundant, direct daylight, the university's lobbies, hallways, and atypically positioned hovering staircases all became places for socializing, producing a sense of spaciousness, airiness, and free, unobstructed movement. In this way, the entire interior space became activated in a network of informal circulation. The overriding sense of harmony and order throughout the complex was attained via the repetition of a single module that the architects systematically applied in the design of all spatial and structural elements. It could be argued that such an approach in turn anticipated some of Team 10's later innovations, such as the "mat-building," an informal structure of circulation networks and occupiable spaces that can be repeated horizontally to form something akin to a carpet or a mat.

In the university architecture, Nikšić and Kučan strove to achieve a timeless, rational expression based on contrasts—between the transparent, glazed single-floor volume and the opaque mass of the cinema hall, between the white walls and the black marble-clad columns, between the white floor and the hovering black staircases, and between the geometrical forms and the natural materials (wood and leather) used in the custom-made furniture designed by architect Bernardo Bernardi.

Tamara Bjažić Klarin

Translated from Croatian by Irena Šentevska.

---

1   Moša Pijade, painter, writer, and the first translator of Marx's *Das Kapital* into Serbo-Croatian, was a Yugoslav Communist leader and Partisan officer during World War II. He died in 1957 while serving as the President of the Federal Assembly of Yugoslavia.

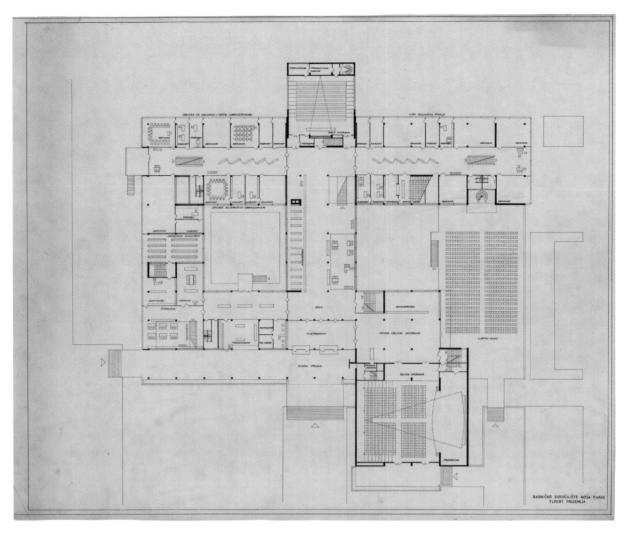

Fig. 2

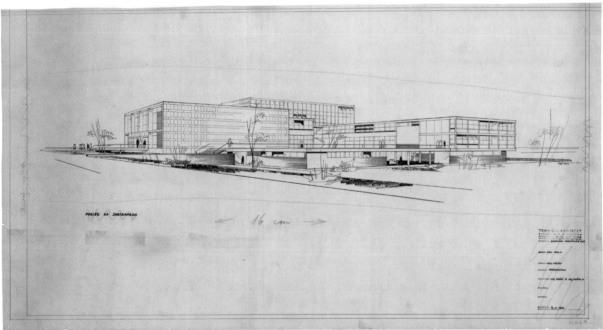

Fig. 3

Fig. 2 Ground floor plan, conceptual design phase. 1:200.
Ink on vellum, 24 × 29¹⁵/₁₆ in. (61 × 76 cm). Archive of
the Faculty of Architecture, Zagreb

Fig. 3 Perspective drawing, conceptual design phase. 1956.
Ink on vellum, 17¹¹/₁₆ × 34¹/₁₆ in. (45 × 86.5 cm). Archive
of the Faculty of Architecture, Zagreb

Fig. 4 Ground floor plan, sketch. Felt-tipped pen and pencil on
paper, 11¹¹/₁₆ × 16⁹/₁₆ in. (29.7 × 42 cm). Radovan Nikšić
Archive. Croatian Academy of Sciences and Arts

Fig. 5 Aerial view. Croatian Museum of Architecture,
Croatian Academy of Sciences and Arts. Photograph:
Krešimir Tadić

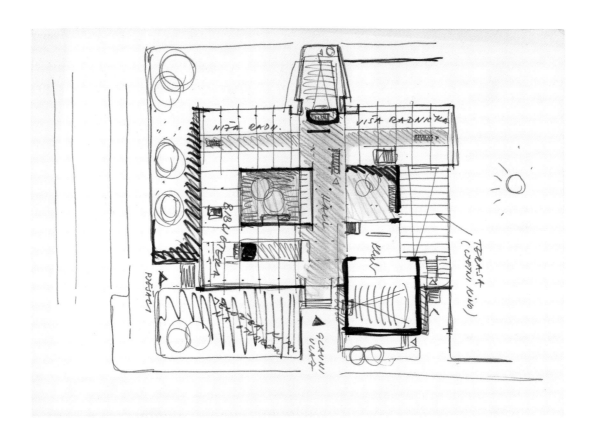

Fig. 4

Fig. 5

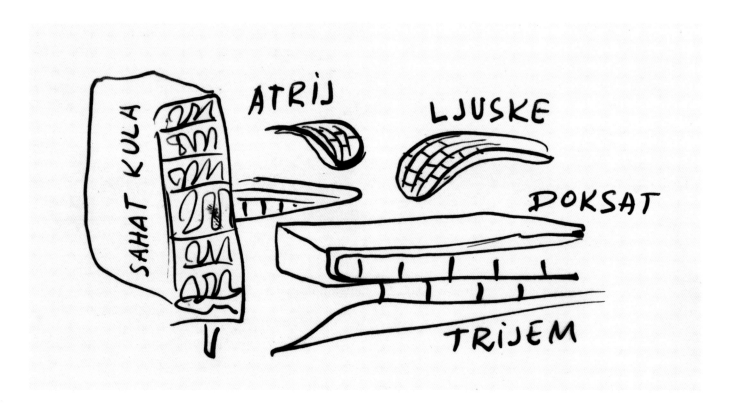

Fig. 1

Fig. 2

Fig. 3

Fig. 1	National Assembly of Bosnia and Herzegovina. 1954–79. Juraj Neidhardt (1901–1979). Sketch of the Assembly's elements. Ink on tracing paper, $5\frac{1}{2} \times 7\frac{1}{16}$ in. (14 × 18 cm). Private archive of Juraj Neidhardt
Fig. 2	Jacket cover of Dušan Grabrijan and Juraj Neidhardt, *Arhitektura Bosne i put u suvremeno/Architecture of Bosnia and the Way to Modernity* (1957).
Fig. 3	"Imaginary impression composed by the elements of Bosnian architecture," 1950–55. Juraj Neidhardt (1901–1979). Collage, $14 \times 14\frac{9}{16}$ in. (36 × 37 cm). Private archive of Juraj Neidhardt

"ARCHITECTURE OF BOSNIA AND THE WAY TO MODERNITY"

Authors   Dušan Grabrijan (1899–1952)
                  and Juraj Neidhardt (1901–1979)

Published   1957

In 1953, Le Corbusier wrote an unusually elated foreword, for a manuscript written by two Yugoslav architects, Dušan Grabrijan and Juraj Neidhardt. The distillation of a long-term ethnographic-architectural research project, their text documented the particularities of the vernacular built environment in Bosnia with the goal of defining principles of contemporary design practice. Grabrijan and Neidhardt's almost two-decades-long study had focused on the traditional architecture and spatial organization of society in this mountainous Yugoslav region, where centuries of Ottoman rule had left a strong imprint of Islamic culture. The resulting book, *Architecture of Bosnia and the Way to Modernity*, was finally published in 1957, five years after Grabrijan's death. In his foreword, Le Corbusier praised the authors' achievement for highlighting "continuity of spirit and continuity of evolution, including also revolutions that may mark the way."[1]

Neidhardt and Grabrijan had begun their research in the 1930s, turning to the native communities of the Balkans and the materiality of their everyday life as resources relevant to contemporary architecture before similar ideas would gain currency in the mainstream of the Modern Movement and before the emergence of a discourse on "critical regionalism." Their diverse formative experiences—Grabrijan's absorption of his teacher Jože Plečnik's classically minded interpretation of the national architectural tradition, and Neidhardt's extensive design practice, which had begun in Peter Behrens's and Le Corbusier's offices between the wars—predicated such an approach. While Grabrijan's early study on the congruence of modern architecture and the "Oriental House in Sarajevo"[2] inspired the project, it was Neidhardt's design-informed contribution that presented Bosnian vernacular as a paradigm for an integral design practice specific to the region. Grabrijan's erudite text, which praised the comfort, functionality, and simplicity of this ubiquitous building tradition in the Balkans, leaned on Neidhardt's conceptual organization of the book, which placed architecture in its environment on a range of scales, from the region and the city to the neighborhood and the house. Neidhardt was adamant that the visual experience of the book should match the "truth" of the Bosnian region, and he meticulously produced the stream of images and controlled the colors, contrast, and fonts within a carefully arranged layout the better to immerse the reader in the specificities of Bosnia's architectural legacy.

The book's subtle subversion of the Modern Movement's universalizing logic and its claims for the inherent modernity of the Oriental House anticipated subsequent attempts to destabilize Western hegemony in modern architectural culture, epitomized by Bernard Rudofsky's 1964 exhibition *Architecture without Architects* at The Museum of Modern Art in New York. In turn, the endorsement from Le Corbusier, which paid tribute to his own formative encounter with the Balkan vernacular (recorded in his legendary notebooks, published in 1911 as *Voyage d'Orient*), tied the book to modernism's own roots. Indeed, this method of attending to "continuity of spirit" remained essential to Neidhardt's design practice and provided the groundwork for an architectural regionalist movement in Yugoslavia.

Mejrema Zatrić

1   Dušan Grabrijan and Juraj Neidhardt, *Arhitektura Bosne i put u savremeno / Architecture of Bosnia and the Way to Modernity* (Ljubljana: Državna založba Slovenije, 1957), 6; translation by the author.

2   Dušan Grabrijan, "Orientalska hiša v Sarajevu – s posebnim ozirom na sodobno" [The Oriental House in Sarajevo—with Special Regard for the Contemporary Situation], *Arhitektura*, nos. 23–24 (1949): 44–61; translation by the author.

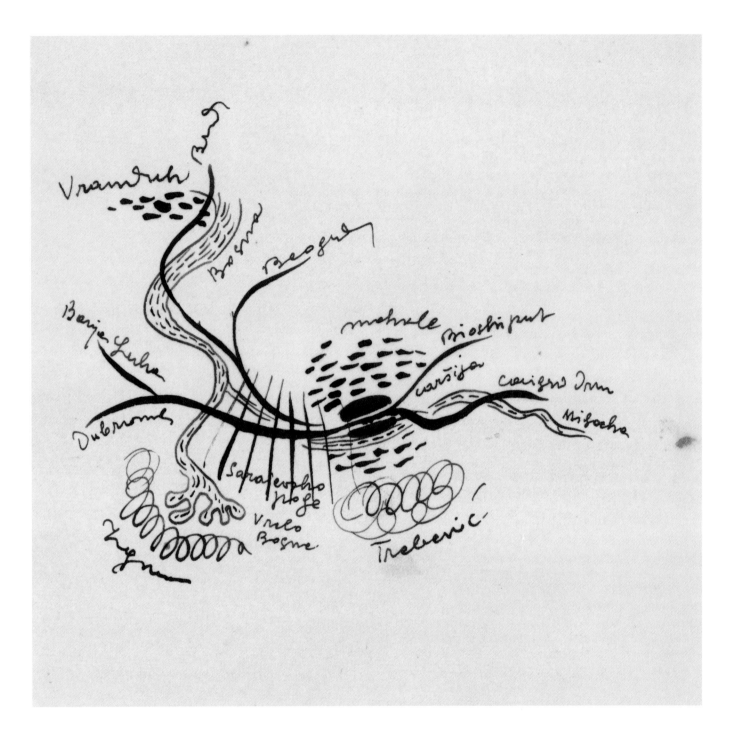

Fig. 4

Fig. 4   "Areas studied in the book," 1954–57. Juraj Neidhardt (1901–1979). Ink on tracing paper, 7²⁄₁₆ × 11¹³⁄₁₆ in. (18 × 30 cm). Private archive of Juraj Neidhardt

Fig. 5   "Composition of the old Bosnian architectural elements," 1955. Juraj Neidhardt (1901–1979). Collage and ink on paper, 7²⁄₁₆ × 11¹³⁄₁₆ in. (18 × 30 cm). Private archive of Juraj Neidhardt

Fig. 6   Double-page spread from Dušan Grabrijan and Juraj Neidhardt, *Arhitektura Bosne i put u suvremeno/ Architecture of Bosnia and the Way to Modernity* (1957), 416–17.

Fig. 5

Fig. 6

Fig. 1

YUGOSLAV PAVILION AT EXPO 58

Architect   Vjenceslav Richter (1917–2002)
Built   1958
Location   Brussels

The first World's Fair to open after World War II, Expo 58 in Brussels offered the young Yugoslav socialist state a prominent platform in which to articulate a position of openness within the bifurcated Cold War political order. The 1958 Yugoslav pavilion—designed by Vjenceslav Richter, a Croatian artist and architect who created several prominent exhibition pavilions abroad—was intended to serve as a conduit in educating the Expo's international public about the distinct brand of Yugoslav socialism, one that represented a progressive political ideology wholly different from the more rigid and bureaucratized Soviet Communist system.

The pavilion itself lacked any of the ornamental flourishes associated at the time with Soviet Socialist Realism, thereby tacitly communicating to visitors the split between Yugoslavia and the USSR. Nor was the Yugoslav structure placed with Warsaw Pact states around the Soviet Pavilion; rather, it stood near the British and Portuguese Pavilions, alongside a wooded patch of trees that emphasized, by contrast, the modernity of Richter's design. The distinctly avant-garde building, with four cascading galleries arrayed across two split-level stories, was sheathed in ceiling-height glazing, which made the transparent box appear to glow at night. Richter initially proposed a monumental central column meant to carry the entire weight of an elevated gallery volume, but, to his regret, this radical structural solution was abandoned at the behest of skeptical engineers. The realized scheme instead rested on twelve columns arranged along the perimeter (so as to preserve the open ground-floor plan) and featured, adjacent to the building, a detached sculptural 115-foot steel obelisk, which gestured at the original idea, demarcated the pavilion, and represented the six constituent Yugoslav states with a motif of six curvilinear steel elements.

Yet the built structure retained several of the exceptional features of Richter's original competition scheme—its free circulation, for example. Visitors to the pavilion were completely uninhibited by doors, either internal or external, including on the ground-level plaza, which was elegantly paved with twelve multicolored varieties of polished Yugoslav marble.

Ultimately, Richter's architecture was the single most successful element of the Yugoslav Pavilion in Brussels, earning praise from leading newspapers and trade magazines such as *Architectural Review*, which dubbed it one of the six best national pavilions at Expo.

In a noteworthy postscript, Richter's building continues to serve a didactic function today, though both the socialist Yugoslav state and the 1958 World's Fair have run their respective courses. After the fair, a Belgian contractor purchased the Yugoslav Pavilion and reconstructed it as the College of Saint Paulus in the nearby town of Wevelgem, where the building still stands.

Anna Kats

Fig. 2

Fig. 1   Yugoslav Pavilion at Expo 58, Brussels. 1958. Vjenceslav
            Richter (1917–2002). Competition model (unrealized
            version). 1956. Vjenceslav Richter Archive, Museum of
            Contemporary Art, Zagreb
Fig. 2   View of the front facade. 1958. Archives of Yugoslavia
Fig. 3   Interior view. 1958. Archives of Yugoslavia
Fig. 4   Longitudinal section. 1:100. 1957. Diazotype,
            $17^{11}/_{16} \times 35^{1}/_{16}$ in. (45 × 89 cm). Archives of Yugoslavia

Fig. 3

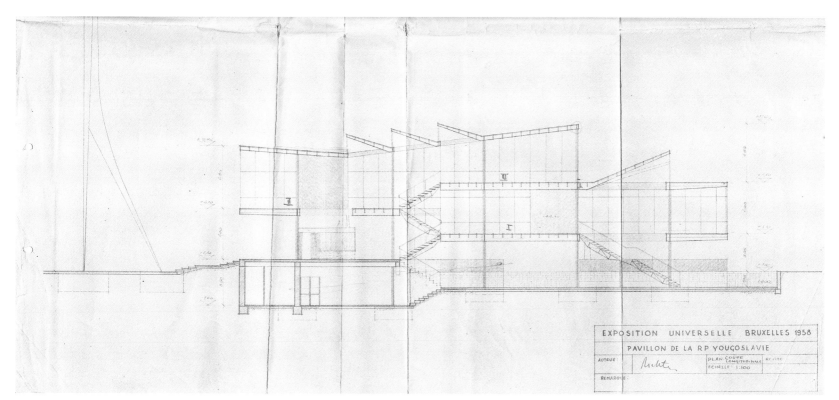

Fig. 4

Fig. 1

Fig. 1   Museum of Contemporary Art, Belgrade, Serbia.
1959–65. Ivan Antić (1923–2005) and Ivanka Raspopović
(1930–2015). Interior view during a retrospective
exhibition of the work of Olga Jevrić. 1981. Museum
of Contemporary Art, Belgrade

MUSEUM OF CONTEMPORARY ART

Architect   Ivan Antić (1923–2005) and
                     Ivanka Raspopović (1930–2015)
Built   1959–65
Location   Belgrade, Serbia

The significance of the Museum of Contemporary Art in Belgrade lies not only in its possession of the most comprehensive collection of Yugoslav modern art, but also in its original contribution to the typology of the modern art museum. Its founder and longtime director was the prominent Belgrade painter, art critic, and curator Miodrag B. Protić, a tireless promoter of modernism who actively participated in the public discussions that inaugurated cultural liberalization in the early 1950s, after the country's departure from the Soviet bloc. Although funded by the city of Belgrade and the government of Serbia, the new institution exceeded local scale: Protić's ambition was to cover twentieth-century artistic production in all of Yugoslavia and to establish Belgrade's place within international artistic networks, an endeavor he steadfastly pursued until his retirement in 1980.

The museum was to be built in New Belgrade, the new capital of socialist Yugoslavia, close to the confluence of the Danube and Sava Rivers. Ivan Antić and Ivanka Raspopović won the 1959 competition for the building design. (They would later collaborate on another exceptional museum building, located in the October Memorial Park in Kragujevac.) In their competition entry, the two young architects proposed a system of interconnected volumes rotated forty-five degrees in relation to the main structural grid. Somewhat akin to a honeycomb, the system allowed for expansion through additional units, though in the end this potential was never realized. The building's zigzagging skylights echo the jagged contours of the plan to produce a strong, iconic image that informed the museum's logo, thus anticipating more famous instances of modern buildings being deployed as branding symbols, such as the Sydney Opera House and Paris's Centre Pompidou. Inside, the cellular structure dissolves to generate dynamic and greatly varied exhibition spaces, through which the visitor ascends via interconnected half-levels from the open ground floor to a taller second story (with spectacular views of the Sava and old Belgrade) to the low, intimate, skylighted galleries at the top. Antić and Raspopović originally proposed modest, "brutalist" materials, with an exposed concrete skeleton and red brick infill, but Protić later lobbied for additional funding to upgrade the infill to polished white marble. Nevertheless, the tectonic coding of the original proposal survived.

In 1962, Protić spent two months in New York on a Ford Foundation grant, studying the curatorial strategies and organization of The Museum of Modern Art and the Solomon R. Guggenheim Museum. From Alfred H. Barr Jr., MoMA's founding director, he absorbed the philosophy of exhibiting a large and complex collection of modern art. Protić's concept for the permanent exhibition in Belgrade was for the modern art of Yugoslavia what MoMA's was for international modernism: an authoritative, canonical view. Again influenced by MoMA, Protić steered his museum to become the first in Yugoslavia to feature permanent departments for documentation, public outreach, education, and international exchange, thereby creating a comprehensive research institution that actively promoted art.

Vladimir Kulić

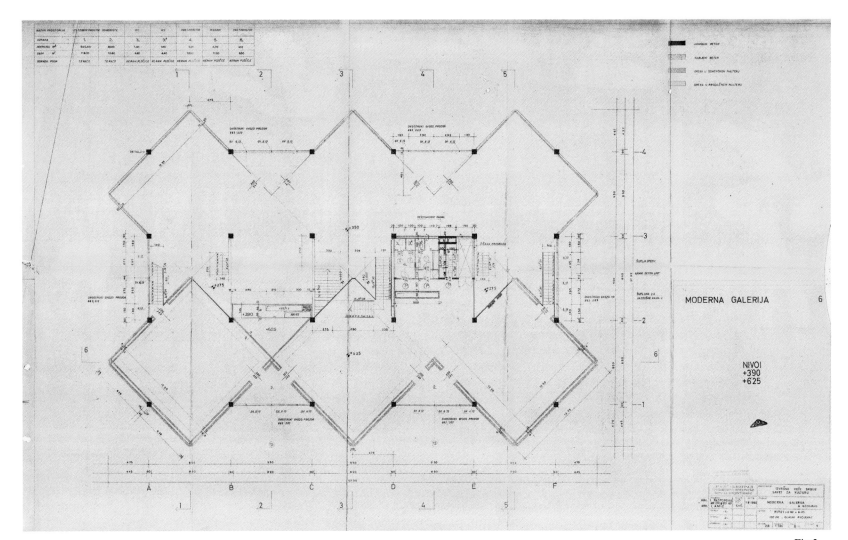

Fig. 2

Fig. 2   Floor plan. 1960. Diazotype, 22⁷⁄₈ × 37³⁄₁₆ in.
             (58.1 × 94.4 cm). Historical Archive of Belgrade
Fig. 3   Exterior view. Museum of Contemporary Art, Belgrade

Fig. 3

Fig. 1

Fig. 1   Partisan Memorial Cemetery, Mostar, Bosnia and
         Herzegovina. 1959–65. Bogdan Bogdanović (1922–2010).
         View of the path and masonry walls. 2010. Photograph:
         Wolfgang Thaler

PARTISAN MEMORIAL CEMETERY

Architect   Bogdan Bogdanović (1922–2010)
Built   1959–65
Location   Mostar, Bosnia and Herzegovina

Bogdan Bogdanović called it the "most opulent work of my architectural youth." For anyone other than the surrealist-leaning Serbian memorial maker, this might seem an odd description for a city of the dead. His Partisan Memorial Cemetery in Mostar, completed in 1965, is at once a graveyard of fallen World War II Partisan soldiers, a city park, a pilgrimage site, and an urban-scale statement on collective memory. As Bogdanović described the project's dramatic mise-en-scène, two "cities" rise up to face one another on opposing hillsides and "look face to face, eye to eye—the city of the dead antifascist heroes ... and the city of the living, for which they lost their lives." [1]

Entering the cemetery complex, one begins an ever-steepening ascent. Built in gray stone and concrete, the necropolis is monochrome, but its textures and contours are multifarious, lending it an uncanny intensity. At first the path marks an axis pointing toward the grail of this pilgrimage—an elevated, quasi-cylindrical fountain in the distance—but the trail soon breaks into a serpentine curl, winding through curves that are sometimes open, with low parapets, and sometimes labyrinthine, with high walls and blind turns. The pilgrim eventually reaches the highest of six grassy terraces, and the path's unsteady cobblestone is replaced by the stable ground of the heroes' graves. Each terrace is lined with scores of flat, strangely shaped gravestone slabs, and at the center of the top terrace the pinnacle fountain suggests both water well and baptismal font. When it still flowed, the water would trickle over the brim and then follow a razor-straight line down the hillside, passing the 810 tombstones to reach a freestanding circular pool. Emerging from the rear wall of the top terrace, a concentric stone relief stands like a sacramental ornament at a pagan mass. Turning to the fountain, the visitor finds himself in the place of a cleric at an altar, presiding over a rite for the assembled dead, their headstones lined up and attentive, the city of the living beyond.

In the Mostar necropolis, Bogdanović created a Yugoslav pilgrimage—one that seems not manufactured but found, rediscovered through the remnants of some prehistoric ritual. The cemetery invokes the scale of epic cycles and sedimentary layering, with each round of forgetting and remembering, burial and recovery, enriching its elusive resonance. Today, Mostar is divided, Yugoslavia is gone, and the necropolis is an untended, graffiti-stained memorial not only to the fallen heroes but also to the fallen country.

Matthew Worsnick

---

1   Bogdan Bogdanović, "Grad mojih prijatelja"
     [The City of My Friends], *Mostarska informativna
     revija* (May 1997): 38–40.

Fig. 2

Fig. 3

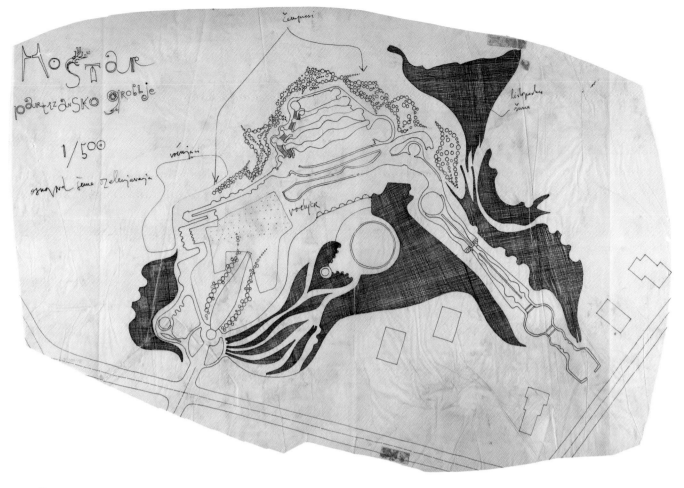

Fig. 4

Fig. 5

Fig. 2   View of the six terraces. 2008. Photograph: Wolfgang Thaler
Fig. 3   Detail of the stone walls. 2008. Photograph: Wolfgang Thaler
Fig. 4   Schematic drawing. 1:500. Ink on tracing paper,
         22½ × 32½ in. (57.2 × 82.5 cm). Architekturzentrum
         Wien, Collection
Fig. 5   Conceptual sketch. Ink and pencil on tracing paper,
         13¼ × 36⅝ in. (33.6 × 93 cm). Architekturzentrum Wien,
         Collection

Fig. 2

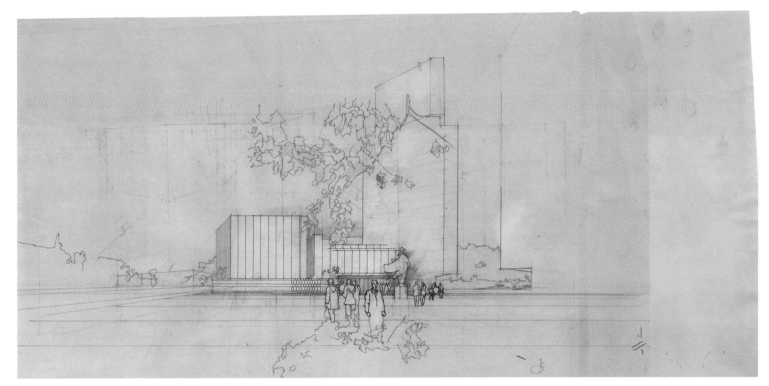

Fig. 3

Fig. 4

Fig. 2   Revolution Square, Ljubljana, Slovenia. 1960–74.
         View of the West Office Tower. 2008. Photograph:
         Wolfgang Thaler
Fig. 3   Perspective drawing of the Ivan Cankar Cultural Center
         and the West Office Tower. 1977. Ink and tempera
         on diazotype, 24 × 40⁵⁄₁₆ in. (61 × 102.4 cm). Museum
         of Architecture and Design, Ljubljana
Fig. 4   Detail of the entrance of the West Office Tower. After 1977.
         Museum of Architecture and Design, Ljubljana.
         Photograph: Damjan Gale

The Right Point of Meeting.

Fig. 1   Kiosk K67. 1967–99. Saša J. Mächtig (b. 1941). *The Right Point of Meeting* leaflet. 1967. Color print on paper, 27 9/16 × 9 15/16 in. (70 × 25.2 cm). Museum of Architecture and Design, Ljubljana

KIOSK K67

Architect   Saša J. Mächtig (b. 1941)
Built   1967–99
Location   Slovenia

Over three decades, starting in 1968, around seventy-five hundred of Saša J. Mächtig's fiberglass-reinforced polyester kiosks were trundled out of the Imgrad Ljutomer factory in Slovenia, ending up as far afield as Japan, Iraq, the United States, and Kenya, as well as scattered throughout Yugoslavia and the Soviet bloc. With their bright colors, rounded space-age forms, and sturdy modern materials, the kiosks became emblematic of both Yugoslavia's physical and ideological transformation, and of a new generation of industrial products showcased in BIO, Ljubljana's international design biennial, established in 1964.

      Plopped down where needed and used in inventive, open-ended ways, the modular K 67 kiosks provided a rhythm and identity to Yugoslavia's rapidly evolving town and cityscapes. For Mächtig, the kiosk K 67 was "the core and the starting point for a comprehensively organized microlocation" that could be developed as required through the addition of further kiosks and features such as information displays, advertising graphics, lighting, greenery, and public benches. While some kiosks were customized to suit a particular function before leaving the factory, the future use of most was left indeterminate. Operating as self-contained units or linked together in a variety of configurations, the kiosks were activated through use—as fast-food stands; newspaper and lottery kiosks; stalls for flowers, key-cutting, and shoe repair; temporary offices; parking-attendant, airport, and ski-lift booths; copy shops; border-patrol stations; soundproof shelters; or storage areas inside factories. This flexible yet systematized approach to urban planning allowed nodes of commercial activity and social interaction to emerge organically.

      The genesis of the kiosk K67—as it had been for Dutch designer Gerrit Rietveld's iconic Red Blue Chair and American architect and inventor Buckminster Fuller's geodesic dome—was experimentation with a joint (in this case the intersection of two plastic tubes) that could generate a flexible constructional system. Mächtig's approach reflected his training in Edvard Ravnikar's influential but short-lived Course B (1961–63) at the Architecture Faculty of the Ljubljana Academy of Fine Arts. The first kiosks were molded in a single piece, but the design was modified after 1971, dividing the structure into two sections for ease of transport and installation. The kiosk K67 was soon attracting international attention and, had it not been for a disastrous fire at Imgrad, would have been used at the 1972 Olympic Games in Munich. Its modular, sculptural form, technological sophistication, and embrace of informal social patterns appealed to MoMA curator Emilio Ambasz, who acquired a K67 for the Museum's collection after spotting it in the April 1970 issue of the British magazine *Design*.

Juliet Kinchin

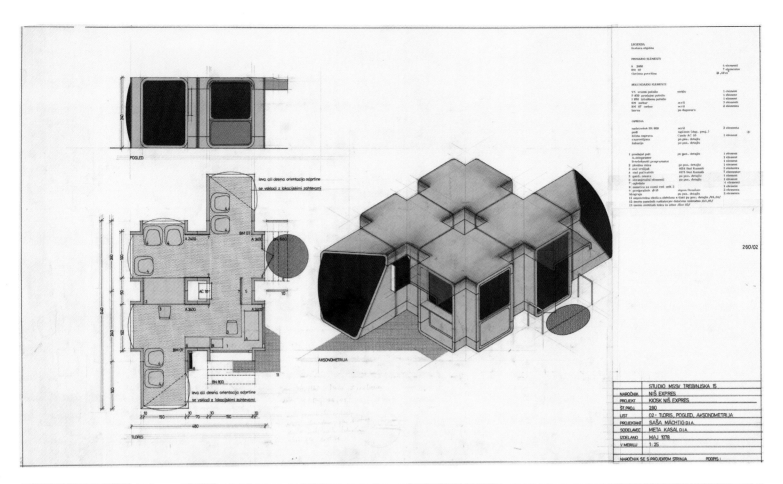

Fig. 2

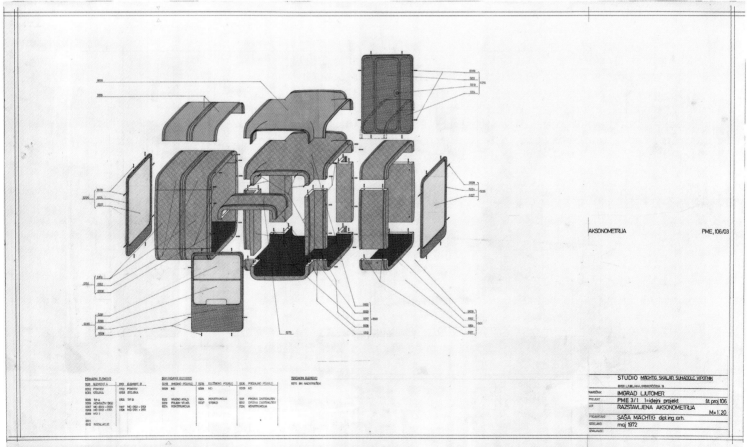

Fig. 3

Fig. 2   Plan, elevation, and axonometric view of K67 for Niš Ekspres. 1967. Collage on tracing paper, 23³⁄₄ × 41⁵⁄₈ in. (60.3 × 105.7 cm). Museum of Architecture and Design, Ljubljana

Fig. 3   Exploded axonometric view of K67 components. 1967. Collage on tracing paper, 24¹⁵⁄₁₆ × 42¹³⁄₁₆ in. (63.4 × 108.8 cm). Museum of Architecture and Design, Ljubljana

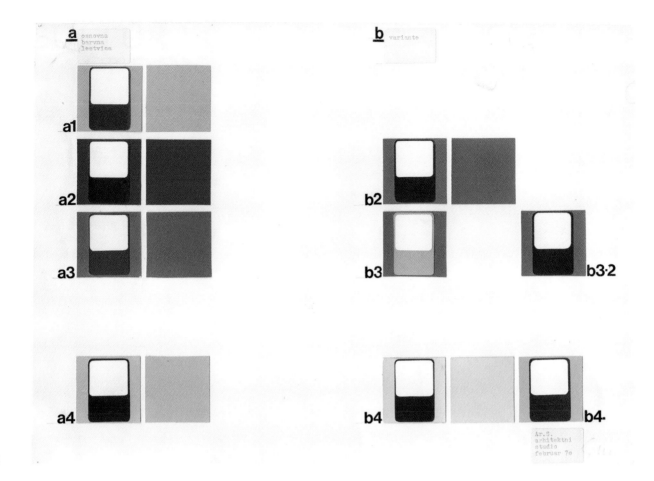

Fig. 4

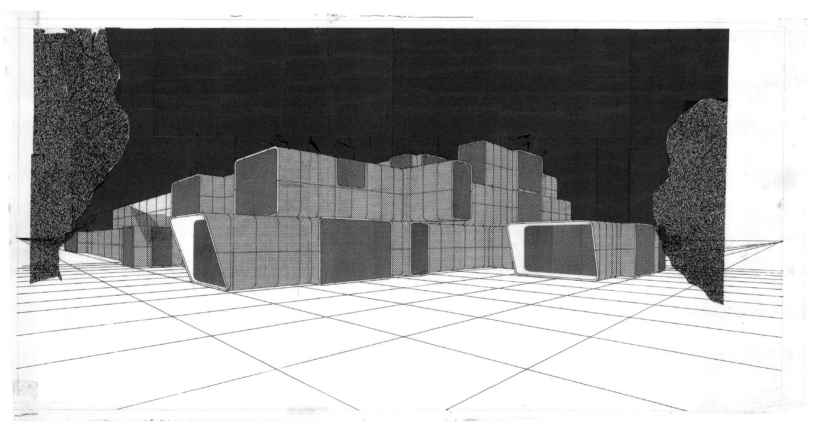

Fig. 5

Fig. 4   Studies of different color combinations. 1967–69. Collage
          on paper. Museum of Architecture and Design, Ljubljana
Fig. 5   Universal mounting system. 1972. Saša J. Mächtig (b. 1941).
          Study for vertically assembling block units. Collage
          on tracing paper. Museum of Architecture and Design,
          Ljubljana

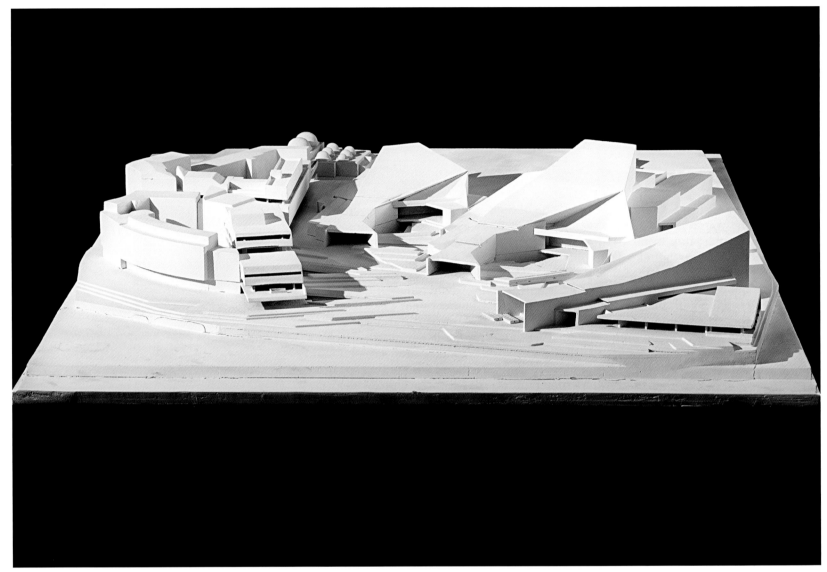

Fig. 2

Fig. 2   Model. 1:500. 9 ¹³⁄₁₆ × 59 ⁷⁄₁₆ × 72 ¹³⁄₁₆ in. (25 × 151 × 185 cm).
          Macedonian Opera and Ballet, Skopje.
          Photograph: Vase Amanito
Fig. 3   Aerial view. 2009. Photograph: Wolfgang Thaler

Fig. 3

Fig. 1

SPLIT 3

Architect   Vladimir Braco Mušič (1930–2014) with
                 Marjan Bežan (1938–2017) and Nives Starc (b.1937)
Built   1968–early 1980s
Location   Split, Croatia

The project to expand the Croatian industrial city of Split in the 1970s, known as Split 3, pushed Yugoslav urban design beyond the orthodox modernist planning paradigm that shaped New Belgrade and New Zagreb. The Slovenian architect and planner Vladimir Braco Mušič, a disciple of Edvard Ravnikar, a fellow of the Harvard Graduate School of Design (1963–64), and a prominent Yugoslav theorist of urbanism, was key to the project's conception.

Transforming a large unurbanized territory southeast of the city's historical center, the ambitious plan created several residential neighborhoods for fifty thousand inhabitants—as well as schools, department stores, public garages, sports and business centers, and a university campus—and was meant to be executed in a mere seven years. The Yugoslav People's Army, alongside local, collectively owned companies and the municipality, was a major investor.

Mušič and his colleagues Marjan Bežan and Nives Starc from the Urban Planning Institute of Slovenia won the national competition for the project in 1968. They proposed a blend of theoretical models and urban planning practices drawn from domestic and international sources—Japanese megastructures, the planimetric structures of Team 10, and the hierarchies of urban landmarks and spaces based on urban theorist Kevin Lynch's ideas about the mental mapping of cities. Carefully inserted into the existing terrain, the basic urban unit was a pair of parallel building blocks of differing heights that delimited narrow pedestrian paths. Streets referred to the structure of old Dalmatian cities, while their grid followed the existing traces of the ancient Roman centuriation or stood in relation to nearby Diocletian's Palace. Such orientation also introduced views of the surrounding natural landscape, further linking the architecture, noted for its incorporation of local materials such as vernacular stone, to the immediate context. The "street concept," as the designers termed it, paid meticulous attention to public space, providing identity for its numerous individual units and generating a distinct urbanity.

Split 3 was also exemplary in its organization of building processes. Streets were conceived by a group of gifted local architects—including Marjan Cerar, Dinko Kovačić, Ivo Radić, and Franjo Gotovac, among others—and built up in several phases by different construction companies. In this way, a homogeneous planning scheme produced a markedly heterogeneous architecture.

By the early 1980s, more than half of the program was realized, but further construction was suspended because of changes in development priorities. Nevertheless, Split 3 represents an exceptional achievement: the transformation of modernist mass housing into a planned environment nevertheless marked by the diversity and spontaneity typical of vital urban neighborhoods. The project turned a new page in Yugoslav urban planning, influencing the design of collective housing in Kosovo, most notably that of the Kurrizi development in Pristina. Split 3's lively street life and human scale—lauded internationally by critics such as Jane Jacobs and Giancarlo De Carlo—persist unabated to this day.

Luka Skansi

Translated from Croatian by Irena Šentevska.

Fig. 2

Fig. 3

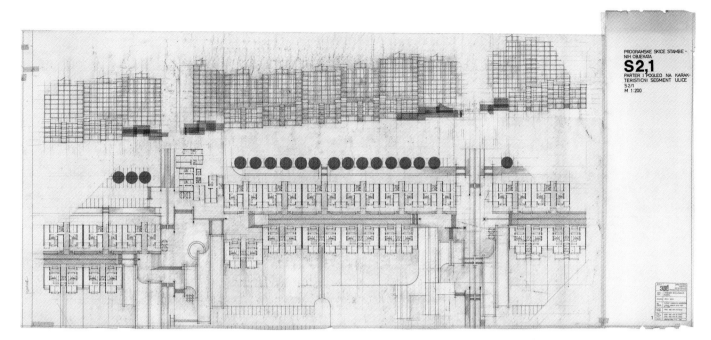

Fig. 4

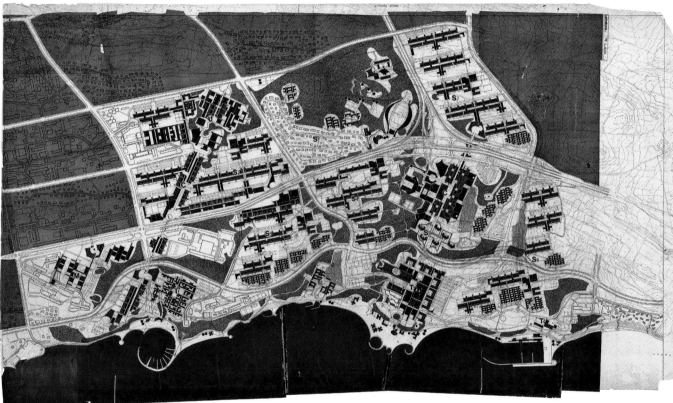

Fig. 5

Fig. 1   Split 3, Croatia. 1968–early 1980s. Urban plan by
        Vladimir Braco Mušić (1930–2014), Marjan Bežan (1938–
        2017), and Nives Starc (b. 1937). Street view of neigh-
        borhood S3 Radoševac. 1970–77. Ivo Radić (1930–2006).
        2010. Photograph: Wolfgang Thaler
Fig. 2   Exterior view of the Braće Borozan building block.
        1974–76. Dinko Kovačić (b. 1938). 2009. Photograph:
        Wolfgang Thaler
Fig. 3   South view of neighborhood S3 Radoševac. 1970–77.
        Ivo Radić (1930–2006). 2009. Photograph: Wolfgang
        Thaler
Fig. 4   Neighborhood S2/1, elevation and ground-floor plan.
        1:200. Marjan Cerar (1938–2017). 1969. Ink and pencil
        on paper, 37 3/8 × 80 11/16 in. (95 × 205 cm). Archives
        of the Republic of Slovenia, Ljubljana
Fig. 5   Competion drawing, site plan. 1968. Ink on paper with
        adhesive and stencil, 41 5/16 × 72 13/16 in. (105 × 185 cm).
        Archives of the Republic of Slovenia, Ljubljana

Fig. 1

GOCE DELČEV STUDENT DORMITORY

Architect   Georgi Konstantinovski (b. 1930)
Built   1969–77
Location   Skopje, Macedonia

Georgi Konstantinovski's Goce Delčev Student Dormitory is bold in its expression, daring in its structure, and powerful in its forms. On the one hand, the design reveals the influence of American brutalism and the experience Konstantinovski acquired in the 1960s, first as a graduate student at Yale University, where he studied with Paul Rudolph, and later as an employee in the office of I. M. Pei. On the other hand, it betrays the impact of Japanese Metabolism, which arrived in Skopje with Kenzō Tange's master plan to rebuild the city center after the devasting earthquake of 1963.

      Konstantinovski was awarded the dormitory commission after a competition at the beginning of 1969. Construction began that same year and was conducted in two phases, owing to the size and the complexity of the endeavor. The first phase was completed in 1971, the second in late 1977. Enabling inexpensive (almost free) accommodation for twelve hundred students, the building should also be appreciated as an important social project.

      The dormitory was to be situated on a square plot within the newly planned part of the city. Four identical housing blocks were built on nearly one hectare (100 × 100 m). Each unit was sited at a ninety-degree angle to its neighbor, so that together they form a dynamic spatial composition around a central open public space. Each of the four blocks is composed of a conjoined five-story building and a thirteen-story tower that share an elevator and staircase. Groups of residential units are arrayed along the central corridor of each block, in the manner of late-modernist experiments in minimal housing standards. On the sixth floor, the four dormitory blocks are connected by "flying bridges," thus forming a "sky square" that contains spaces for entertainment and social interaction (recalling the "streets in the air" proposed in the 1950s by the British architects Alison and Peter Smithson). The residential areas in the complex are complemented by an adjacent low-rise restaurant and student store; a sports hall was planned but never built.

      The student dormitory (named after the Macedonian anti-Ottoman revolutionary leader Georgi Nikolov Delčev, known as Goce Delčev) is one of the many examples from the late 1960s and early 1970s in Skopje of sculptural form expressed by means of exposed concrete. The exclusive use of that brutalist material par excellence subverts the conventional modernist distinction between structure and enclosure, resulting in an ascetic reduction in terms of materiality and color. Nevertheless, strong rhythms of "serving spaces" and pronounced textures—fluted surfaces, embossed geometric ornaments—ultimately generate a highly aestheticized building.

Vladimir Deskov, Ana Ivanovska Deskova, and Jovan Ivanovski

Fig. 1

Fig. 2

Fig. 1 Šerefudin White Mosque, Visoko, Bosnia and Herzegovina.
1969–79. Zlatko Ugljen (b. 1929). Aerial view. 1983.
Aga Khan Award for Architecture. Photograph:
Jacques Betant

Fig. 2 Drawing of west elevation. Pastel pencil on paper,
23⅝ × 26⅜ in. (60 × 67 cm). Personal archive
of Zlatko Ugljen

ŠEREFUDIN WHITE MOSQUE

Architect   Zlatko Ugljen (b. 1929)
Built   1969–79
Location   Visoko, Bosnia and Herzegovina

In panoramic views of the historic guild town Visoko, near Sarajevo, the Šerefudin White Mosque dominates less by its scale than by its imposing presence. Designed by Zlatko Ugljen in 1969, the project is an early epitome of his signature regionalism, an idiosyncratic, in situ elaboration of the natural and cultural contexts inspired by Croatian-born architect and theorist Juraj Neidhardt's concern for regional, "unwritten laws" of design.

 The building is situated in Visoko's densely built town center, its prayer hall and minaret sunken below street level and behind an elongated wing containing offices and a library. The sacred space is accessed by a ramp curving from the courtyard gate to the front porch, which accommodates ritual washing, providing a humble interlude for visitors before they enter the immersive prayer hall. A sculptural concrete shell pierced by carefully placed skylights defines the sparsely furnished interior and contributes greatly to its subtle spatial intensity. The mosque's unconventional dome, the formal centerpiece of the project, is structured by a sophisticated geometric operation: the sectioning of mutually penetrating truncated pyramids.

 Ugljen's studies reveal the conceptual rigor with which the seemingly amorphous form emerged, loaded with symbolic value: the pyramid evokes the ascension of the prayers to the heavens, the five roof segments suggest the five duties of Islam, and the five skylights choreograph the light differently for each of the five daily prayers. What defies representation by any medium, however, is the architecture's dynamic performance: only after the vistor makes the slow descent from street level to the subterranean level of the mosque—a descent that removes her not only from the chatter of the surrounding market but also from her everyday preoccupations—can she fully appreciate the dignified austerity of the light-bathed interior.

 The pyramidal composition of the structure was Ugljen's sole explicit concession to the conventions of the typical Ottoman mosque in Bosnia. His liberal interpretation of that tradition was bound to strain the imagination of the local Muslim community, and indeed the building took more than a decade to be realized. Nevertheless, the project garnered significant professional acclaim, winning the Aga Khan Award for Architecture in 1983.

 Ugljen's contextual and topological approach to this project remains a rarity in contemporary mosque architecture in the Balkans, which is overwhelmingly reliant on typological interpretations linked to imperial tradition and literal citations of Islamic geometric ornamentation. His design strategies, exemplified by the disarming modesty of the Šerefudin White Mosque, demonstrated a way in which architecture could channel Yugoslavia's multiethnic traditions to enrich its broader culture.

Mejrema Zatrić

Fig. 1

Fig. 1   National and University Library of Kosovo, Pristina,
Kosovo. 1971–82. Andrija Mutnjaković (b. 1929).
Aerial view. 2017. Photograph: Agon Nimani

NATIONAL AND UNIVERSITY LIBRARY OF KOSOVO

Architect   Andrija Mutnjaković (b.1929)
Built   1971–82
Location   Pristina, Kosovo

The National and University Library, created with the express goal of preserving and promoting the intellectual heritage of Kosovo, came into being with the establishment of the University of Pristina in 1970, the first Albanian-language institution of its kind within the Socialist Federal Republic of Yugoslavia. The new university engaged some of the most eminent Yugoslav architects to design the proposed campus, including Kosovo's first architect with a university degree, Bashkim Fehmiu, as a lead designer, and Bogdan Bogdanović as a consultant. Other notable members of the design team were Miodrag B. Pecić, Ranko Radović, Dimitrije Mladenović, and Rexhep Luci. The involvement of so many prominent architects demonstrates the importance attached to the endeavor, not only within the context of Pristina but for all of Kosovo. And at the center of this urban project was the library building, designed in 1974 by the Zagreb-based architect Andrija Mutnjaković.

Mutnjaković's design combined a visionary perspective with references to the architectural traditions of the Balkans. That the architect was steeped in the ethos of Zagreb's neo-avant-garde circles and their explorations into systemic art is evident in the building's basic compositional elements: the cube and the hemisphere, repeated on varying scales throughout the project. However, as both Byzantine and Ottoman architecture employ these shapes, seen frequently in Kosovo, the design, in a local context, thus came to represent as well the region's two main religious affiliations, Serbian Orthodoxy and Islam—an unmistakable gesture of inclusion in a multiethnic society such as Kosovo's.

Seventy-four domes placed on an equal number of cubes of varying sizes are scattered dynamically on a grid, along both horizontal and vertical axes, creating the impression that the structure can be replicated endlessly without sacrificing compositional integrity. The hexagonal aluminum grillwork that covers the building's facade—and is echoed in its geodesic domes—filters direct natural light and resembles filigree. Here that traditional technique, cultivated for centuries by Kosovar master craftsmen, is given a highly technologized interpretation. The result is a captivating dynamism, wrought by a reconciliation of vernacular and contemporary building traditions that binds the structure to the modern present and a transhistorical past.

Arber Sadiki

Translated from Albanian by Elidor Mëhilli.

Fig. 2

Fig. 2   Interior view. 2009. Photograph: Wolfgang Thaler
Fig. 3   Ground-floor plan, conceptual design phase. 1:200.
             Ink, letraset, and letraton on vellum, 25⁹⁄₁₆ × 38³⁄₁₆ in.
             (65 × 97 cm). Private archive of Andrija Mutnjaković
Fig. 4   Study sketch of massing, conceptual design phase.
             Ink and pencil on paper, 8¼ × 11¹³⁄₁₆ in. (21 × 30 cm).
             Private archive of Andrija Mutnjaković

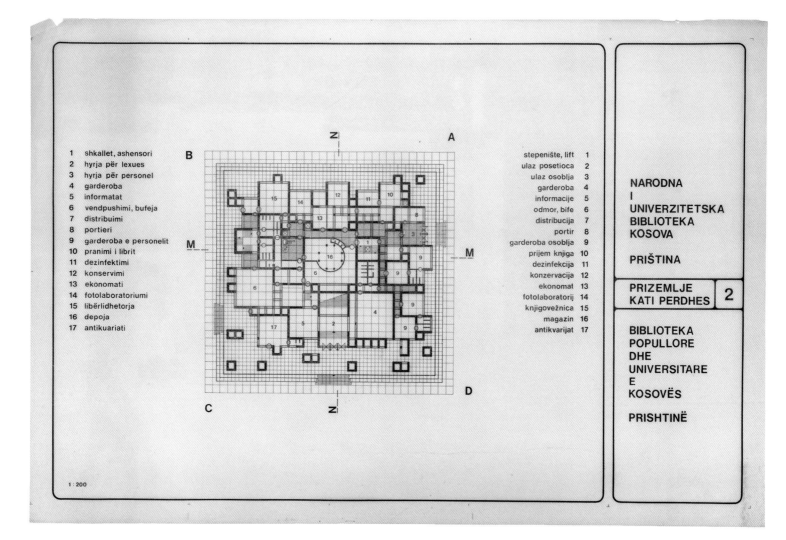

1 shkallet, ashensori
2 hyrja për lexues
3 hyrja për personel
4 garderoba
5 informatat
6 vendpushimi, bufeja
7 distribuimi
8 portieri
9 garderoba e personelit
10 pranimi i librit
11 dezinfektimi
12 konservimi
13 ekonomati
14 fotolaboratoriumi
15 libërlidhetorja
16 depoja
17 antikuariati

stepenište, lift 1
ulaz posetioca 2
ulaz osoblja 3
garderoba 4
informacije 5
odmor, bife 6
distribucija 7
portir 8
garderoba osoblja 9
prijem knjiga 10
dezinfekcija 11
konzervacija 12
ekonomat 13
fotolaboratorij 14
knjigovežnica 15
magazin 16
antikvarijat 17

NARODNA
I
UNIVERZITETSKA
BIBLIOTEKA
KOSOVA

PRIŠTINA

PRIZEMLJE
KATI PERDHES | 2

BIBLIOTEKA
POPULLORE
DHE
UNIVERSITARE
E
KOSOVËS

PRISHTINË

1 : 200

Fig. 3

Fig. 4

Fig. 1

Fig. 1   City Stadium Poljud, Split, Croatia. 1976–79.
         Boris Magaš (1930–2013). View of the roof structure.
         c. 1980. Private archive of Boris Magaš

CITY STADIUM POLJUD

Architect   Boris Magaš (1930–2013)
Built   1976–79
Location   Split, Croatia

In 1945, the war's tank tracks had barely washed away when the nascent Yugoslav government called for volunteers to build new athletic stadia. And build they did: just two years later, Yugoslav workers erected or renovated eighty-six athletic facilities, both modest and grand.[1] Stadia were the perfect focus for an impoverished, nationally fragmented, war-torn socialist state. They served as places for collective spectacle, tools of physical fitness, local landmarks, and venues for sports teams that fostered apolitical, urban-level identities. Yugoslavia took pride in each stadium, as object and experience.

By the time City Stadium Poljud was built for the 1979 Mediterranean Games, professional planning and construction teams had replaced volunteers, but the genre of the Yugoslav city stadium remained a socialist endeavor, rallying point, and international exemplar. From a thousand points in Split, Poljud Stadium is visible and legible: it sits low, half-embedded in the earth, with the gestural scoop of its outer edge seemingly drawn by a single curved stroke of architect Boris Magaš's pen. From a distance, as Magaš himself has described, the concrete structure resembles a delicately worked saucer. On one axis, the rim is pressed down; on the opposite axis, the two sides have been coaxed upward. At the upturned flanks, paperlike sheets bend over the interior, forming two awnings that shade spectators from the Adriatic sun. Early drawings show Magaš supporting the rim's distinctive geometry with bulky angled columns, but he eventually arrived at a graceful solution: tension cables circumscribe the rim and tie it together, using the structure's own weight to counterbalance the cantilevered stands and eliminating the need for exterior buttresses.

Inside, the building's iconic coherence dissolves, and its components separate with diagrammatic clarity. The roof appears nearly detached from the concrete saucer, with astonishingly slim space-frame trusses springing from the edge of the stands to support translucent glazing. Its two canopies mirror one another to form a partial shelter that largely covers the stands while leaving the playing field open to the sky and framing glimpses of the city and surrounding landscape. Marjan Hill, a public park and sailors' landmark, and socialist-era housing blocks—markers of the city's past and present—are prominently visible from spectator seats and even from the playing field. But the concrete stands themselves, with elaborate public sport facilities hidden below, are the arena's real substance. Designed and originally built only with bleachers and no individual seats, the stadium forced the city's fans to negotiate, shuffle, engage—to become participants in a socialist experiment, manufacturing daily life with every interaction and urged along by the infrastructure under their feet.

Matthew Worsnick

1   Richard Mills, "Laying the Foundations of Physical Culture: The Stadium Revolution in Socialist Yugoslavia," *International Journal of the History of Sport* (2017): 3–8; <http://doi.org/10.1080/09523367.2017.1391221>.

Aga Khan Award for Architecture: 164 [fig.1], 166 [figs.3, 4];
© Vase Amanito: 154 [fig.2];
Architekturzentrum Wien, Collection: 104 [figs.1, 2], 143 [figs.4, 5];
Archive of the Faculty of Architecture of the University of Zagreb: 44 [fig.10], 126 [figs.2, 3];
Archives of the Republic of Slovenia, Ljubljana: 159 [figs.4, 5];
Archives of Yugoslavia: 134 [fig.2], 135 [figs.3, 4];
© Associated Press: 21 [fig.13];
Association of Architects Belgrade: 49 [fig.15], 58 [fig.2], 67 [fig.3], 88 [fig.7], 98 [fig.4];
Association of Croatian Architects: 40 [fig.3], 60 [fig.5], 120 [fig.1];
Courtesy of Zoran Bojović: 10 [fig.1], 84 [figs.2, 3];
Courtesy of Branko Brnce: 90 [figs.1, 2];
© Jacques Betant: 164 [fig.1], 166 [fig.4], 167 [fig.5];
CCN-Images: 78 [fig.4], 80 [figs.5, 6];
Croatian Academy of Sciences and Arts (HAZU): 64 [fig.2], 78 [fig.1];
    Bernardi Collection: 40 [fig.4];
    Croatian Museum of Architecture (HMA): 64 [fig.1], 78 [fig.3], 93 [fig.6];
    Department of Prints and Drawings: 14 [fig.6];
    Boris Magaš Archive: 174 [fig.2], 175 [figs.3, 4];
    Radovan Nikšić Archive: 127 [figs.4, 5];
    Ivan Vitić Archive: 93 [fig.4];
Croatian State Archives: 82 [fig.9];
Private collection Milena/Dušan Debeljković in deposit at National Library of Serbia: 122 [fig.2];
Personal archive of Ana Ivanovska Deskova: 76 [fig.7];
Energoprojekt Archive: 23 [fig.17], 101 [fig.6, 7];
© Damir Fabijanić: 44 [fig.8];
© F.L.C./ADAGP, Paris/Artists Rights Society (ARS), New York 2018: 14 [fig.3];
Damjan Gale Archive: 94 [fig.8], 147 [fig.4];
© Nenad Gattin: 110 [fig.11];
© Getty Images: 115 [fig.4];
gta Archives, Institute for the History and Theory of Architecture at the Swiss Federal Institute of Technology (ETH) in Zurich: 21 [fig.16];
Zofia and Oskar Hansen Foundation: 76 [fig.9];
© Andrew Herscher: 115 [fig.2];
Historical Archives of Belgrade: 64 [fig.1], 138 [fig.2];
Institute for the Construction of Belgrade: 60 [fig.3];
Personal Archive of Jovan Ivanovski: 75 [all], 152 [fig.1];
France and Marta Ivanšek Foundation: 23 [fig.17];
© Valentin Jeck: i–xliv, 55 [fig.22];
© Dušan Jovanović: 102 [fig.8];
© Janez Kališnik: 43 [fig.7], 67 [fig.4], 69 [fig.7], 93 [fig.5], 94 [fig.7], 144 [fig.1];
Aleksandar Karolyi Archive: 43 [fig.6], 104 [fig.3], 109 [fig .9];

Private Archive of Georgi Konstantinovski: 163 [fig.3];
Macedonian Opera and Ballet: 154 [fig.2];
© Damjan Momirovski: 76 [fig.8];
Archive Damjan Momirovski and Mitko Donovski: 76 [fig.8];
Museum of Architecture and Design, Ljubljana: 14 [fig.4], 43 [fig.7], 52 [fig.18], 69 [fig.7], 93 [fig.5], 94 [fig.7], 102 [fig.9], 115 [fig.5], 144 [fig.1], 147 [figs.3, 4], 148 [fig.1], 150 [figs.2, 3], 151 [fig.4];
Museum of Arts and Crafts, Zagreb: 40 [fig.2];
Museum of the City of Zagreb: 63 [fig.7];
Museum of Contemporary Art Belgrade: 17 [fig.7], 136 [fig.1], 139 [fig.3];
Museum of Contemporary Art Zagreb: 17 [figs.8, 9], 32 [all], 110 [fig.10];
    Tošo Dabac Archives: 14 [fig.6], 40 [fig.1], 124 [fig.1];
    Vjenceslav Richter Archive: 51 [fig.16], 132 [fig.1];
Museum and Galleries of Ljubljana: 36 [fig.16];
Museum of Macedonia: 96 [fig.2];
The Museum of Modern Art Archives, NY: 18 [all];
Museum of Science and Technology, Belgrade: 63 [fig.6];
© Vladimir Braco Mušič: 108 [fig.6];
NIP Štampa: 35 [fig.10];
© Agon Nimani: 168 [fig.1];
© Vesna Pavlović: 28 [all];
Svetlana Kana Radević Legacy Collection, Faculty of Architecture, University of Podgorica: 98 [fig.5];
© Edvard Ravnikar Family Archive: 14 [fig.5], 94 [fig.8], 144 [fig.1], 147 [figs.3, 4];
© Ante Roca: 64 [fig.2];
Sena Sekulić Gvozdanović: 63 [fig.7];
Courtesy of the Serbian Orthodox Eparchy of Raška-Prizren: 115 [fig.3];
SSNO Uprava vojnog građevinarstva, Direkcija za izgradnju i održavanje stambenog fonda JNA: 47 [fig.13];
© Łukasz Stanek: 88 [fig.6];
© Krešimir Tadić: 127 [fig.5];
Kenzō Tange Archive. Gift of Takako Tange, 2011. Courtesy of the Frances Loeb Library, Harvard University Graduate School of Design: 72 [figs.1, 4];
Wolfgang Thaler: 13 [fig.1], 31 [fig.6], 35 [fig.11], 36 [figs.13, 14], 43 [fig.5], 55 [fig.20], 70 [fig.8], 82 [figs.7, 8], 96 [fig.1], 107 [fig.5], 123 [fig.3], 140 [fig.1], 142 [figs.2, 3], 146 [fig.2], 155 [fig.3], 156 [fig.1], 158 [figs.2, 3], 160 [fig.1], 162 [fig.2], 170 [fig.2];
United Nations Archives and Records: 21 [fig.15];
Urban Planning Institute of Belgrade: 58 [fig.1];
Estate of Lebbeus Woods: 112 [fig.1], 116 [figs.5, 6];
© Matthew Worsnick: 108 [fig.7];
© Miodrag Živković: 109 [fig.8].

Published in conjunction with the exhibition
*Toward a Concrete Utopia: Architecture in
Yugoslavia, 1948–1980*, at The Museum of
Modern Art, New York, July 15, 2018–
January 13, 2019. Organized by Martino Stierli,
The Philip Johnson Chief Curator of
Architecture and Design, The Museum of
Modern Art, and Vladimir Kulić, Associate
Professor, Florida Atlantic University, with
Anna Kats, Assistant Curator, Department of
Architecture and Design, The Museum of
Modern Art.

Major support for the exhibition is provided by
The International Council of The Museum of
Modern Art.

Generous funding is provided by the Graham
Foundation for Advanced Studies in the
Fine Arts.

Additional support is provided by the
Annual Exhibition Fund.

Support for the publication is provided by
the Jo Carole Lauder Publications Fund of
The International Council of The Museum
of Modern Art.

Produced by the Department of Publications,
The Museum of Modern Art, New York

Edited by Stephanie Emerson
Designed by Bruno Margreth and
Martina Brassel, Zurich
Production by Matthew Pimm
Color separations by t'ink, Brussels
Printed and bound by DZS Grafik, Ljubljana,
Slovenia
This book is typeset in in Times NR Seven MT.
The paper is 150 gsm Magno Satin and
130 gsm Schleipen Fly.

Library of Congress Control Number:
2018936426
ISBN: 978-1-63345-051-6

Published by The Museum of Modern Art
11 West 53 Street
New York, NY 10019-5497

Distributed in the United States and Canada by
ARTBOOK | D.A.P.
75 Broad Street, Suite 630
New York, NY 10004
www.artbook.com

Distributed outside the United States and
Canada by Thames & Hudson Ltd

181A High Holborn, London WC1V 7QX
www.thamesandhudson.com

Front cover:
West Gate of Belgrade (Genex Tower),
Belgrade, Serbia. 1977–80.
Mihajlo Mitrović (b. 1922). Photograph:
Valentin Jeck, 2016.

Back cover:
Sinturbanizam (Synthurbanism). 1962–63.
Vjenceslav Richter (1917–2002).
Perspective section of Ziggurat.
Exhibition copy, 43⅜ × 39⅜ in.
(110 × 100 cm). Vjenceslav Richter Archive,
Museum of Contemporary Art, Zagreb

Printed and bound in Slovenia

SOCIALIST FEDERAL REPUBLIC OF YUGOSLAVIA

AUSTRIA

Ljubljana

Socialist Republic of
SLOVENIA

● Zagreb

Socialist Republic of
CROATIA

Socialist Republic of
BOSNIA
AND
HERZEGOVINA

Venice

ITALY

● Zadar

Split

Adriatic Sea

● Rome

100 km